Flags of Alaska and British Columbia

CRUISING ALASKA 2019-20

A Guide to Alaskan Waters

CONTENTS

INTRODUCTION

Alaska, the largest of the American states, is like a world unto itself. It is detached from what they call "The Lower 48, as travel to Alaska must be either by air, sea or by land through a large portion of the Canadian west. Alaska is truly the last frontier of the United States. It is vast, much of it near to or above the Arctic Circle. And it experiences cold, dark winters with few to no hours of daylight, but long to endless and cool summer days.

The coastal region, which is what most visitors see, especially those who are cruising, is the most spectacular part of the state. The deep-water fjords, high mountains, glaciers and thick forests make this one of the continent's most majestic of landscapes. It is also a region that holds a hidden danger. The coastal region sits along a very active plate boundary in the earth's crust. Earthquakes, potentially catastrophic, do occur at infrequent intervals. At the time this update was being prepared in late 2018, Anchorage experienced an especially strong earthquake, but fortunately it was not as disastrous as the great 1964 earthquake – second strongest every recorded on earth. The most severe earthquakes can trigger dangerous tsunami that are capable of devastating coastal areas. The mountains of the Alaska Peninsula and Aleutian Islands are predominantly of volcanic origin, and still active. Periodic eruptions are of tremendous magnitude and can even divert or shut down air traffic. But it is these Titanic forces that have helped to create the magnificent scenery that is coastal Alaska.

This is not your typical tour book such as Frommer's or Fyodor's. Those books provide every minute detail regarding where to stay or camp, to dine and to shop along with even providing suggestions for sightseeing tours or local walks. This is not one of those books. My cruise guide is designed to provide you first with a broad overview of Alaska and Western Canada to set the stage for your cruise since the majority begin or terminate in Vancouver and cruise through the inside passage of British Columbia and the Alaska Panhandle. There is then a chapter on each of the major ports of call that will tell you about the geography and history of the town to make your visit more enlightened. I do provide you with details on the major sights that are worth seeing in each port. It is not possible for this book to comment on the nature or quality of the hundreds of individual tours offered by each cruise line since the details are best left to the itinerary of your particular cruise. And depending upon the nature of your cruise, some tours may be highly specific to one particular company or even to one given ship. I provide information regarding the major sights to be seen in each port of call, the important sights in the immediate surrounding area and where to dine on shore to be able to sample local cuisine. Most people either return to their ship for lunch or simply have a quick snack so as to not waste time, but in so doing, they miss a great opportunity to sample the culinary flavors of Alaska. Some of the full day cruises do offer lunch, but there is no choice as to venue or even meal. As noted before, this is not the typical guidebook that is designed to detail every last nuance about shopping or dining. The purpose is to offer a concise outline of the nature and history of each port of call. The majority of the tour books on the market are oriented toward visitors who will be traveling on their own and spending more than part of a day in the ports you will be visiting. And those books also devote a lot of their space to the vast interior of Alaska, which cruisers can only hope to do either before or following their cruise, and of course on their own. Some of the larger cruise lines do offer pre

or post cruise rail journeys to Denali National Park or to Fairbanks, but these programs are pre planned and you will not have much, if any, free time for personal exploration.

Each chapter has loads of personal photos to help bring the destination alive. But unfortunately due to the high cost of printing in color based upon total pages, including text, this book is presented in black and white, but there is a full color edition that is more far more costly. The maps presented are from OpenStreetMaps,org and you can use your smart phone, tablet or laptop to open these maps and greatly enlarge them for more detail than can be seen on the pages of this book.

I trust you will find this book to be useful as a guide in preparing you for your Alaska cruise. But if you want more detail in the areas of lodging, dining and shopping, then I would highly recommend one of the more standard guidebooks.

Dr. Lew Deitch,
January 2019

CRUISING THE ALASKA COAST

Almost all major cruise lines offer summertime Alaska itineraries. These cruise lines vary in price and of course in the levels of quality service and cuisine being offered. Most of the itineraries are very similar with the major ports of Vancouver, Ketchikan, Sitka, Juneau, Skagway, Glacier Bay, Hubbard Glacier, Prince William Sound and Anchorage included in the one week to 10-day cruises. The length of the itinerary and the number of ports visited is commensurate with the quality of the cruise line and the price for the cruise. The most commonplace itinerary is a seven-day cruise from Vancouver, returning to the same port, traveling as far north as Glacier Bay or Skagway. Some cruise lines offer seven to 10 day cruises that are one way, starting or ending in either Vancouver or one of the two ports for Anchorage - Whittier or Seward. In the spring and fall there are the repositioning cruises between Hong Kong/Tokyo and Vancouver, eastbound in spring and westbound at the end of the Alaska summer season. These cruises include ports along the Kenai Peninsula and Aleutian Islands as well as on Russia's Kamchatka Peninsula, in Japan, South Korea and China. They are much longer, consisting of itineraries that vary from 16-days to a full month.

The higher end cruise lines offer smaller ships and their staterooms are generally larger and better appointed than the mega ships belonging to the major mass market companies. There is also a higher ratio of crewmembers to passengers, thus giving more personalized and attentive service. Likewise the cuisine on the smaller up market lines is gourmet oriented. But because these ships are smaller and carry fewer passengers their theaters and casinos are likewise less grand and the entertainment is not as lavish. One must choose between having a more sedate and elegant atmosphere or "glitz" and glamour of the larger vessels.

The higher end cruise lines also have a price schedule that is more all-inclusive, resulting in there being no additional charges for bar service, bottled water, shuttle transfers in ports and in end of cruise gratuities. One up market line even includes all tours in the fixed price of the cruise. And with less than 1,000 passengers and in many cases less than 500 passengers, the total experience is far more satisfying.

For those who are new to cruising, here are some basic tips that will help to maximize your voyage:

*** Always book an outside cabin if traveling on one of the larger ships that offer less expensive interior cabins that have neither a window nor a veranda.**

*** To economize, book an outside cabin with a window, as these are generally on the lower passenger decks. One advantage in rough seas is that being lower down in the ship equals more stability when the ship begins to pitch or roll. If having the opportunity to enjoy fresh air at any time is important to you, then it is wise to book a cabin with a veranda.**

*** Whenever possible book a cabin in mid ship, as when a ship begins to pitch the midsection acts like the fulcrum in that it experiences far less movement than either forward or aft cabins.**

*** If you should become queasy during periods of rough weather and pitching or rolling sea, it is best to go up on deck and breath some fresh air. Also by staring off at the horizon the body surprisingly is less stressed by motion. But if you are unable to go out on deck because of the danger presented during really inclement weather, it is still possible to sit near a window and from time to time look out to sea, toward the horizon.**

*** Starving one's self when feeling queasy will only make the condition worse. Dry crackers or toast along with hot tea is one way to calm an irritated stomach. And there are patches, pills or injections available from the ship's medical office to calm extreme discomfort.**

*** In Alaska be prepared for sudden changes in the weather. During summertime, the average temperatures in Alaskan waters are between 15 and 25 degrees Celsius or 69 and 77 degrees Fahrenheit. Occasional summer rainstorms can drop temperatures and it is easy to become chilled or soaked if not properly dressed or carrying an umbrella. Dressing in layers is the best way to accommodate the changes that can occur on a given day. And yes there are occasional warm days when the sky is blue, the sun feels strong and temperatures can climb up over 30 degrees Celsius or 88 degrees Fahrenheit.**

*** Do not over indulge in eating or drinking. It is best to pace yourself and try and eat normally, as you would at home. Overindulgence only leads to discomfort and added weight gain.**

*** When in port, weight the option of going on organized tours against freelancing and visiting on your own. If you have any sense of adventure, a local map, local taxi information and the names of basic venues make it possible to see as much, if not more, in a relaxed atmosphere in contract to being shepherded around as part of a tour group.**

*** When starting a cruise, arrive at least 36 hours ahead of the departure and spend a minimum of one night in the port of embarkation. This enables you to recover from any jet lag and to become acclimated to a new environment.**

*** When disembarking, it is also recommended that you spend at least one night in the final port of call before flying home. Two nights is preferable, as most cruises end in either Vancouver or Anchorage where there is a lot to see and do.**

*** When on shore in Alaska or Canada, it is safe to eat without fear of gastrointestinal upset. Local restaurants maintain a high degree of freshness in their summer seafood. And of course local water supplies are safe.**

*** Violent crime in Alaska or Canada is absolutely minimal. The ports of call on the itineraries are exceptionally safe. However, pickpockets are found almost everywhere that tourists will be seen in greater numbers. So wise precautions always apply regarding not keeping a wallet in a back pocket, not showing large sums of money and for women to keep a tight rein on their handbags.**

*** The use of credit cards is widespread at all major restaurants and shops. If using cash, remember than while in Vancouver, you will need to have Canadian currency, as most places will not accept American Dollars, Euros or other foreign banknotes.**

*** Returning to the ship is normally expedited by having your cruise identification card handy to be swiped by the security officers. Packages and large handbags are generally put through an x-ray machine similar to what is used at airports. And passengers pass through an arch to screen for any major metal objects.**

*** Most ships offer hand sanitizers at the gangway and recommend that you sanitize your hands upon return. This is not mandatory, but it never hurts to be cautious. The Baltic Sea region is one of the cleanest parts of the world, but still a bit of extra precaution is a good policy.**

*** Passports are necessary for all cruises that will either begin or conclude in Vancouver. The United States and Canada both require the carrying of a passport for all visitors. If you are holding a passport other than American or Canadian, you must check with your cruise line or the nearest American or Canadian consulate as to the possibility of needing a visa for entry into either country.**

*** In Alaska, the official currency clearly is the U. S. Dollar. And while in Canada, the Canadian Dollar is the official currency. Major hotels generally can exchange U. S. Dollars, Euro or U. K Pounds for Canadian Dollars. If you are traveling beyond Alaska on one of the repositioning cruises, you will need to have other currencies available for small purchases or tips. In Petropavlovsk, the currency is the Russian Ruble while in Japan you will need Japanese Yen. In South Korea you will need the Korean Wan while in China the currency is the Yuan. And if you are going as far as Hong Kong, the currency is the Hong Kong Dollar.**

ALASKA/CANADA
THE BIG PICTURE

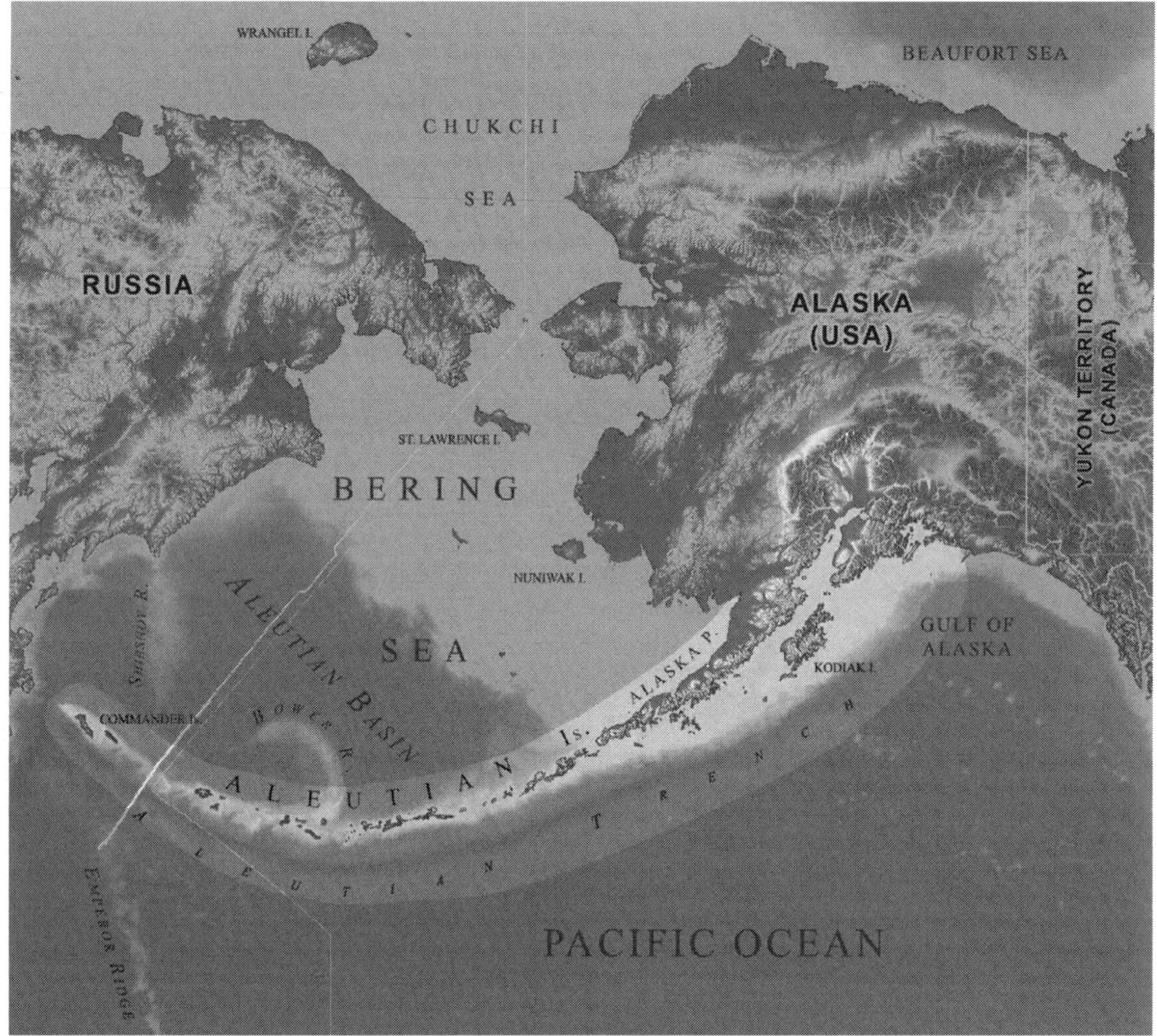

A map showing the scope of Alaska (Work of Gretarsson, CC BY SA 2.0, Wikimedia.org)

SIZE AND SCOPE: Big is the adjective that describes both Alaska and Canada. The state of Alaska is larger than the majority of world nations. Alaska covers 1,717,656 square kilometers or 663,268 square miles, making it by far the largest American state in land area. It is larger in area than Texas, California and Montana combined. And those are the next three largest states in land area. If you superimpose a map of Alaska over the lower 48 states, it would stretch from the northwestern tip of Washington clear across the country down to Florida. Years ago Alaska included four time zones, but given its far northern latitude where summer days are up to 24 hours in length and winter plunges it into darkness, all of the time zones were merged two. The majority of the state is within the Alaska Time Zone (GMT-9) and the westernmost Aleutian Islands are in the Hawaiian-Aleutian Time Zone (GMT-10). In actuality, the western Aleutian Islands extend farther west than the 180th degree of longitude, which is officially the International Dateline, but the actual calendar change

occurs within the Eastern Hemisphere beyond the island chain. Likewise, the International Dateline bends into the Western Hemisphere in the Bering Sea to accommodate a small piece of Russia, which is technically within our calendar sphere. One geographic question I used to ask my students in university was for them to name the easternmost state in the United States and the westernmost state. They would all state that Alaska was the westernmost but would fall into my trap by claiming that Maine was the easternmost state. This is a naturally expected answer because beyond Maine is the Atlantic Ocean and ultimately Europe. However, the far western Aleutian Islands of Alaska are so far west that they extend beyond the 180th degree of longitude, which divides the Eastern Hemisphere from the Western Hemisphere on one side of the globe. The Prime Meridian, which runs through Greenwich, England is where the two hemispheres meet on the other side of the world. So Alaska is thus the westernmost and easternmost state in the United States.

The core area of British Columbia (© OpenStreetMap contributors.org)

In physical size Canada is the second largest nation on earth. In size, it is second only to Russia with 9,984,670 square kilometers or 3,851,788 square miles. If you look at the North American continent, you will notice that it continues to widen as you move north. Thus to cross Canada by road or rail entails a longer journey than crossing the United States.

Whitehorse in the Yukon Territory is over 1,120 kilometers or 700 miles farther west than San Francisco while St. John's, Newfoundland is nearly 1,600 kilometers or 1,000 miles farther east than Boston. This greater expanse gives Canada two more time zones than the lower 48 states. They love to tell a story in Canada regarding its size. According to the story, a young man living in Vancouver (on the Pacific coast) receives a telegram from his father in England saying, "Son your brother is coming to visit you. His flight arrives in St. John's on Saturday. Please pick him up at the airport." Now St. John's is the capital of Newfoundland (on the far Atlantic coast). Of course the parents are not aware of the fact that it is over 8,000 kilometers or 5,000 miles east of Vancouver. So the son writes back via e-mail, "Dear dad, you pick him up since you are closer." St. John's is 1,600 kilometers or 1,000 miles closer to London than it is to Vancouver. This anecdote may give you some appreciation of the size and scope of Canada.

Alaska only has 736,742 people living in its vast expanses, with more than half living in the greater Anchorage area. This is still a wild and rugged state that possesses few roads, only one railway line and has its panhandle population totally cut off by land from the rest of the state. The only way for the capital city of Juneau to have access to the core of the state is by a combination of ferryboat and road but with much of the distance by road being through Canada. Nowhere else in the United States does one need to carry a passport to travel by boat and road when going from the capital to the core of the state.

THE ALASKA LANDSCAPE: The physical geography of Alaska is very dramatic. The highest mountains in North America parallel the coast, providing an incredible spectacular backdrop. These mountains formed through uplift and volcanic activity along a major plate boundary just offshore. The subduction of one plate under the other created great reservoirs of molten material that spewed forth in massive eruptions, creating many of the highest peaks. At the same time, internal pressures caused ongoing uplift of the land, culminating in Denali Peak (Mt. McKinley), which is the continent's highest mountain topping out at 6,194 meters or 20,320 feet. Earthquake and volcanic activity continue to the present day, and often the results can be catastrophic. On Good Friday in April 1964, a magnitude 9.1 earthquake shook the central coast around Anchorage. This was the world's second most powerful measured quake on the Richter scale. It also created a massive tsunami that caused damage as far as the northern California coast. Since 1964, several volcanic eruptions have caused great hazards to air navigation, but fortunately they have occurred in isolated regions. And these forces will continue. And just recently in late 2018, Anchorage experienced a magnitude 7 earthquake with the epicenter very close to the city, and it caused widespread damage, but fortunately no fatalities were reported.

The panhandle region has what is called a fjord coastline, very similar to that of Norway where the word originated. A fjord is a deep channel that was carved by glacial ice during the Pleistocene (Ice Age). After glaciers began their rapid melt back to today's levels, the sea rose and flooded well inland into these channels. Where the glaciers had converged, as they melted away and sea level rose, the result was the creation of large offshore mountainous islands. Thus the panhandle is a blend of deep interior channels of calm water and a barrier of large, mountainous islands just offshore. It is not only beautiful to sail through the Inside

Passage, but the waters are exceptionally calm, protected by the mountainous islands to the west.

From the central coast, two peninsulas extend south, one being the Kenai Peninsula that terminates in the vicinity of the town of Seward, the other being the great Alaska Peninsula that has been broken by rising seas into the elongated curved archipelago of the Aleutian Islands. The smaller Kenai Peninsula is the result of uplift along a series of fault lines similar to those that created the great mountains of the Alaska Range. The Alaska Peninsula is comprised primarily of very high and powerful volcanic mountains that continue out into the Aleutian Islands. These volcanic mountains are active, and violent eruptions are not uncommon.

The entire coastal region experiences what is called a Marine West Coast climate. Here water from a relatively warm ocean current evaporates and is carried inland by the prevailing Westerly Winds. As the moist air rises, it rapidly cools resulting in heavy rainfall and snow at elevations that range from sea level to an average of 457 meters or 1,500 feet. The coastal towns can receive up to 254 centimeters or 100 inches of rainfall while in the mountains snow is measured in meters or feet per year with totals being extreme in many areas. The resulting forests are exceptionally rich in varied species of conifers including Douglas fir, hemlock, cedar, spruce and larch. There are large ferns and a thick understory of shrubs and herbs. This is one of the most magnificent of the northern forests. The rivers are filled with migratory salmon; the sea abounds in crab, black cod, whales and dolphins. The skies are often filled with bald eagles. The great land carnivore is the grizzly bear. Many consider this to be the closest environment to what could be called Eden.

North of the Alaska Range lies the great lowland drainage basin of the Yukon River, a massive waterway many of whose tributaries rise along the northern slopes of the Alaska and Coast Ranges in both Canada and Alaska. The land is flat to gently undulating, often covered in marshes and lakes, the result of the departing glacial ice over 10,000 years ago. Being exposed to more blasts of cold Arctic air, and being farther north where winter days are shorter, this is a land covered in spruce forests, as the Douglas fir, cedar, hemlock and other maritime species cannot thrive in the intense cold of Arctic winters. As you travel farther north, reaching the Arctic Circle, the forest begins to thin and become stunted woodland. Eventually you reach that point where the summer temperatures are not sufficient enough for tree growth and the landscape turns to tundra. By definition tundra is often spoken of as a polar desert because moisture is scant due to the intense cold. Only the smallest lichens, mosses and leafy herbs along with grass can thrive in the short and cool summer season.

The Brooks Range is of uplifted origin, considered by many American geologists to be the northernmost Rocky Mountains. However, Canadian geologists believe the Rocky Mountain cordillera begins in the central Yukon. Whether or not they are part of the Rockies is insignificant with regard to their appearance. They are uplifted mountains that were heavily glaciated and have their maximum high peaks topping out at around 2,740 meters or 9,000 feet. There are a few small clusters of spruce in sheltered coves, but the more common trees are the poplar, related closely to aspen that grow farther south. The entire region is home to

roaming herds of caribou, and they in turn are followed during summer by grizzly bear. Eagles are also found, as they are primarily fish eaters and during the summer they thrive on the open waters and have little competition from man. This is one of the most remote and unknown regions in all of the United States. It lacks roads and settlements, left primarily to nature.

The northern slope of the Brooks Range and the Arctic coast plain are especially barren, only sprouting grasses and wildflowers during the six weeks of summer. It is to these shores that the caribou migrate to forage. And it is in these grasslands that tens of thousands of migratory geese are found during the summer months. And on these shores the polar bear can be seen during the late summer and early autumn months before the ocean freezes over and they can then return to the ice to hunt seals. But with summer lasting longer and being warmer, the delay in the refreezing of the Arctic Ocean may cause the polar bear to eventually become extinct lest it turn to alternate food sources like the caribou. But then it would compete with the grizzly bear. One of the great tragedies of nature would be the extinction of wild polar bears, but at the present rate of climate change, they may be one of the first victims.

CANADIAN LANDSCAPES: Western Canada is also essentially an empty land. With a population of approximately 33,000,000, Canada has an average density of only 3.7 people per square kilometer. With 318,968,000 people and having 3,717,813 square miles, the population density of the United States is 88.6 people per square mile, and this includes the vast emptiness of Alaska, so it is clear that Canadians have a lot more legroom than do Americans (here at the outset of discussing Canadian landscapes, I did not convert American miles to kilometers simply to illustrate the fact that Canada as a nation uses the Metric system of measurement). The western Canadian provinces of British Columbia and Alberta and the Yukon Territory and Northwest Territories contain many of the same landscapes as do Alaska. The only difference is that southern British Columbia has milder winters and more sheltered interior valleys where summers are relatively warm and the land is especially productive. Across the Rocky Mountains, the Canadian Prairie extends north to the edge of the Yukon Territory. This is the great grain-producing region of the country. But in the far north of both provinces and extending into the territories, the land is dominated over by the great boreal forest of spruce and willow and dotted with thousands of lakes. And like Alaska this is a very empty land.

The coastal mountains of British Columbia are geologically an extension of the Cascade Range of the lower United States. They consist of uplifted and dissected plateaus topped with many ancient volcanic peaks. There are also sections of mountain that simply result in uplift, as do much of the Alaska Range. And along the border of the Yukon and the Alaska panhandle the Canadian Coastal Ranges merge into the Alaska Range. And like the Alaska panhandle, this is a region of heavy coastal rainfall and interior mountain snowfall. Thus the thick and rich forests of Douglas fir, cedar, hemlock and larch predominate. And they are equally rich in the wildlife noted for coastal Alaska. However, around the great city of Vancouver, a major urban development has altered the landscape, replacing much of the forest with cities, towns and farmland. And the wildlife has been forced to retreat deeper into the interior or to higher altitudes.

The Rocky Mountains are found hundreds of miles farther inland, the country in between being a mix of dissected plateau and uplifted ranges. Many of the peaks reach elevations of 3,050 meters or 10,000 feet and their peaks were glaciated, producing sharp and angular features. The inland forests are more open, consisting of both pine and spruce, but not containing the large coastal trees that are so moisture dependent. Farther to the north the vegetation grades slowly into a forest environment of spruce, willow and birch, the great boreal forests of the north. The interior plateau region has warm, mild summers in the south and short, cool summers to the north. And of course winters are cold throughout.

Both the Columbia and Fraser River systems rise along the edge of the magnificent Rocky Mountains, their waters flowing west to the Pacific. On the eastern side of the Rocky Mountains the waters flow together into the great Saskatchewan River system that empties into Hudson Bay. And farther north in the Yukon and Northwest Territories the rivers converge to form the great Mackenzie River system. The Rocky Mountains result from sedimentary rock layers having been uplifted and then glaciated, producing a landscape similar in flavor to the Swiss Alps to which they are often compared.

Despite the fact that Canada has so much legroom, most Canadians live in the major cities of the country, the majority of which are less than a day's drive from the American border. Some wise guy American once said that if the border were not there, most Canadians would be living even farther south. He must have been from Florida as his reference was to the intense cold of the northern winters. Even though winter can be brutal, Canadians love their land and would not choose to live in the United States, although they do envy those who live in Florida or Arizona during the winter months. And many do spend the winter months south of the border in either Florida or Arizona, but that is only an interlude, as most Canadians would not want to live permanently in the United States. These are two different countries with two distinctly different lifestyles, so for Canadians living in the United States or for Americans living in Canada requires quite an adjustment.

ALASKA AS A STATE: Alaska is the second youngest state in the United States, having been admitted in 1959 as the 49th state. Like all American states, it sends two members to the Senate and at present based upon its population it sends only one member to the House of Representatives. Thus it has little impact in the House of Representatives, but is equal to the most populous of states in the Senate.

The state government of Alaska is similar to the majority of American states in that it has a bicameral legislature with a Senate and House of Representatives. The populace elects a governor and lieutenant governor apart from its legislature. Laws are passed by the legislature, but can be vetoed by the governor. The governor is the head of the state, but still can experience a veto being overturned.

Law enforcement over all of the vast landscape is provided by the Alaska State Troopers, and only Anchorage maintains its own city police forces. The state is divided into 19 boroughs that function somewhat like counties in lower mainland states, yet have no sheriff's office. Where a major town exists, the borough and town combine to form a single governmental

unit. In the middle of the state there is one massive unorganized country that is larger than the state of Texas but only has a population of 78,000 residents. Its local functions are administered directly by the state government.

One unique characteristic of the state is its Alaska Permanent Fund. This fund consists of oil revenues that have been invested. Each year there is a payment made to every citizen of Alaska from the permanent fund and it can amount to as much as $3,000 in a given year. However, now in 2015 with oil revenues taking an economic hit, the fund will probably pay out a small sum until revenues increase.

Alaska does not have sales or use tax, but local municipalities can impose a sales tax of their own. And as would be expected, there is no state income tax in Alaska. But offsetting these tax advantages is the cost of goods. Because of its physical isolation necessitating that goods not produced locally be shipped in primarily by boat, the cost of daily shopping in Alaska can average as high as 25 percent more than in the lower mainland states.

The capital city of Juneau is totally isolated from the rest of the state. There are no roads connecting Juneau with the rest of Alaska. To get to Anchorage or Fairbanks requires a journey partly by ferryboat and then a long overland drive in part through Canada before reaching the core of the state. Several decades back a referendum was held on moving the capital to Anchorage, but surprisingly the voters rejected the idea partly because of cost, but also out of a sense of history since Juneau had been the territorial capital. So it appears that Alaska will remain a state with a capital city that remains cut off from the rest of the state. Also the borders of the Borough of Juneau extend to the border of Canada on the east, making it the only state capital city bordering another nation.

CANADIAN DIFFERENCES: Canada is divided into ten provinces and three federal territories. A Canadian province is like a state, but it has a greater degree of internal autonomy and more political clout than U. S. states. For example, provinces can negotiate directly with foreign governments regarding the development of resources; they have a total say in the development of health care programs and they own most of the land within their boundaries whereas in the United States, most land that is not privately owned is federal land. Most of the provinces are much larger than their American counterpart states because they are fewer in number.

Canada's national capital straddles the border between the provinces of Ontario and Québec. The main seat of government is in the city of Ottawa, Ontario, however, many important government offices are located across the Ottawa River in the sister city of Hull-Gatineau in the province of Québec. As a nation that is bicultural and bilingual, the location of the national capital was deliberate, chosen in 1867 by Her Majesty Queen Victoria to be a center that would bind the two primary cultures together.

If you spend any time in Vancouver, Americans watching the news on television or reading a newspaper suddenly realize that Canada is very different politically. The entire system of governing Canada is based upon the British parliamentary system. And you will find in a news broadcast that there are many distinct aspects of government or culture that will be

quite different from that of the United States. For example when a high ranking government official meets with reporters, it is not called a news conference or briefing, it is a "scrum."

The head of state for Canada is Her Majesty, Elizabeth II, Queen of Canada. However, since the queen cannot live in Canada a representative is chosen by the Canadian Government to act on the queen's behalf. This individual is selected for a five-year term, normally from the ranks of prominent citizens, and is known as the Governor General. The Governor General is the physical embodiment of Queen Elizabeth, serving in all official capacities where the queen would normally function. The Governor General has the ultimate power of veto over the parliament, and in the event of a deadlock within the legislative body, has the power to call for a national election. The present Governor General of Canada is Her Excellency Julie Payette, Canada's first woman astronaut.

A legislative body known as the Canadian Parliament governs Canada. It is divided into two houses, and patterned after the British Parliament.

* The Senate – Upper House: This body is composed of Senators who are chosen rather than elected. There are 104 seats in the Senate apportioned by province on the basis of population. It is primarily a ceremonial body and the members are prominent citizens, selected for their contributions to the nation. The ruling party in the lower house names new senators when vacancies occur. Senators represent the various political parties of the nation, and debates are conducted according to the same rules as in the lower house. The function of the Senate is to review legislation passed by the lower house and make recommendations to the Governor General with regard to giving royal assent or issuing a veto. The Senate can also send a bill back to the Lower House with suggested changes. There are limited occasions when the Senate may initiate legislation with regard to the welfare of the people of Canada so long as the bill does not involve taxation. The Senate may also form special committees to investigate matters that could lead to new legislation.

* The House of Commons – Lower House: This is the primary body of the parliament. Although it is called the lower house, it is where the real power of government rests. The House of Commons represents the people. There are 338 seats, apportioned by province on the basis of population. After each national census, the seats are reapportioned and the number of seats may be increased to enable each member to represent approximately the same number of people from the district they serve. Districts are known as Ridings. The member representing a riding is known as a Member of Parliament or abbreviated as "MP."

At present, Canada has four major political parties that are represented in the House of Commons.

* Liberal Party: The Canadian Liberal Party is similar in its outlook to the Democratic Party in the United States. This party supports labor, is strongly oriented toward an effective welfare net for the public and tends to favor the role of larger government. It had been the party in power in the House of Commons continuously now since 1991, but lost in 2006. In the 2015 national election, the Liberal Party regained a majority and today The Right

Honourable Justin Trudeau is the Prime Minister of Canada. The next election is slated for October 2019.

*** Canadian Conservative Party: This is essentially a new party that was created in November 2003 after a long rift in the Canadian right. They were been in power since 2006, first as a minority government, winning again as a minority government in 2008 and finally becoming a majority governing party in 2011. Today they are the leading party of the opposition, having lost power in the 2015 national election.**

*** New Democratic Party: This is a party that has represented a more socialistic viewpoint on the left. It originated in the Prairie Provinces and has had strong support from the agricultural sector of the economy. Although it has won various provincial elections, it is not strong enough to win a national election. But in the 2011 election, it gained the second highest number of seats and headed up Her Majesty's Loyal Opposition. They had high hopes of winning a majority in 2015. It is doubtful in the 2019 federal election that they will come anywhere close to gaining a majority.**

*** Bloc Québecois: This party has represented the separatist movement within the province of Québec. Given that Québec is the second most populated province, thus having a large number of seats in the House of Commons, the Bloc has from time to time been a significant force politically. The issue of separatism for Québec has been laid to rest, as the province has received special recognition status and in many ways governs its internal affairs as a nation within a nation. In the 2011 election, the Bloc won only two seats, as its power had been predicated upon agitation for separation, a topic presently put to bed. In the 2015 federal election it fared somewhat better, but is not presently a force to be reckoned with at the national level.**

National elections must be held once every five years at the maximum, but can be held at any time the ruling party chooses to call one, or in the event of a deadlock in the debates of the House of Commons when at least 51 percent of the members vote no confidence in the ruling party. Once the Governor General calls for a national election, approximately six weeks are allowed for campaigning prior to the vote. Citizens will vote in their respective Riding for the candidate who represents the party they wish to see rule. During the campaign period, the leader of each party is the person whom most media attention focuses upon. The next election will take place in 2019.

Once the votes are counted, the party that receives the greatest number of votes is then called upon by the Governor General to form a government. This means that the party leader will become the Prime Minister. He or she will then designate top ranking party members to hold the portfolios of the various government ministries such as external affairs, defense, labor, etc. These members then comprise the cabinet and along with the Prime Minister they represent The Government.

The opposition parties collectively constitute Her Majesty's Loyal Opposition and the leader of the party with the second highest number of seats becomes the Leader of the Opposition.

His or her role is to challenge the party in power at every turn, thus representing those citizens who did not vote for the party now holding the power.

If there are more seats held by the opposition, then it is said that the country has a minority government. In such instances, which are rare in Canada, the ruling party must satisfy the opposition or it will be brought down by a vote of no confidence. In such a scenario, the House will be dissolved and a new election will be called. Generally speaking, minority governments last only a few months at best, but the Conservative Party under Prime Minister Stephen Harper managed to survive as a minority government from 2004 to 2011. In 2015 it lost its hold on power and now the Liberal Party led by Justin Trudeau formed the government, and is quite popular with the public. It is too early to tell if this popularity will translate to another major victory in the 2019 federal election. It is, however, doubtful that the Liberal Party will return with anything less than enough seats to form a minority government. But in Canadian politics there are always surprises.

It is so important to understand the basic characteristics of Canadian culture and everyday life so as to appreciate the country when visiting Vancouver. Those who say that Canada is just like the United States are absolutely wrong. Yes there are many visual similarities and the two countries share a commonality in their standards of living, but behind these similarities is a vast array of differences. Even the perceived visual similarities are superficial, as there is a decidedly Canadian architecture. But on the whole the sight of gasoline stations, strip malls, large shopping malls, housing tracts and other such facets do create a degree of similarity until one looks deeper. As for overall standards of living, Canada and the United States are visually similar. But the big difference lies in the fact that approximately 80 percent of Canadian families would be placed in the broad middle class category. There are is a fair smaller percentage of extremely poor Canadians than there are poor Americans, and large urban slums are essentially absent. Likewise there is only a small segment of the population that would be classified as especially wealthy. Canada is more of a middle ground nation with regard to wealth distribution, and this has a great positive impact upon the level of crime and violence. Canadians often describe their culture as being gentler than that of the United States.

Unlike their American counterparts, Canadian cities are exceptionally clean, very vibrant and relatively crime free. Urban blight and decay are not the ongoing problem that most American urban centers must contend with. The question raised is why? It is not easy to answer without a major discourse. Essentially Canadian cities owe their greater economic success, a large middle class, strong government, a good social welfare net and a level of pride that is innate to the culture itself.

The downtown core of Canadian cities like Vancouver is the center of economic and social life. Flight to the suburbs does not have to mean an abandonment of the inner city, and Canada is proof of that fact. However, as young families move to the suburbs, working singles and many executives choose to live in and around the downtown core, thus breathing great life into the city's hub. The downtown of any Canadian city is a mix of high-rise office buildings, major hotels, large department stores, theatres, concert halls, restaurants and museums. It is the place to go for retail services and entertainment. But above all, it is the

focus of high-rise apartment or condominium living with rents or sales prices maintained at high levels due to demand. There is also the factor of fast and efficient public transportation. The major cities of Toronto, Montréal, Vancouver, Edmonton and Calgary all possess a subway, light rail and/or commuter train service into the downtown core. In all other cities, busses and electric trolleys connect downtown with the rest of the city. Hopefully on your Alaska cruise you will allow yourself a couple of days in Vancouver. You will find it so unlike any American city in that it is safe, spotless and so vibrant. It has a skyline that belies its nearly 3,000,000 metro area population. The Vancouver skyline is more comparable to that of Chicago than to any other American city. And greater Chicago is three to four times more populated than Vancouver.

Next we will briefly look at the history of Alaska and western Canada so you can appreciate how both political entities came into existence. And knowing something of the history helps you to better appreciate the landscape. The visual scene is partly the result of the building of the layers of history over the past.

Mike Dunleavy, Governor of Alaska (Photo by Alaska Senate Majority)

The Alaska House of Representatives Chamber

Her Majesty Elizabeth II, Queen of Canada (Open Government License v3) andHer Excellency Julie Payette, Governor General of Canada (Work of Sgt. Johanie Maheu, Government of Canadda),

The Right Honourable Justin Trudeau, Prime Minister of Canada

BRIEF ALASKAN HISTORY

Alaska has a rich and fascinating history. In this book I present a brief sketch of the state's formation, but in the individual chapters on the ports of call I offer a more localized history to help you understand the local architecture and customs, which have resulted from the evolution and growth of each community.

Four distinct native cultural regions have existed in Alaska since long before the first Europeans arrived. Today remnants of those native cultures still exist and there are villages where the traditions and values of each is still found:

*** Inuit or Eskimo culture is found along the Arctic shores of far northern Alaska. Their ancestors are believed to have been among the later arrivals coming across the Bering Sea land bridge from Siberia. In Alaska the term Eskimo is appropriately used, but across the border in Canada they are known as Inuit. Living in the cold Arctic, their culture has been predicated upon hunting seal, whale and in summer caribou. They were primarily hunters, and today are still allowed to hunt species that are off limits for the rest of us. Government subsidies and alcohol have had an impact upon Eskimo life, but they have retained much of their pride and still maintain many traditional values. One of the most important contributions to the settlement of Alaska by Europeans was the use of the dog sled, a piece of Eskimo technology.**

*** The mid portion of Alaska, namely the Yukon River plain was settled by scattered hunting tribes, many speaking Athabascan languages. This is the same linguistic family found in Arizona and New Mexico among the Navajo and Apache who were an offshoot of the Yukon River tribes that migrated into the American Southwest around 800 years ago.**

*** The coastal region of Alaska was inhabited by the most sophisticated people, tribes that lived in villages of wood houses, carved elaborate poles detailing their mythology and history and basing their livelihood upon fishing the coastal waters primarily for salmon. These tribes such as Tlingit, Haida, Salish and others thrived until the middle of the 19th century when disease and alcohol introduced by Europeans disrupted their social order.**

*** Out on the Aleutian Islands, a hardy people called the Aleut developed a lifestyle based upon fishing the treacherous offshore waters, and many of these people are little changed today because the Europeans found it too difficult to settle.**

The Russians were the first Europeans to attempt settlement in Alaska, coming across the Bering Sea from their outposts in Siberia's far eastern reaches. The first Russian village is believed to have been the result of sailors having been blown ashore by a gale in 1648, but this story is still disputed. The most accepted belief is that Shestakov and Pavlutsky were the first navigators to explore the coast in 1732. But the most celebrated expedition was that of Vitus Bering who explored the coast in 1741. He brought back a wealth of fine quality sea otter pelts and this began what was akin to a gold rush of colonists. By 1784, a small settlement was established on Kodiak Island, later moved to present day site of the town of Kodiak. And in 1799, Sitka was founded, later to become the capital of Russian Alaska.

Bering's accomplishments are the ones lauded in world history, yet other Russian explorers pre dated him and still other followed and were the ones who opened up Alaska to colonization. Bering's expedition was the first official naval voyage. He did found the port of Petropavlovsk on the Kamchatka Peninsula of Russia prior to sailing across the sea that would ultimately carry his name. And he did recognize the potential for exploitation of resources in Alaska, especially from his second voyage, which the Russians kept to themselves for a long while following his death in Alaska.

Spain, which had settled coastal California, attempted to counter Russian settlement in Alaska, and established a few trading and trapping outposts of their own between 1774 and 1800. There are place names such as Valdez and Cordova that attest to Spanish attempts. But ultimately the Russians came to dominate, trapping and fishing and sending Eastern Orthodox priests to bring Christianity to the coastal tribes. To this day from the Aleutian Islands to the panhandle towns, Russian Orthodox churches still minister to the people of the coastal towns, many a cross between Native American and European bloodlines. In no other part of the United States did the Russians play such a major role as the first European settlers.

Russia found it difficult to colonize Alaska. It was too distant from the core of the empire, requiring a long overland journey across Siberia just to get to the Pacific coast. And Siberia itself was so vast and unexplored that there was really no need for further expansion into North America. By the late 1860's, Russia was ready to sell its Alaska holdings to the United States. Secretary of State William Seward managed to negotiate a transfer of the territory for the sum of $7,200,000, which may appear to be insignificant today, but which was a large amount of money to pay for essentially what amounted to wilderness. Many Americans referred to Alaska as either "Seward's Ice Box" or "Seward's Folly" for years afterwards.

At first Alaska fell under military jurisdiction, later in 1884 it became a district with an appointed governor, and in 1912 it achieved full territorial status with a measure of home rule. What brought Americans to Alaska was the great Klondike Gold Rush of 1898. Most of the gold was discovered in Canada, but it did help establish the port of Skagway where people began their climb over Chilkoot Pass or White Pass into Canada. And prospectors eventually discovered gold in Juneau and other sites along the panhandle, thus bringing ultimate settlers. Until the gold rush, the few Americans who had come to Alaska were on Baranof Island around the former Russian capital of Sitka. In 1906, because of its gold discoveries, Juneau replaced Sitka as the capital of Alaska.

In addition to seeking gold, logging and fishing soon proved to be the real gold of Alaska. Agriculture has always been limited by geography, as the summers are too short and cool and the topography restricts the amount of level land. Farmers did ultimately grow vegetables for local consumption in the fertile Matanuska Valley north of Anchorage, capitalizing on the long summer days to offset the shortness of the season.

When Japan began to emerge as a great military power in eastern Asia, the security of Alaska became a major concern. Military bases were expanded in Alaska to strengthen the

territory's defenses in the event Japan should ever turn its attentions northward. Ultimately the Japanese did attack and occupy Attu, Agattu and Kiska Islands in the Aleutians and they bombed the naval base at Unalaska Island's Dutch Harbor.

Also during the war, U. S. aircraft being lent to the Soviet Union were flown via Whitehorse to Fairbanks, on to Nome and then flown by Soviet pilots across the Bering Straits into the U. S. S. R. The war brought more focus upon Alaska and it did connect the territory with the lower mainland via the Alcan Highway, built primarily through Canada, but constructed by the U. S. Army Corp of Engineers.

The wartime focus upon the strategic importance of Alaska is what ultimately helped the people in their bid for statehood. Not every resident was in favor of the change in status, but Congress approved statehood on July 7, 1958 and on January 3, 1959 President Dwight Eisenhower signed the official proclamation.

Two catastrophic events have occurred since statehood. The first was the Good Friday Earthquake that spawned a massive tsunami. At 9.2 on the Richter scale, it was the second most powerful earthquake ever recorded on earth, having shaken the coastal region for over five minutes. The combined devastation from both the earthquake and tsunami was considerable, but fortunately the Anchorage area was not heavily populated at the time. On March 24, 1989, the Exxon Valdez came aground and the rip in its hull resulted in the worst oil spill to have occurred in the history of the United States. The cleanup effort did fortunately restore much of the land to nearly pristine levels, but it drove home the point that as an oil producing state, Alaska is vulnerable to ecological disasters. Alaskans today are divided over expansion of oil drilling as opposed to maintaining greater protection of the state's environment. And with regard to the importance of tourism, the natural landscape is Alaska's greatest asset.

Crossing White Pass during the Klondyke Gold Rush

Skagway in 1900 - gateway to the Klondike Gold Fields

After a Japanese bombing raid on Dutch Harbor, Unalaska Island

Defending Alaska during World War II

The aftermath of the Good Friday Earthquake in Anchorage

The heart of downtown Anchorage after the great 1964 earthquake

SETTLING WESTERN CANADA

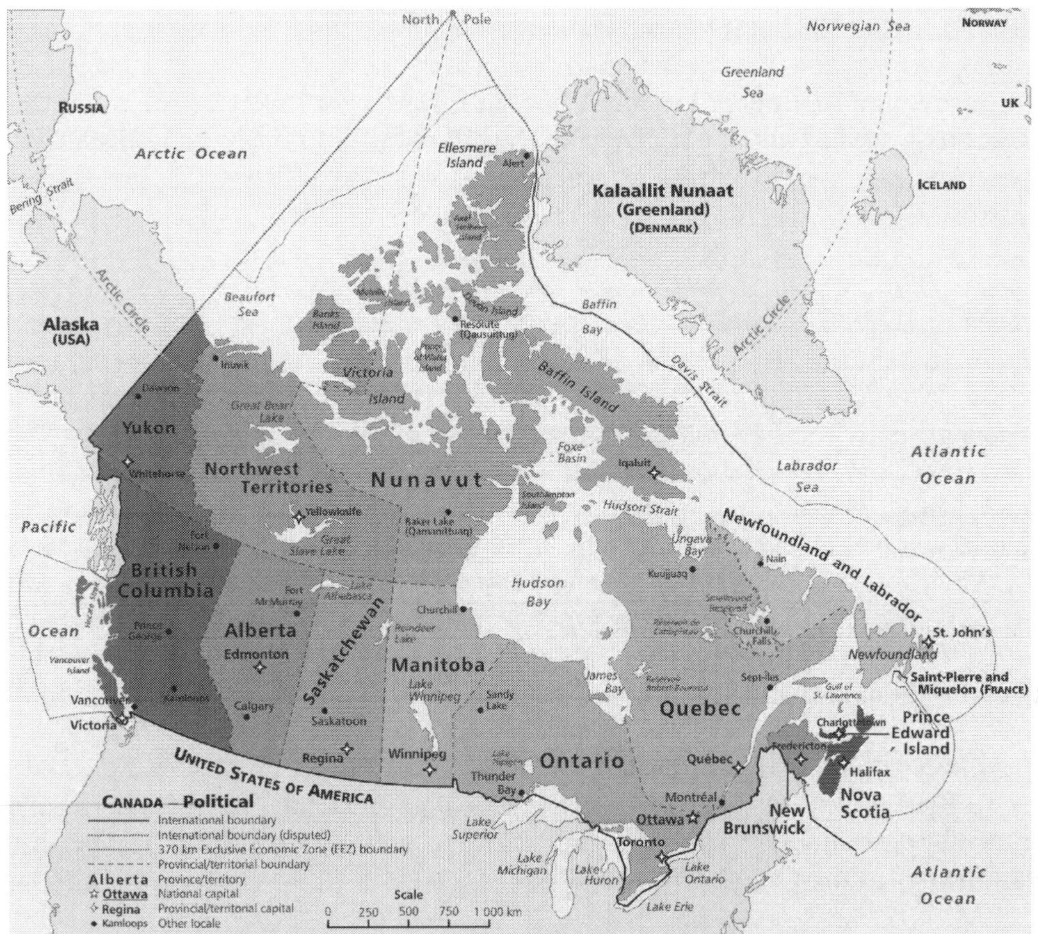

A map of the Canadian provinces and territories

The history of any nation tells us much about the present day landscapes and the cultural makeup of the people. Canada has a rich and colorful history, one that has interacted with that of the United States on several occasions, but by in large, has evolved on its own. It is the history of Canada that gives the nation its distinct qualities and makes it a very different country from its neighbor to the south. The way in which western Canada was settled is very different from that of the United States in that there was very little violent confrontation between the Native American tribes and Canadians pushing west. The Yukon Territory's history combines with that of Alaska in that the great Klondike Gold Rush actually involved both territories.

To set western Canada into context, I think it is very important to just see briefly how Canada as a nation came to be. This helps you understand how Vancouver differs so greatly from Seattle or other northwest Pacific cities.

FRENCH COLONIAL PERIOD: The French initially settled Canada in 1608, 12 years before the Pilgrims landed at Plymouth Rock. Ville de Québec was the first settlement, founded by Samuel de Champlain and built on a high bluff overlooking the St. Lawrence River. It is now the oldest and most historic city in Canada. Montréal was the second major colony established in 1642 at the head of navigation on the St. Lawrence River.

French explorers and trappers ventured out into the Great Lakes country and down the Mississippi River to the Gulf of Mexico, claiming all of the land for King Louis XIV, thus the name Louisiana. Other explorers ventured west into the Prairies as far as the Rocky Mountains by 1748, establishing regular trade contacts with tribes all across this immense region.

The British attempted to box in French colonial holdings by establishing a fur-trading company in the Hudson Bay region in 1670, and later by seizing the Atlantic colony of Acadia, later guaranteed by a peace treaty in 1713. Both the French and British attempted to ally various native tribes, which ultimately led to conflict over the vast Ohio River territories. Here is one event shared in the history of both the United States and Canada. The war lasted from 1754 to 1763. This was more than just a war for the valley of the St. Lawrence; it was a contest between two great powers over the future control of the interior of North America. The British government inherited a vast colonial territory with over 60,000 French subjects, living mainly in Québec, who were now cut off from their homeland. In a gesture of magnanimity the French people were allowed to maintain their language, customs and religion intact without interference from British authorities.

To keep from losing their vast Louisiana holdings to the British, France gave control of the territory to Spain, only to later receive the territory back at the time of the American Revolution. They ultimately sold the vast interior holdings in what became known in American history as the Louisiana Purchase.

The colony of Québec changed drastically at the time of the American Revolution. Prior to 1776, there were a handful of British subjects living in the St. Lawrence Valley. They did not interact with the French colonists, thus Québec maintained its distinctly French flavor. When the Declaration of Independence was issued and the 13 Colonies began to prepare for war, British Loyalists knew that their lives would be in danger if they remained. A mass exodus of over 40,000 fled to the British held territories to the north, primarily into Nova Scotia, but some 7,000 chose to carve out a new home on the northern shores of Lake Erie and Lake Ontario in the region of Québec that was unsettled. Thus the bicultural seed for Canada was sewn as now there were settlers representing two cultures and languages.

A DUAL CULTURAL REGION DEVELOPS: In 1791, Québec was divided into two separate colonies to enable each culture to exist in its own territory. The English dominated area around the Great Lakes became known as Upper Canada, while Québec was renamed

Lower Canada. By the first decade of the 19th century, Upper Canada had a population of over 80,000, most having come from the United States, claiming to be Loyalists, although some were just eager to seek out new lands for settlement.

Conflicts over the border between the new United States and the British along with British harassment of American ships at sea led to the War of 1812, and this worried British officials as much of the population of Upper Canada claimed to be loyal to the Crown, but their pledges had yet to be tested. The war dragged on into 1814 when both sides agreed to a declaration of peace. In actuality, the war was a stalemate as neither side could claim victory. But events left their mark for years to come. British forces had invaded Washington, burning the White House and other government buildings. In retaliation, American forces burned Fort York (present day Toronto).

In 1840, Upper and Lower Canada were unified, an event that turned out to be unsuccessful as the English and French politicians could not agree on issues, literally paralyzing the colonial government. The union was broken and when the two colonies reemerged, the names Ontario and Québec become recognized.

The American Civil War had a drastic impact upon the future of Canada. In 1862, the United States and Britain almost went to war when a Union warship stopped a British vessel to remove two Confederate diplomats en route to London. This so outraged the British that they sent reinforcements to Canada. In 1864, Confederate raiders attacked St. Albans, Vermont via Québec, and despite being later captured by British forces, they were set free to the dismay of American settlers living along the border. Other such incidents only served to inflame public opinion in the United States.

CANADA BECOMES A NATION: In the United States, there had been pre Civil War agitation to fight the British to settle the western border at 54 degrees 40 minutes north latitude, but in 1849, a compromise was reached that set the border at the 49th parallel of latitude from Lake of the Woods to the shores of Puget Sound. Now at the end of the War, there was agitation in the Congress to annex all of Canada, which would have meant a war with the British. But given the fever of "Manifest Destiny," there were many in the American government willing to risk such a war.

Since 1864, representatives of the Canadian colonies had held various meetings on the possibility of creating a federal union. Under the threat of American invasion, the meetings took on a new meaning. At Charlottetown, Prince Edward Island, agreement was reached on a confederation, and in 1867, the British Parliament passed the British North America Act, creating the Dominion of Canada. This was the first time in the history of the British Empire that independence was voluntarily granted to a grouping of colonies. By enabling independence, the British government removed the threat of a United States takeover. An invasion of a sovereign nation would have brought the Americans condemnation from the world community.

The newly formed Canada did not include all of what we see today. Initially, the confederation consisted of only Ontario, Québec, New Brunswick and Nova Scotia. Prince

Edward Island, Newfoundland and British Columbia chose to stay apart from the new nation, remaining as British colonies. The three Prairie Provinces had as yet not even come into existence. Thus the vast Prairie region and the west remained in the hands of the British, most of it being administered by the Hudson's Bay Company.

THE CANADIAN NATION GROWS: At the time of Canadian confederation, the west was an empty wilderness containing only some 15,000 settlers, mainly of mixed blood, combining French and Native American, known as the Métis. The Métis were concentrated primarily along the banks of the Red River in what is today Manitoba. In 1869, Canada purchased the land that is Manitoba from the Hudson's Bay Company for $1,500,000. A later purchase added the entire Hudson's Bay Company territory, extending westward from Manitoba to British Columbia and northward to the shores of the Arctic Ocean and the border with Alaska. In landmass, these acquisitions made Canada the second largest nation on earth, a title it still holds to this day. The Métis were uncertain as to Canadian intentions, thus they rebelled unsuccessfully against the takeover. Their terms for union with Canada were guarantees for protection of the French culture, language and religion, terms that the federal government initially agreed to negotiate. In 1870, Manitoba joined Canada as a province.

Unlike the Wild West of the American Frontier, the Canadian government negotiated treaties with the Native American tribes of the Prairies and Rocky Mountains, guaranteeing reservations, schools, cash payments and tools in exchange for the vast tracts of land the natives once roamed. To insure law and order in the west as settlers moved out onto the Prairies, the government established the North West Mounted Police in 1873, today better known as the Royal Canadian Mounted Police. By adhering to treaty agreements and through vigilant enforcement of the law by the Mounties, Canada was spared the intense bloodshed that characterized the American expansion into the Great Plains and far western regions. The Mounties earned the respect of Native American and settlers alike for their diligence. Even today in a world where police are often taunted or maligned by many in the community, in Canada there is great respect for the RCMP.

British Columbia, a colony rich in minerals, timber and fish, was reluctant to join the Canadian confederation, given the distance between the west coast and Manitoba, which was the nearest Canadian province. Their price was a guarantee of a transcontinental railroad. In 1871, British Columbia joined confederation and work began on the building of the Canadian Pacific Railroad. The line opened in 1885, connecting Vancouver with the east. This not only tied the expanding nation together, but it opened up the Prairies for settlement. By 1905, Saskatchewan and Alberta had sufficient population to become provinces. The railroad was built by a private company, but heavily subsidized in land grants and capital by the federal government. In later years, the government itself entered into competition with Canadian Pacific, developing the Canadian National Railway system, which extended a transcontinental line west to Prince Rupert on the northern British Columbia coast, with an additional line southwest to Vancouver.

Prince Edward Island, which had hosted the important confederation conference, held out on joining Canada until 1973. Newfoundland, on the other hand, refused to become a part of Canada, remaining as a British colony until 1949. After World War II, the British

government forced a referendum upon the people of Newfoundland, the end result being union with Canada. But to this day, many in Newfoundland claim that the British rigged the vote in that the majority had not voted to join with Canada.

Western Canada never grew to where the Native Americans became totally displaced, although many did loose portions of their land, and definitely the plains tribes lost the freedom to roam the prairies hunting buffalo. White hunters, as in the United States, did not decimate Canada's herds but they lost much of their range when wheat farmers plowed up large tracts of the prairies. Relations on the prairies were far more peaceful, but the end result was that First Nations people ended up on tribal reserves. And to this day, they are among the poorest and least served communities in the country. The Liberal Government has been attempting to rectify many of the ills of the past, but still has a long way to go.

GATEWAY TO ALASKA: British Columbia, the Yukon Territory and the Alaska Territory carried out trade even after the depletion of the goldfields. Fishermen plied the waters of both countries for salmon and halibut, and the railroad between Skagway and Whitehorse continued to function into the mid 20th century carrying lumber, minerals and some grain to Skagway for onward shipment. Today tourism ties these three entities together even more closely. Vancouver is the primary gateway for summer cruises to Alaska, with tens of thousands of passengers making the journey each year. And for others it is the terminus of the reverse journey southbound. The city of Vancouver is a world-class destination, and it is the Pacific window to Canada, giving visitors a glimpse into the true nature of what it means to be Canadian.

For those who wish to drive into Alaska, there are two alternatives. They can drive through British Columbia to its northern port of Prince George and link up with the Alaska Ferry to take them as far north as Skagway or Haines, continuing on by road into the core of Alaska. Or they can drive the entire route on the now paved Alaska Highway, the improved version of the World War II Alcan Highway. British Columbia and the Yukon Territory offer the same majestic scenery as Alaska, and visitors do take advantage of the Canadian landscape as well as the Alaskan scene.

Kwaikutl and Clayoquot First Nations at the turn of the 20th century

Downtown in Vancouver in 1912

Building the Alaska Highway thru Canada's Yukon Territory during World War II

The Canada U. S. border atop White Pass

VANCOUVER,
BRITISH COLUMBIA

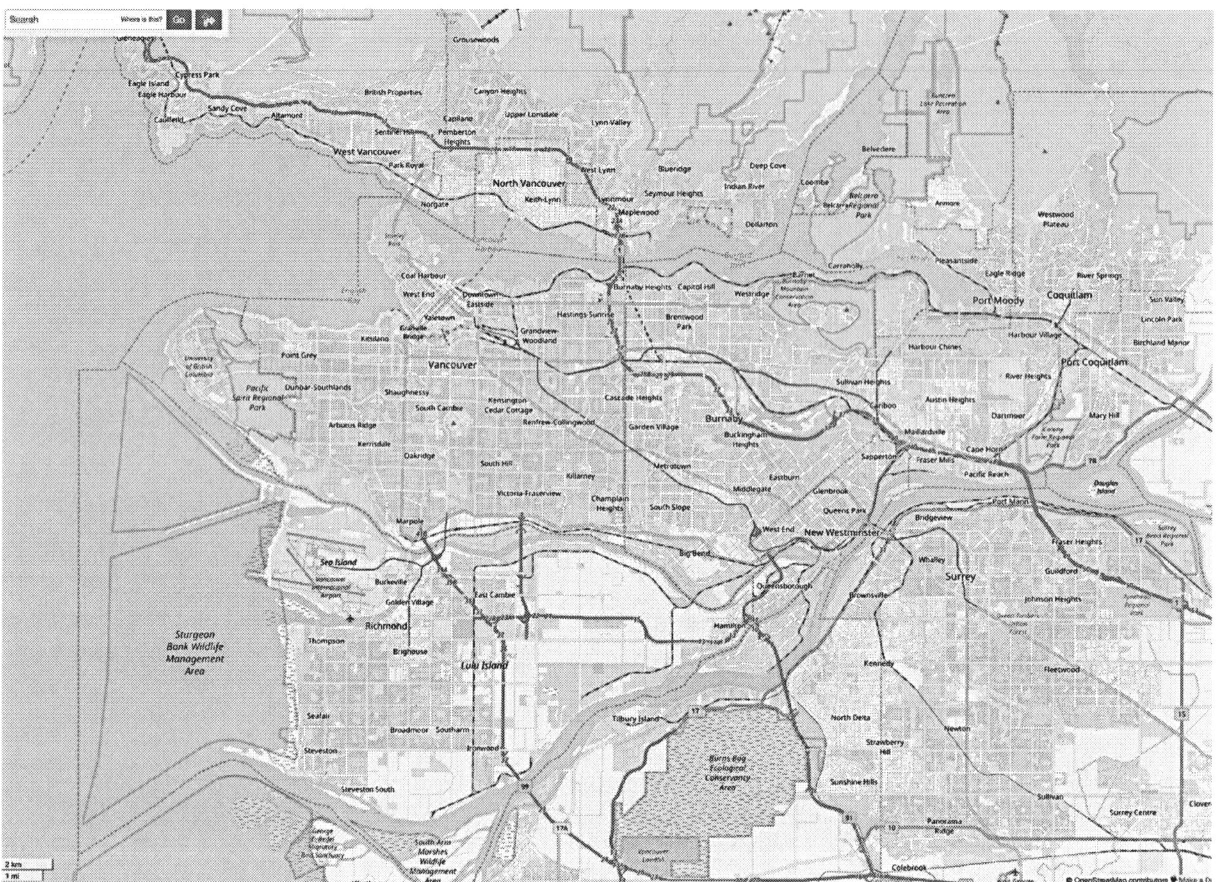

A detailed street map of central Vancouver (© OprnStreetMap contributors)

When you take an Alaska cruise, it will most likely either begin or end in Vancouver. There are a handful of Alaska cruises that begin or end in either Seattle or San Francisco, but they comprise a very small minority of cruise itineraries for Alaska.

Vancouver is truly the gateway to Alaska for cruise passengers. The question arises as to how much time to spend in Vancouver. My recommendation is clearly that you will be doing yourself a great injustice if you do not spend at least three days in this incredible city. As a former resident of the city, I say with confidence that Vancouver is the most dynamic and exciting city on the entire west coast of North America. It is one of the five most vibrant cities on the continent, one that you should not miss. Vancouver has far more than just a brash and bold skyline. This is a city with a character like no other. Yes it is Canadian. But it is also very Asian in flavor. And at the same time it has an international sophistication and cosmopolitan atmosphere akin to that of any major European city. No west coast city in the United States comes even close to having so many positive attributes as does Vancouver. So plan to do more than take a taxi between the airport and ship. Stay and become acquainted with this amazing and beautiful city of 2,900,000 people, Canada's third largest.

AN INCREDIBLE SETTING: The setting for Vancouver is spectacular. The city occupies a peninsula of land between the Fraser River to the south and the deep waters of Burrard Inlet to the north while fronting on the sheltered Georgia Straits to the west. The downtown area, West End and Stanley Park occupy a secondary peninsula that juts north like the thumb from a mitten. Snow-capped, thickly forested mountains rise immediately to the north of the inner harbor, presenting a magnificent backdrop for the city whose land area is rather hilly and still has many original stands of conifers, in particular the more than 2,023 hectares or 5,000 acres of Stanley Park. Vancouver, like Toronto, has been selected on several occasions by the United Nations as one of the world's five most livable cities. There is a true sense of drama to Vancouver. It is a city dominated over by its snow-covered mountains, rimmed by sparkling water and scented with cedar and hemlock forests. Yet it is an exceptionally cosmopolitan city.

The Vancouver-Victoria environment, however, is deceptive in its beauty for this region is part of the Pacific Rim. Just off the coast of Vancouver Island is a major subduction zone that runs the full length of the coast from northern California to southern Alaska. Every few hundred years, major slippage along this fault zone sets off a catastrophic earthquake. Geologists say it is presently overdue, and when it occurs, the impact will be quite devastating to cities from Portland, Oregon northward to Vancouver. So natural beauty often comes with a terrible price tag. What makes the earthquake prediction even more ominous is the intensive urban development of Vancouver with its major high-rise skyline. But Canadian building codes do consider fire, earthquake and other potential disasters.

Vancouver's climatic drawback to being a perfect Eden is the winter weather. The coastal region is part of the Marine West Coast climatic regime, which translates to long, chilly and gray winters with drizzly rain that can last for days, and sometimes weeks on end. I remember one rainy winter when we did not see the sun for just over four weeks. For some people, this is simply too much 'gloom." And on occasion, rain turns to snow for a day or so and then back to rain. But during summer the weather is almost perfect, if any location can be said to be so. Temperatures are in the upper teens and 20's Celsius or 70's and 80's Fahrenheit and most days are bright and sunny, with cool breezes coming off the water.

Vancouver is an impressive city in ways apart from its natural setting. The skyline is second only to that of Toronto. The downtown area is quite large and is bordered on the west by an area of dense high-rise apartments and condominiums, fronting on Stanley Park known as "The West End." The density of residential towers is intense, comparable to Manhattan, but with a more modern architectural flair and with plenty of green spaces between the high rise towers. Elsewhere in the city, there are neighborhood clusters of high-rises, thus giving Vancouver the same look as Toronto – a city of towers extending from the central core out into the suburbs. The downtown is noted for its major retail and entertainment districts as well as its selection of hotels and dining establishments. This is a city in which downtown is truly the focal hub of all major activities, making it exceptionally inviting. And with the large West End and Yaletown populations living within walking distance, the downtown caters to both local and tourist populations on an equal basis. For American visitors who remember the days when downtown was the focal hub of their cities, Vancouver brings back a level of nostalgia.

Vancouver is also a city of fine parks and public gardens, the most noted of which are Queen Elizabeth Park and Stanley Park, a 2,023 hectare or 5,000-acre reserve of natural woodland that was set aside in the very early years of the city's development. On the tip of the main peninsula that houses the bulk of the city lies The Domain, a major forest preserve that totally separates the campus of the University of British Columbia, located on Point Gray, from the rest of the city is even far larger than Stanley Park. The Domain is a bit of wild British Columbia located between the campus of the University of British Columbia and the Point Grey residential district.

In its ethnic composition, Vancouver shows a mix of European communities, especially German and Austrian plus the largest East Asian population in Canada. Because of the large exodus from Hong Kong prior to the 1997 takeover by Mainland China, the city of Vancouver now has over 500,000 Chinese residents, enabling some journalists to dub Vancouver as "Hongcouver." But since it has been seen that the Chinese government is not abusing personal rights in Hong Kong, many of those who fled to Vancouver have either returned to Hong Kong or share in the lives of both cities on an equal basis. Thus there is frequent air traffic between Vancouver and Hong Kong. There are also many European ethnic groups living in Vancouver. One of the largest is the German community, which gives the city some incredible bakeries and restaurants.

The city is a major manufacturing center, in particular wood products and food processing. It is also Canada's largest seaport, its trade being primarily oriented toward the Asian mainland. The commercial and industrial activities give Vancouver a good mix between industrial, retail and wholesale trade, transport services and financial activities. It is truly a well-rounded economic base that supports Vancouver.

THE DOWNTOWN CORE: Downtown Vancouver shares much in common with Toronto; however, it is not as large as its eastern counterpart. The true downtown of Vancouver occupies approximately three square kilometers or almost two square miles on the inner harbor side of the thumb that juts north from the main body of the city. Despite the potential for devastating earthquakes, downtown Vancouver displays an array of ultra-modern high-rise buildings with maximum heights of 50 stories. Given the dark winter days, buildings utilize a great amount of glass to provide interior light. In an earthquake environment there is a potential danger inherent in extensive glass use. But putting that potential danger aside, downtown Vancouver sparkles on sunny days and especially at night when the buildings are all lit up.

The retail component of downtown Vancouver is very significant, especially with the large numbers of professional people living adjacent to the core in both the West End and Yaletown. Downtown is still the best single venue for the variety of goods and services. The Pacific Centre Mall offers more diversity than any regional shopping mall. And the Hudson's Bay Company store is an exceptional example of the old fashioned complete department store that has been forsaken in most United States cities. A new Nordstrom store is quite striking and is one of the five largest stores in that exclusive chain. There are regional shopping centers, but many people still enjoy the downtown shopping experience.

In addition to the retail component, Vancouver's downtown is also home to the city's large convention center and in turn to all of the major international hotel chains. When it comes to restaurants and cafes, Vancouver's city center has a tremendous selection, including a wide variety of ethnic foods. Robson Street is the center for much of the downtown's gastronomy and nightlife. It would take a visitor many months of continuous dining to even begin to make a dent in the number of fine restaurants in the city center.

As the largest city in western Canada, and as the nation's great Pacific seaport, the financial component of downtown is especially important. The western regional offices of all of Canada's major banks, brokerage houses and insurance companies will be found in downtown Vancouver. The many large office blocks also are home to major law firms, accountant services, medical offices and other service organizations. Thus there is a major white-collar workforce that travels into and out of the city's downtown every day. Commuter rail connects downtown with suburbs in the far eastern Fraser Valley. And the city's Sky Train is a primarily elevated inter urban system connecting southern and near eastern suburbs with the city center while fast ferries link North Vancouver with downtown.

Entertainment venues are a final component of downtown Vancouver. There is the Queen Elizabeth Theater, many small playhouses and cinemas all within the downtown core. BC Place and Rogers Arena are the downtown areas two major sports facilities, hosting a varied menu of athletic events. In 2010, the city did play host to the winter Olympic games with the opening and closing ceremonies taking place at BC Place.

A BRIEF HISTORY: The Spanish were the first to explore what is now coastal British Columbia, possibly as early as 1579. But it was British explorer Captain George Vancouver who conducted detailed studies of the coastline, affixing many of the place names still used today. And of course the city is named in his honor. The first one to set foot on what is now land occupied by the city was the Scottish trader Simon Fraser who traveled down the river now named for him all the way to the western tip of what is presently Point Grey.

The first community to develop was New Westminster, one of today's major suburbs just east of the city along the Fraser River. In 1858, a small gold rush brought the town into being. It was not until 1862 that a sawmill was built in what is today North Vancouver, followed by mills on the south shore of the inlet. A mill located on the south shore in 1867 is the first known set of buildings in what would become Vancouver.

What would be called Gastown grew up outside of the Hastings Mill and by 1870 a proper town site was surveyed and named Granville. Because of the excellent anchorage for ships, the Canadian Pacific Railway chose it to become the western terminus for the transcontinental railroad, a choice that upset the residents of New Westminster who had planned that their town would become the major city of the far west. The City of Vancouver became official on April 6, 1886 just prior to the arrival of the first train from the east.

The city was constructed primarily of wood and in June of the same year as incorporation it suffered from a major conflagration, burning most of the buildings. Later construction included stone and brick to give the city more stability with regard to fire.

Vancouver and Seattle both became major trade centers and ports partly because of the impact of the Klondike Gold Rush of 1898. By the end of the first decade of the 20th century Vancouver's population had reached 100,000. And growth has been steady ever since, as the city has been a magnet for young eastern Canadians who have dreamed of making a name for themselves out west.

As a port, Vancouver developed trade ties with Asia. And it also became a major center for processing lumber. False Creek, which today is the center of fashionable residential districts, was once the focus of timber milling with logs jamming the waterway. With close ties to Asia, the city saw an influx of Chinese and Japanese immigrants, and Canadians did not show any more tolerance than did Americans in the cities of the west. During World War II, Japanese residents were also removed from coastal areas, as was true across the border to the south.

During the 1960's, Vancouver began to experience rapid growth in all of its economic sectors, especially with increasing trade abroad. It became a major financial center and attracted young Canadians as well as European immigrants. By 1970, it has well over 1,000,000 residents and it began to exhibit a dramatic high-rise skyline as its eastern counterpart city of Toronto. Today both cities unofficially vie with one another to see whose skyline is more dramatic. So far Toronto is winning in both height and overall size of its downtown, but it does have twice the population of Vancouver.

SIGHTS TO EXPLORE: Vancouver will either be your port of embarkation or the termination of your Alaska cruise. I strongly recommended a visit rather than simply taking a taxi or shuttle to the airport. This is just too grand and exciting a city to miss. Sightseeing in Vancouver can be accomplished in numerous ways. These include:

*** Hiring a car and driver/guide – This is the most personalized, yet most expensive way to see the city. All four and five-star hotel concierges can take care of booking the car and will charge the fee to your room account. There are so many companies that offer the service, making it difficult for me to recommend one, whereas in the small ports there are generally one or two limousine companies that offer this service.**

*** Renting a car – I have lived in Vancouver in the past and thus I know my way around. But I do not recommend it if you have never visited the city before. Traffic is rather heavy and with the many waterways that dissect the urban landscape, it is a bit difficult to get around unless you are familiar with the street and bridge accesses.**

*** Hop on hop off busses – Vancouver does offer hop on hop off bus services that will take you to most of the major sightseeing venues. Your hotel concierge can advise you as to where you can board the bus. Tickets are generally purchased at the time you board. For more detail you can click onto their web page at *<u>www.westcoastsightseeing.com</u>*.**

*** Public transit – Getting around Vancouver without an automobile is not too difficult. There are busses and electric trolley busses providing coverage on all major streets. There is no rail service for passenger use west of Granville Street, which includes approximately half of Vancouver proper. Vancouver does have a Metro called the Sky Train. Apart from in the immediate inner city and a portion of the southern residential area around Queen Elizabeth Gardens, it runs above ground on elevated concrete causeways. This affords the visitor some great views of the city, but it does not provide access to many outer residential and suburban venues. The main line operates between downtown and the far southeastern suburb of Surrey across the Fraser River. A second line runs south and branches to the Vancouver International Airport and the suburban city of Richmond. There are numerous tourist venues than can be accessed via the Sky Train. Your hotel concierge should be able to provide you with maps and information for the city's Trans Link bus and sky train lines. You can also click onto their web page at *www.translink.ca.***

There are many specific venues for visitors within the central core of Vancouver. The most important ones are listed alphabetically below with a brief description and opening/closing hours where needed:

*** BC Place – This is the large indoor stadium used for sports events, concerts and major political gatherings. It is located in Yaletown, which is a newer community development south of the downtown core. For event information check their web page to see if anything is scheduled during your visit to the city. Their web page is *www.bcplace.com.***

*** Canada Place – This combination hotel, shopping and dining complex, IMAX theater and cruise ship terminal sits at the foot of Howe or Burrard Streets in the downtown waterfront district. The building's unique architecture is reminiscent of sails on the water and has become an iconic symbol of the city in the same way that the Sydney Opera House has in Australia. The various venues maintain separate opening and closing hours, but the building is accessible seven days per week.**

*** Chinatown - Similar in nature to Chinatown in Toronto, Pender Street is a working Chinese community that is not specifically oriented toward tourism. It is here that one can get a bit of the feel of Hong Kong. Shops and restaurants are open most evenings as well as during daylight hours.**

*** Dr. Sun Yat Sen Gardens – Located in Chinatown at 578 Carrall Street, this classical garden in the old Chinese tradition honors the great cultural leader. It is a beautiful place for meditation or to just relax and soak in its flavor. The garden is open from 10 AM to 4:30 PM Tuesday thru Sunday and is a must see venue when visiting Chinatown.**

*** Edgewater Casino – Located in Yaletown along False Creek, this is a major gaming establishment comparable to the Casino de Montréal. It is open 24 hours a day.**

*** Gastown – A restored waterfront district south of the main Sky Train terminal, the buildings and street lamps (gas fired) take one back to the 19th century Vancouver. This**

district is filled with cafes, gift shops and other venues that cater heavily to visitors. Most shops and cafes stay open into the mid evening hours.

*** Granville Island – Located in False Creek, Granville Island and the entire creek once was heavily a part of the lumber industry. Today the shops and markets of the island offer the finest in gastronomy that the city has to offer for both take home and local dining. The entire False Creek shoreline is today high value commercial and residential real estate. The Granville Market is open daily from 9 AM to 7 PM and is the crown jewel of the island.**

*** Robson Street – This major street stretches from the Yaletown area all the way to Stanley Park. It is a focal part of the downtown core, lined with restaurants, bistros, bakeries, boutiques, hotels and apartment blocks. It was once the heart of the German community, and traces of Germanic culture are still integrated into its character.**

*** Rogers Arena – The smaller sports venue in Yaletown, home to Vancouver's hockey team, The Canucks. Rogers Arena does offer tours when there are no events scheduled. For tour details or tickets for events, check their web page at *www.rogersarena.com.***

*** Science World at TELUS – This is the Vancouver science museum and interactive center located at the upper end of False Creek. It is open Monday thru Friday 10 AM to 5 PM, Saturday until 6 PM and Sunday only until 1 PM.**

*** Stanley Park – The largest city park in Canada, covering over 5,000 acres of mostly natural maritime rain forest. There are many special venues within this massive park that occupies the tip of the thumb on which the downtown core and the high-rise apartment and condominium neighborhood called the West End is located. The sub venues include:**

**** Brockton Point Lighthouse – at the eastern most tip of the park where one gets a great view of the downtown skyline and the entire inner harbor. The lighthouse is open 24 hours per day every day of the week.**

**** Park Drive – The outer road that runs around the entire five-mile perimeter of the park. If you have a car and driver or take one of the city bus tours, you will have a chance to experience this beautiful forest drive in the very heart of the city.**

**** The Sea Wall – A pedestrian walkway that runs around the outer edge of the park, following the natural shoreline.**

**** The Teahouse – A famous landmark on the western shore of the park where tea and light refreshments can be enjoyed. When locals partake of the entire sea wall walk, it is often customary to stop into the teahouse for refreshments. It is open daily from 10:30 AM to 10 PM.**

****Totem Poles – Just prior to reaching Brockton Point there is a large collection of native British Columbia tribal totem poles. The totem poles are outdoors and always accessible.**

*** Vancouver Aquarium – This spectacular exhibition is located within Stanley Park. It is open from 10 AM to 5 PM daily. It does showcase the marine life of the Pacific Coast. And the research facility is engaged in a variety of projects to protect the marine environment.**

*** Vancouver Art Gallery – On Georgia Street in the former old Law Court, the gallery houses a diverse collection of art. It is open from 10 AM to 5 PM daily with extended evening until 9 PM on Tuesday. Their web page provides valuable details regarding special shows and events as well as providing basic information regarding the regular collection. Visit them on line at *www.vanartgallery.bc.ca.***

*** Vancouver Convention Centrer – Located along the harbor at the foot of Burrard Street in Canada Place, the center extends out over the water and is noted for its spectacular modern architecture. Their web page presents an ongoing calendar of events. Visit them at *www.vancouverconventioncentre.com.***

*** Vancouver Lookout – Perched high atop the 555 West Hastings Street, this revolving lookout gives one a fantastic view of the entire city and its surrounding mountains and waterways. On a clear day it is possible to see the mountains of Vancouver Island across the Georgia Straits and even far off Mt. Baker, the snow covered volcanic peak just across the border in Washington state. The lookout is open daily from 9 AM to 9 PM and advanced reservations are not necessary.**

Vancouver is a city of distinctive neighborhoods, however, most do not have a strong ethnic component. The Vancouver neighborhoods are based more upon location and economics. The manner in which the physical geography separates the urban area, it is not difficult to see defined neighborhoods separated from one another by geography. The major neighborhoods are (shown alphabetically):

*** East End is probably the least seen part of Vancouver by visitors, as this is the lower income blue-collar part of the city. Here the houses, built mainly out of wood or unpainted gray stucco, and they are rather tightly packed and lack more of the unique architectural elements seen in the more fashionable neighborhoods. There is also a relatively strong mixed ethnic component to the East End, yet there are no real distinctive ethnic districts.**

*** Kitsilano Beach is one of the trendiest neighborhoods in the city. In the early 20th century, smaller late Victorian bungalows were built within the first few blocks of the beach, as this was a very popular summer venue and many people decided that they wanted to live here year around. As the city grew in the 1960's, and as the West End skyline developed, the views from Kitsilano Beach became exceedingly popular, only adding to the value of this very distinctive neighborhood. Today many low-rise condominiums and town houses are being built in Kitsilano, giving this area its especially high degree of trendy real estate value**

*** Point Grey is a somewhat hilly residential district that is located east of Kitsilano Beach, and bordering The Domain, that vast forest preserve that separates the city from the University of British Columbia. Property values in Point Grey have gone off the chart. Once**

again it is the views that many properties have combined with proximity to the University of British Columbia that has made this a most favored neighborhood.

*** Shaughnessy – Located about 1.5 kilometers south of False Creek, the land rises along a short ridge starting at 15th Avenue. Here many early 20th century mansions, often with very strong British architectural styles, were built, as the views over the city and harbor made this choice real estate. The neighborhood was developed by the Canadian Pacific Railroad as an alternative to the residential development of the West End. Today the magnificent old homes of Shaughnessy Heights are highly sought after properties, selling in the millions of dollars.**

*** West End is one of the most geographically distinct neighborhoods in the city. It is located between the landward border of Stanley Park and the downtown core. Having developed in the late 19th century, there are still a few surviving old Victorian mansions left in the West End. But essentially this is the city's most sought after high-rise neighborhood because of its walking distance proximity to downtown, its beautiful English Bay Beach and the recreational advantages of Stanley Park right on its doorstep. Apartments and condominiums are expensive, thus this is not a favored location for young families. Most people living in the West End are young or seniors. The apartments and condominiums are not overly large, thus not compatible for families. Denman Avenue is the primary shopping street, offering many fine quality gourmet food shops, bakeries, cafes and other essentials. Many who cannot afford to live here or for whom it is not practical due to family commitments tend to envy the residents of the West End.**

*** Yaletown is a newly developed district bordering on False Creek, and like the West End its boundaries are distinct. It has False Creek forming a natural boundary and then to the west and northwest it merges with downtown. Yaletown has developed with an exceptionally high density of apartment and condominium blocks, giving it a highly congested appearance. Like the West End this is a neighborhood favored by the young white-collar community.**

The major suburban communities of interest are (shown alphabetically):

*** Burnaby and New Westminister are among the earlier suburban areas to develop immediately east of the city. They were also characterized by the same type of housing as seen in the east end of the city, but today there is a strong emphasis upon high-rise apartments and condominiums, especially along the Sky Train route. Burnaby Town Centre is a major area for retail shopping and high-rise development, as it is the midway point on the Sky Train between downtown and New Westminster. Despite today being a suburb, New Westminster, located on the Fraser River, predates the founding of Vancouver.**

*** North Vancouver and West Vancouver are the two suburban cities that occupy the North Shore, reached via Lion's Gate Bridge or from the far eastern side via the Second Narrows Bridge. With only a short foreshore the land rises rapidly uphill toward the mountains. Thus most housing in these two suburban communities has views out over the central city. West Vancouver also has a very significant shoreline of expensive high-rises that offer waterfront living with a view of Stanley Park. There are also very elegant and exceptionally expensive**

homes in West Vancouver and above it in a development called British Properties. Many years ago, the Sultan of Brunei wanted to buy a large waterfront home in West Vancouver, lending the prestige of his royal title to the city's residents. However, he wanted a variance to be allowed to have a helipad on his property. The city council members turned him down and the sultan went elsewhere. This shows the tenacity of high-end residents in Vancouver when it comes to their peace and quiet.

There are many other neighborhoods that comprise greater Vancouver, but the ones presented thus far cover a good portion of the city, especially areas where visitors might either deliberately visit or pass through en route to major suburban venues. These important suburban venues include the following major sites that should not be missed (shown alphabetically):

*** Capilano Suspension Bridge – Located in North Vancouver and spanning Capilano Creek, this bridge that was originally made of hemp rope dates to 1889. But over the years it has been rebuilt and strengthened with steel cable, spanning 430 feet and at 230 feet above the rushing waters of the creek. The bridge is open from 8 AM to 8 PM daily during summer, 9 AM to 6 Pm starting September 1.**

*** Grouse Mountain – This peak above North Vancouver is 4,000 feet high and contains an extensive series of ski runs. Grouse Mountain is the nearest ski facility, literally within the city, as residents living in the West End can watch skiers with binoculars. To reach the top of the mountain, the popular Sky Ride is a traditional gondola that was built in Austria. It makes the nearly 61-meter or 2,000 foot climb in a matter of minutes. For those who just wish to enjoy the view at all seasons, there is excellent dining at the top. The Sky Ride to the top is open daily from 8:45 AM to 10 PM, weather permitting.**

*** Metropolis at Metrocentre – One of the larges shopping malls in Vancouver, surrounded by a massive high-rise residential complex. Metropolis can be reached from downtown Vancouver in 20 minutes via the Sky Train. It is open from 10 AM to 9 PM daily, 11 AM to 6 PM Sunday.**

*** Pacific Spirit Regional Park – Separating the city from the campus of the University of British Columbia, this massive park composed primarily of native forest was once crown land. The park is open daily from 7 AM to 5 PM.**

*** Queen Elizabeth Gardens – Located off Cambie Street south of the city center, a one-time rock quarry has been turned into a beautiful Asian style botanical garden. There is also a glassed in conservatory that features a tropical rainforest environment replete with a myriad of birds.**

*** Simon Fraser University – This very modern campus located atop Burnaby Mountain with spectacular city views has been the site of the filming of many science fiction movies or episodes, especially for Star Trek. The futuristic architecture of the campus is worth any visitor's attention, as it is totally unique and even now in the 21st century, it is still futuristic.**

SIGHTS OF IMPORTANCE OUTSIDE OF THE CITY: There are many interesting places to visit outside of greater Vancouver, but you will need several extra days. This is why even though I recommended at least three days in Vancouver, if you can afford more time, a week is a more logical approach to seeing the city and its surroundings. Many travelers make Vancouver a destination in its own right. I can well understand that when you have booked an Alaska cruise, it is a matter of time and added cost to include a lengthy stay in Vancouver. But for those of you who are combining the two destinations, here are my recommendations for the most significant locations to visit outside of the city:

*** Harrison Hot Springs – Located in the mountains east of Vancouver, this popular lakeside community with its hot springs is a popular weekend getaway for local residents. If you have a rental car or a car and driver/guide, a day trip to Harrison Hot Springs gives you a chance to enjoy some of the spectacular scenery of the Lower Mainland of British Columbia. You will motor through the Fraser River Valley, a lush agricultural region under the shadow of the coastal mountains to the north and Mt. Baker, the lofty volcanic peak just across the border on the south. It takes around two hours to reach Harrison Hot Springs where you can walk the waterfront promenade, have a nice lunch in one of its small cafes or at the Harrison Hot Springs Hotel before motoring back to the city. En route you can take the Trans-Canada Highway and on the return follow the slower Lougheed Highway, which is provincial route seven.**

*** Victoria: A one-day outing to Victoria, the provincial capital of British Columbia, is also an enjoyable experience. Even without a car, it is possible to take a motor coach from downtown Vancouver, easily arranged by your hotel. The coach will proceed to one of two ferryboat crossings and then take the approximately two-hour boat crossing from Tsawwassen Point to Vancouver Island and proceed on to the city of Victoria. Surprisingly it is not easier and faster to go with a car, which you can rent from one of several agencies in downtown Vancouver. A scheduled motor coach is given top priority in boarding the ferryboat whereas a car is not given any special consideration. But if you do decide to make the trip by car, which I have done many times, be sure to leave in the morning, as it takes about 30 minutes to drive to the southern crossing at Tsawwassen Point. Upon arrival, you will be directed to one of several large parking lots where cars will be lined up in rows. Each lot represents the number of cars capable of being placed on one ferryboat. If you are fortunate, you will be in the first lot. That is why I recommend a morning crossing. From Tsawwassen it takes about one and a half hours to cross and then another 20 minutes to reach the city. You can still enjoy the day in Victoria, but remember that you need to do the crossing in reverse on the way back to Vancouver, so it will be a long day.**

With a short time in Victoria, I recommend the following sights (shown alphabetically):

**** Beacon Hill Park - Be sure to visit Milepost Zero of the Trans-Canada Highway in the park, which is open 24-hours a day. This is also one of the most beautiful of city parks.**

**** British Columbia Parliament Building and its beautiful grounds. You will not have time to take a tour without sacrificing other sights to see in the short time you are in Victoria.**

**** Butchart Gardens - If you have an hour or more to spare, you can stop at Butchart Gardens, one of the world's most magnificent botanical garden and one of the highlights of any visit to western Canada, just off the main road back to the ferry terminal at Swartz Bay. Some people will make the crossing just to visit the gardens rather than the city of Victoria. The gardens are open daily from 9 AM to 9 PM. If gardens are important to you, my recommendation is to make this your focus of the visit rather than the city of Victoria.**

**** Government Street - Walk a few blocks and take in all the fancy English china shops on this main shopping street of Victoria. Government Street has a very British flavor. Some say it is even more British than England.**

**** Oak Bay - Drive along Beach Avenue in Oak Bay and enjoy the beautiful homes, each elegantly landscaped. Oak Bay is one of the most elegant residential districts in all of western Canada.**

**** Royal British Columbia Museum - This museum is especially well known for its exhibits on the Pacific Northwest tribes, and its totem poles, which also represent the various coastal tribes of Alaska. It is open from 10 AM to 5 PM Tuesday thru Sunday. Closed on Monday.**

The city of Victoria, (© OpenStreetMap contributors)

*** Whistler – This is the most famous ski resort in Canada, and it was home to the ski events for the 2010 Vancouver Winter Olympic Games. It is 121 kilometers or 75 miles from the downtown core, taking approximately 1.5 to two hours travel time depending upon how many times you stop. Whistler is a series of villages composed mainly of vacation properties**

mixed with restaurants, gift shops, ski outfitters and boutiques. It is comparable to America's Aspen or any of the major European ski resorts. The ski slopes are as well-equipped as the finest slopes in Europe. During summer some of the lifts or gondolas operate to take visitors to high overlooks where the views of the coastal mountains are spectacular. In most years there is still spring or summer skiing at the higher elevations.

HOTEL RECOMMENDATIONS: Vancouver will be either the starting point or terminus of your Alaska cruise. I do advise spending a few days in this incredible and beautiful city. I am offering my recommendations for the top four and five star hotels in the city. These are my choices in alphabetical order:

*** Fairmont Hotel Vancouver is one of the most venerable hotels in the city, located at 900 West Georgia Street in the heart of the city. Canadian National Railroad built the hotel, as part of its program to provide luxury accommodation in all of the major cities of the country. The hotel has 557 guest rooms, which Fairmont has been renovating and upgrading as an ongoing project. There is a wide range of categories of guest rooms from standard to deluxe and the hotel does offer special needs accommodation. The Fairmont Gold level offers concierge service, breakfast, afternoon tea and evening canapés long with the privacy and comfort of a traditional club level. I GIVE IT *******

*** Fairmont Pacific Rim is located at 1038 Canada Place just opposite the Convention Centre West Building. Like the Shangri la, this is another gleaming high-rise tower that is quite a dominant feature on the waterfront. All 367 guest rooms and suites are magnificently designed and feature all of the latest high tech amenities. And 70 percent of the rooms offer striking views of the harbor and mountains while the other 30 percent offer vibrant city views. Guest rooms offer a variety of views and all average between 37 and 41 square meters or 400 to 450 square feet. There is also a selection of larger suites with very stunning harbor and mountain views. There is a Fairmont Gold level, which offers full concierge service with breakfast, tea and afternoon libations. The hotel has several fine dining options that include Oru, a gourmet dining room, Giovane Cafe and Market for more casual dining and the Lobby Lounge and Raw Bar for libations and lighter dining options. And 24/7 room service is provided. A beautiful outdoor pool, full service spa and fitness center are available, as are meeting facilities. I GIVE IT ******

*** Fairmont Waterfront is another beautiful property located at 900 Canada Place Way just opposite the Pan Pacific Vancouver Hotel and cruise ship terminal. The hotel is essentially in the very heart of the city and convenient for convention visitors or those either embarking on or returning from a cruise. The hotel offers standard, terrace, partial harbor view, signature harbor and corner harbor views, plus very beautiful suites. The hotel also offers a Fairmont Gold concierge level with breakfast, afternoon tea and evening libations and appetizers. The hotel has one main dining room serving distinctive cuisine and it also offers 24/7 room service. An outdoor pool and fitness center are provided. I GIVE IT ******

*** Four Seasons Hotel Vancouver - Located at CF Pacific Centre, 791 West Georgia Street, this is one of the venerable members of the Four Seasons worldwide chain of five star hotels. Like all Four Seasons properties, this one in Vancouver offers a full array of luxury rooms**

and suites plus excellent dining facilities. Service is always the hallmark of a Four Seasons property. Guest accommodation consists of 372 rooms that are graded from premier to deluxe to superior depending upon size, floor and view. There is no special club level offered, and every guest receives the same level of care. There are two dining rooms with Yew Seafood being the specialty restaurant. There is also 24/7 room service. The hotel also offers a full service spa and an indoor/outdoor pool. There is direct access for guests to the Pacific Centre Mall, the largest downtown shopping center in the city. I GIVE IT ***

* Hyatt Regency Hotel located in the city center at 655 Burrard Street is one of my favorites even though I said I would not make any specific recommendations. This 32-story hotel is another long standing property that has developed a good reputation over the years. Guest accommodation offers a variety of choices from standard to deluxe rooms and suites. And the Regency Club level provides that added attention that many regular guests desire. Given the number of tall buildings in downtown Vancouver, not all rooms have choice views, but those that do are the most in demand, as the views can be quite spectacular. All of the rooms are luxurious and modern, as the hotel is always being upgraded to meet current standards. The Mosaic Grill and the Mosaic Bar offer meal service with the grill being a full service restaurant with an extensive menu. The bar offers light snacks and appetizers. There is 24/7 room service. The hotel offers a heated outdoor pool, fitness room and full service spa. And the property is in the very heart of shopping, dining and entertainment. I GIVE IT *****

* Pan Pacific Vancouver is conveniently located in the Pan Pacific Centre, which also includes the city's large convention center and exhibition hall as well as the major cruise ship terminal. The designated address is Suite 300-999, Canada Place Vancouver. There are three categories of guest rooms that grade from deluxe to deluxe with harbor view to premier that also offer sweeping harbor and mountain views. There are three categories of suites that have both city or harbor views and the largest have panoramic harbor views. There are also large suites that are essentially residential in their size and amenities. The hotel offers several dining options from the Ocean 999 with sweeping views while you dine. Coal Harbour Bar offers libations and snacks. Five Sails Restaurant is a AAA four-diamond dining room and the Patio Terrace offers outdoor dining during the warmer months. And 24/7 room service is provided. A large swimming pool, a full service spa and a fitness center complete the hotel facilities. There are also meeting and banquet rooms. I GIVE IT ****

* Residence Inn by Marriott – This is a more budget friendly hotel, but one with many of the amenities of the higher priced properties. It is located at 1234 Hornby Street just outside the heart of the downtown core. The hotel offers comfortable accommodation, restaurant facilities, breakfast included in the tariff, room service, indoor pool, fitness center and conference facilities. I GIVE IT ***

* Rosewood Hotel Georgia is one of the city's historic hotel properties located at 801 West Georgia Street in the very heart of the city. There is an Old World classic feeling of elegance to the hotel, yet it offers all of the most modern amenities and conveniences. Guest rooms are spacious and fully stocked with all of the extra touches you expect in a first class hotel. Rooms are graded from superior to deluxe to premier executive depending upon their size and location, but even the smallest guest room is much larger than usually found in the newer**

high-rise hotels. There is a range of suites that is sure to please the most discerning guest. There is no club level available. Unlike the more modern high-rise hotels, the Rosewood Hotel Georgia offers several dining options. Prohibition is a lounge and restaurant with a Roaring 20's atmosphere. Hawksworth is a casual restaurant serving breakfast, lunch, dinner and Sunday brunch. Bel Cafe is a casual eatery with delicious soups, sandwiches and elegantly baked pastries and cakes. Room service is available. The hotel also has an indoor pool, full service spa and fitness center. I GIVE IT ****

*** Shangri la Hotel is located at 1128 West Georgia Street between the heart of the downtown and the West End. This gleaming new high-rise towers above the surrounding buildings and this assures you that every room on the middle and upper floors has a superb view of the city, Stanley Park or the inner harbor. The guest rooms are large, especially elegant and are tastefully furnished with a distinct Asian flair, as you would expect from the Shangri la group. And each room has a large picture window. Rooms graduate from superior to deluxe to executive balcony king with a variety of suites offered as well. There is no designated club level in the hotel. The hotel's main restaurant is known as Market, and it offers three-star Michelin cuisine. And 24/7 room service is also provided. The hotel offers an outdoor pool, a full service spa and a fitness center. There are also meeting rooms for special events. I GIVE IT ******

*** Sylvia Hotel – Located in the West End right on English Bay, this is a rather unknown hotel except by its loyal following. If you are looking for a budget friendly hotel with few frills, but one that is especially clean, well-run and has an Old World charm, then I do recommend the Sylvia. I used to live one block away and put up may visiting guests here. The hotel has a nice restaurant and lounge, offers room service, has breakfast included, free parking and does have a small gym and fitness center. You will not find glitz and glamour but you will find comfort at a good price. I GIVE IT *****

*** Sutton Place Hotel Vancouver – At 845 Burrard Street, this hotel offers very good comfort and value for the money. It has a restaurant, room service, indoor pool, spa and fitness center, concierge, banquet and meeting rooms. It is the west coast equivalent of the Sutton Place Toronto, which has a loyal following who expect quality service and comfort I GIVE IT ******

*** Trump International Hotel and Tower – Now the tallest tower in Vancouver, this well-known hotel brand offers luxury with the "glitz" and flair of other Trump hotels. It is located at 1161 West Georgia Street in the city center. Guest rooms and suites have an ultra-modern vibe, but with such distinctive features as hardwood floors and massive floor to ceiling windows to take in the view. The hotel offers all the major amenities of any five-star property such as a stylish restaurant, luxurious spa and fitness center, business center, indoor pool, concierge service, room service and valet parking. The hotel also has meeting and banquet room facilities. I GIVE IT *******

*** Westin Bayshore Vancouver is located at 1601 Bayshore Drive just west of the city center, situated on the harbor just opposite Stanley Park across the marina. It has easy access to The Seawall, the beautiful outer walkway around the park perimeter. The hotel consists of**

the original lower building that was the original Bayshore Inn plus the addition of the high-rise tower. Rooms grade from city view to harbor view and then there are the premium tower rooms with either a city or harbor view. In addition the hotel offers suites. All rooms have large picture windows and all have been designed for modern elegance and comfort. There is no designated club level. The hotel restaurants include Currents, which serves breakfast and the Seawall Bar and Grill open for lunch, dinner and Sunday brunch. And 24/7 room service is provided. The hotel provides workout facilities and has a full service spa. There is a beautiful outdoor pool with surrounding gardens, but this is not utilized during the damp winter months. And there are large meeting and banquet facilities. I GIVE IT **

DINING OUT: Vancouver is a great city for experiencing fresh seafood and also Asian cuisine. There are literally thousands of restaurants and cafes, but I have selected only those that I personally have enjoyed and recommend to you. Here are my choices, listed alphabetically, for great dining in Vancouver with an emphasis upon seafood and Canadian specialties:

* AnnaLena is a distinctive Canadian restaurant with a short, but very delectable menu. The restaurant is located at 1809 West 1st Avenue in Kitsilano just one block west of Burrard Street after coming off the bridge over False Creek. It is necessary to have a private car or take a taxi, as this is too far from the city center for walking. The restaurant is open only for dinner from 5 PM to 12 AM and reservations are necessary.

* Bao Bei Chinese Brasserie is located at 162 Keefer Street, two blocks south of Hastings Street and half a block west of Main Street. It cannot be reached on the Sky Train without a significant walk, thus a private car or taxi is needed. This is a well-known Chinese restaurant with outstanding quality and freshness. Their menu is limited to a select few items and this is not your typical Canadian Chinese restaurant. Each dish here is expertly made and is unique. I suggest checking the on line menu prior to reserving a table, as it is quite unique. It is only open for dinner from 5:30 PM to Midnight (11 PM on Sunday) and you should make a reservation.

* Bacchus Restaurant – In the city center at 845 Hornby Street, this restaurant features a menu that combines Canadian with European cuisine in a very unique and flavorful way. The ambiance and service compliment their delicious menu. Seafood figures prominently along with beef, lamb and poultry dishes combined with the freshest seasonal ingredients. And they most always receive the highest of rave reviews. They serve Monday thru Friday from 6:30 AM to 11:30 PM and on weekends from 7 AM to 11 PM. I would strongly recommend a reservation for the evening meal.

* Bauhaus Restaurant – This fine dining establishment is located at 1 Cordova Street West and is rated as one of the finer restaurants for contemporary European cuisine. There is an emphasis upon German and Central European dishes. And one of their features is a tasting menu where you can experience a variety of flavors. They normally receive rave reviews for the quality and presentation of each dish and have a loyal repeat clientele. They only serve lunch Friday from 11:30 AM to 2:30 PM. Dinner is served Sunday thru Thursday from 5 to**

10:30 PM, Friday and Saturday from 5 to 11 PM. Reservations are strongly recommended and your hotel concierge should call on your behalf.

*** Blue Water Cafe is located at 1095 Hamilton Street in Yaletown, which is on the downtown peninsula just a few blocks north of False Creek. You can take the Canada Line Sky Train from Waterfront Station to Yaletown Roundhouse Station and walk one block west on Davies Street then one block north on Hamilton Street. This restaurant is noted for its quality seafood and the menu is brimming with delectable choices. And there are dishes for meat eaters as well. They only serve dinner between 5 and 11 PM and reservations should be made.**

***Chongqing is a popular chain of Chinese Sichuan restaurants, the most convenient location for visitors being at 1260 Robson Street in the city center and close to the West End, easy walking from all major hotels. They are open daily from 11:30 AM to 10:30 PM, serving lunch and dinner, and they offer a great variety of the typically spicy Sichuan dishes. Reservations should only be made during peak dining hours. They will also deliver to hotel suites in the city center and West End.**

*** CinCin Restaurante is conveniently located at 1154 Robson Street close to all major city center and West End hotels. This is an Italian restaurant with a very traditional Old World atmosphere. It serves in the true Italian style where dinner begins with an appetizer followed by a pasta course, main course of meat or seafood and then dessert. And all dishes are quite authentic. Lunch is served from 11:30 AM to 2:30 PM and dinner from 4:30 to 11 PM. I would recommend a reservation except if you are dining very early.**

*** Fable Restaurant at 1944 West 4th Avenue in Kitsilano is another fine eatery that offers what is considered to be farm to table cuisine. You will need a private car or taxi to reach Fable, as it is too far from the city center to walk. Lunch is rather basic with hearty burgers, sandwiches, eggs Benedict and grilled cheese while the dinner menu offers fish, beef, pork duck and pasta entrees with several distinct Canadian comfort food appetizers and of course some rich desserts. Lunch is served weekdays from 11:30 AM to 2 PM and dinner is from 5 to 10 PM daily. Weekend brunch is served from 10:30 AM to 2 PM.**

*** Forage – Located at 1300 Robson Street, this restaurant specializes in traditional Canadian cuisine, which many visitors find quite unexpected, anticipating that it would be similar to American cuisine. Seafood, wild game, fish soups and local seasonal vegetables offer the diner a real taste of British Columbia. I believe every non Canadian visitor should at least once be exposed to Canadian cuisine, and Forage is one of the best venues. They are open Monday thru Friday from 6:30 to 10 AM for breakfast, Sunday thru Thursday from 5 to 10 PM for dinner, Saturday and Sunday from 7 AM to 2 PM for breakfast and Friday and Saturday from 5 to 11 PM for dinner. Reservations for dinner are recommended.**

*** Joe Fortes Seafood & Chop House is located on the edge of the West End at 777 Thurlow Street just half a block north of Robson Street, easy to reach from all major hotels. Open daily from 11 AM to 11 Pm with reservations suggested. This is a beautiful old style restaurant and oyster bar and it also has a rooftop patio that is nice during the summer months. The specialties are seafood, steaks and chops. The oyster selection is quite extensive**

and even includes those from Prince Edward Island as well as the Pacific Northwest Coast. Clam chowder, lobster bisque, chilled salads, and a great variety of fresh fish and shellfish are available as well as fish and chips, fish cakes and a variety of sides. Steaks and chops are also featured on the dinner menu along with an even larger selection of seafood dishes.

*** Kingyo located at 871 Denman Street is in the heart of the West End's main shopping district. A private car or taxi will be needed, although in good weather it is an enjoyable walk from the city center and takes about 30 minutes. It is open from 11:30 AM to 2:30 PM for lunch and from 5:30 to 11:30 PM for dinner. Reservations are advised. The atmosphere and decor are what you would find in Japan, as is the menu. The menu features an array of appetizers, salads, sashimi, raw tapas, stone cooked meats including Kobe beef, seafood dishes and of course a beautiful selection of sushi. Miso and udon and tan tan noodles are also served.**

*** Maenam is a very beautiful Thai restaurant at 1938 West 4th Avenue in Kitsilano. You will need a private car or taxi to get here from the city center, as it is not close to any Sky Train station. They have a diverse Thai menu for both lunch and dinner that is very traditional and not the run of the mill offerings you will find in so many restaurants claiming to be authentic Thai. Lunch is served Tuesday thru Saturday from 12 to 2 PM. Dinner is served daily from 5 to 10 PM.**

*** Miku is located at 200 Granville Street at the foot of the city center across from Canada Place and Cruise Terminal. They are open daily from 11:30 AM to 10 PM and reservations are recommended. Miku is a traditional Japanese restaurant serving a limited, but very carefully planned menu at lunch and dinner, featuring the freshest ingredients. Their bar bites menu features light dishes including several types of beautifully prepared sushi.**

*** Minami Restaurant is an outstanding seafood restaurant serving in Japanese style. It is located at 1118 Mainland Street in Yaletown. It can be reached on the Canada Line Sky Train from Waterfront Station to Yaletown Roundhouse Station and then one block north on Mainland Street. Open daily from 11:30 AM to 10 PM with reservations recommended. Their lunch menu is not extensive, but each dish is very traditional and expertly prepared, including sushi, soba, Jidori chicken and sashimi. The dinner menu is devoted to sushi, nagiri and sashimi dishes.**

*** Nightingale is adjacent to several major hotels and Canada Place, located at 1017 West Hastings Street. It is open from 11 AM to 12 AM and reservations are recommended. The restaurant features traditional Canadian cuisine served with a modern touch. There is a beautiful selection of vegetable dishes that are primarily roasted or grilled. Distinctly unique pizzas are a specialty as well as an array of small plates of fish, tortelloni, chicken, meatballs and chops. Larger plates of gnocchi, tuna, boar, steak and pork for heartier appetites are available. And there are some lovely desserts.**

*** Oakwood Canadian Bistro is a popular restaurant at 2741 West 4th Avenue in the heart of the Kitsilano main shopping area. You will need a private car or taxi to get to the restaurant, as it is not walking distance from the city center. They are open only for dinner from 5 to**

10:30 PM and reservations are recommended. Their menu is small, but varied and includes choices from the sea and land along with a variety of vegetable garnishes. The flavors are definitely Canadian and if you are a foreign visitor, you will be quite pleased.

*** Royal Dinette is another very popular casual restaurant with a true Canadian flair. It is located at 905 Dunsmuir Street, one block north of Georgia Street and one block east of Burrard Street. The restaurant specializes in what they call "farm to table fare." And the good food comes with great service as well. Their diverse lunch menu offers several pastas, open face and smoked brisket sandwiches, fresh fish, chicken and sirloin and there are side orders of five different vegetable creations. The dinner menu is similar, but with heartier meat dishes and one additional fish entree. And in true Canadian fashion, they have several tempting desserts. They are open from 11:30 to 2 PM and from 4:30 to 10 PM daily.**

*** Salmon n' Bannock is a Canadian favorite at 1128 West Broadway, Suite 7. This is south of False Creek between Granville and Cambie Streets, and requires a private car or taxi. If you feel like a bit of a walk through an interesting and vibrant part of the city you can take the Canada Line Sky Train to Olympic Village, walk south on Cambie and then about a kilometer west on Broadway. The atmosphere and menu feature the Canadian northland with wild fish, game, meat dishes and of course bannock, traditional Canadian bread. Their menu is very extensive and features fresh soups, organic greens, salmon, elk, bison, boar, wild game sausages and much more. This is truly a taste of Canada at its best. They are open from 11:30 to 3 PM and 5 to 9 PM and reservations are always advised.**

*** Sandbar Seafood Restaurant is located on Granville Island at 1635 Johnston Street, Suite 102. This is a very popular nightspot with live music and great seafood, sitting under the Granville Bridge. You will need a private car or taxi to get here. The restaurant is open from 11:30 AM to 10:30 PM and should be a must when you first visit the great public marketplace on Granville Island to work up an appetite. The restaurant is very futuristic with steel beams and glass walls commanding views of False Creek and Yaletown. Lunch or dinner can start with crab cakes, fish tacos and fried oysters as just a few of the starters. This can be followed by clam chowder or crab and shrimp Louie, Kung Pao chicken, wok chicken or squid or prawn flatbread.**

*** Seasons in the Park is one restaurant every visitor should try. It is located in Queen Elizabeth Gardens, a sight in and of itself. Situated on high ground, the restaurant's picture windows offer great panoramic city and mountain views. They are open from 11:30 AM to 10 PM and reservations are always advised. You will need a private car or taxi to get to the gardens. Their menu is very extensive with a full selection of appetizers, main courses including seafood, meat and poultry along with a variety of side dishes as well as tempting desserts. On Sunday they feature a prime rib dinner.**

*** Teahouse in Stanley Park is a Vancouver landmark, located at 7501 Stanley Park Drive along the south side of the Sea Wall. It is open from 11:30 AM to 10 PM, and on Saturday and Sunday serving an amazing brunch starting at 11 AM. Reservations are suggested, especially for brunch. The setting is classic. The building has a rustic charm and is set against a wooded backdrop in the park and fronts on English Bay. Lunch and dinner selections are**

limited but include smoked Salmon, smoked meats and cheeses along with many sides. These are mainly light meals but the brunch menu is truly their specialty and is quite extensive.

*** Wildbeest – Located at 120 Hastings Street this restaurant features Canadian cuisine with an emphasis upon flavors that many have not experienced. Canadian cuisine is different from its American counterpart in that there is more emphasis upon fish, game meats and local vegetables common to the northland. They are open for lunch from 10 AM to 2 PM and for dinner from 5 PM to Midnight daily. I would urge you to have your hotel concierge book a table just to be safe.**

Dessert is very much a part of Canadian life, and anyone with a sweet tooth should try some Canadian confections. So here are a few of my recommendations if you like desserts:

*** Breka Bakery & Cafe is the place to go if you have a sweet tooth and really like to indulge in delicious, rich pastries. There are three locations in the city, but the closest to the downtown hotels is at 812 Butte Street just a few doors south of Robson Street and two blocks west of Burrard Street. In addition to fantastic pastries that you will have a hard time making up your mind as to which one to choose, they also serve quiche, soups and sandwiches in their small cafe area. Best of all for any midnight cravings, they are open 24/7.**

*** Cafe Crepe has a traditional French flavor that is very typical of the overall Canadian food scene. They are located at 1032 Robson Street in the heart of the best vibe in Vancouver. They serve both savory main course crepes and dessert crepes so you can have a complete meal or simply a sweet snack. They are open from 7 AM to 11 PM daily and no reservations are necessary.**

*** Notte's Bon Ton Bakery and Tearoom – This is a Vancouver institution located at 3150 West Broadway. They produce the most amazing cakes, pastries and petit fours that you have ever seen, and this includes Europe. The Bon Ton is to be savored. When I lived in Vancouver, I always had their pastries in my home to enjoy every night. I would highly recommend stopping by just for tea or coffee and dessert. You will definitely want to take some back to your hotel or even home. They are open Tuesday thru Saturday from 9;30 aM to 6 PM in the bakery, but only to 5 PM in the tea room.**

*** Purebread - Located downtown at 150 Hastings Street West, this is a baked goods heaven. They offer up a fantastic array of cakes, cookies, brownies and breads that is quite dazzling and makes selection difficult. They do offer scones, savory baked goods and light fare in addition to satisfying the sweet tooth urge. I am sure in addition to eating there, you will want to take something back to your hotel or for your flight home. They are open daily from 8 AM to 6 PM.**

*** Small Victory – Just south of the city center at 1088 Homer Street, this is another of those baked goods heavens. They offer a great variety of both sweet and savory pastries and breads along with more decadent and creamy cakes. This is a place for breakfast or lunch or just to come in and have something sweet with coffee or tea. Small Victory carries forth the great**

Canadian tradition of baked delights. They are open They are open weekdays from 7:30 AM to 6:30 PM and on weekends from 8:30 AM to 6:30 PM.

*** Thierry Chocolateirie Patisserie Cafe offers delectable pastries and other sweet confections at its downtown location of 1069 Alberni Street, one block south of Robson Street and one block west of Burrard Street. Their cafe offers a variety of sandwiches, quiche and soups. And then to top off the meal, you must have dessert, or you can simply come in to satisfy that sweet craving. They are open from 7 AM to Midnight, but on Sunday they open at 8 AM.**

SHOPPING: Vancouver is the third largest city in Canada, and the metropolis of the west coast, thus shopping is outstanding. And anyone coming from the United States, the United Kingdom or the Eurozone will have the great advantage of currency exchange.

There are of course the usual souvenir shops selling the typical tourist kitsch and post cards, but for serious shopping, especially for clothing with smart appeal, I do recommend the following (in alphabetical order):

*** Hudson's Bay Company - This is the largest retail chain in Canada and it is most historic, dating back to the mid 1600's when it began as a fur trading company. The main Vancouver store, which is quite a complete department store, is located downtown at Georgia and Granville Streets. They are famous for their trapper blankets and heavy winter coats made from the blanket material. It is open weekdays and Saturday from 9:30 AM to 9 PM, Sunday from 11 AM to 7 PM.**

*** Holt Renfrew - This very up market store is comparable to the famous Neiman Marcus in the United States or Harrod's in the United Kingdom. Their Vancouver store is small, but very elegant, located in the Pacific Centre Mall downtown. Hours are from 10 AM to 7 PM Monday and Tuesday, until 9 Pm Wednesday thru Friday, to 8 PM Saturday and only until 5 PM Sunday.**

Nordstrom - This famous American department store has opened a beautiful store in downtown Vancouver opposite Hudson's Bay Company on the southwest corner of Georgia and Granville Streets. Their hours are from 9:30 AM to 9 PM Monday thru Saturday and from 11 AM to 7 PM Sunday.

There are literally thousands of small shops and of course the so called "big box" stores in downtown and suburban malls, but most visitors will be staying downtown, so apart from the big three named above, I do recommend browsing through Pacific Centre Mall in the heart of downtown. The mall is open 10 AM to 7 PM Monday and Tuesday, 10 AM to 9 PM Wednesday thru Friday, staying open until 8 PM Saturday and only 5 PM Sunday.

TRANSPORTATION: Vancouver International Airport is the second busiest in Canada. The city is linked with the rest of the nation, the two major carriers being Air Canada and WestJet. Numerous American carriers plus Canada's two prime airlines offer extensive service to the United States and Mexico. And the city is also linked to Europe and Asia by the principal carriers and several foreign airlines.

Limited double deck commuter rail service is provided along the Canadian National main line to the far eastern suburban towns as far outbound as Mission, providing service to Maple Ridge, Coquitlam, Port Coquitlam and Port Moody. Called the West Coast Express, it is the only commuter rail system in British Columbia, offering primarily service during the morning and evening rush hours.

Vancouver is the western terminus for Via Rail Canada's transcontinental train called "The Canadian" This is the only long distance rail service outbound from Vancouver. The route is via Edmonton, Saskatoon, Winnipeg to Toronto with connections to Montrėal, Ottawa, Quėbec City and Halifax.

VANCOUVER MAPS

THE MAIN CITY OF VANCOUVER

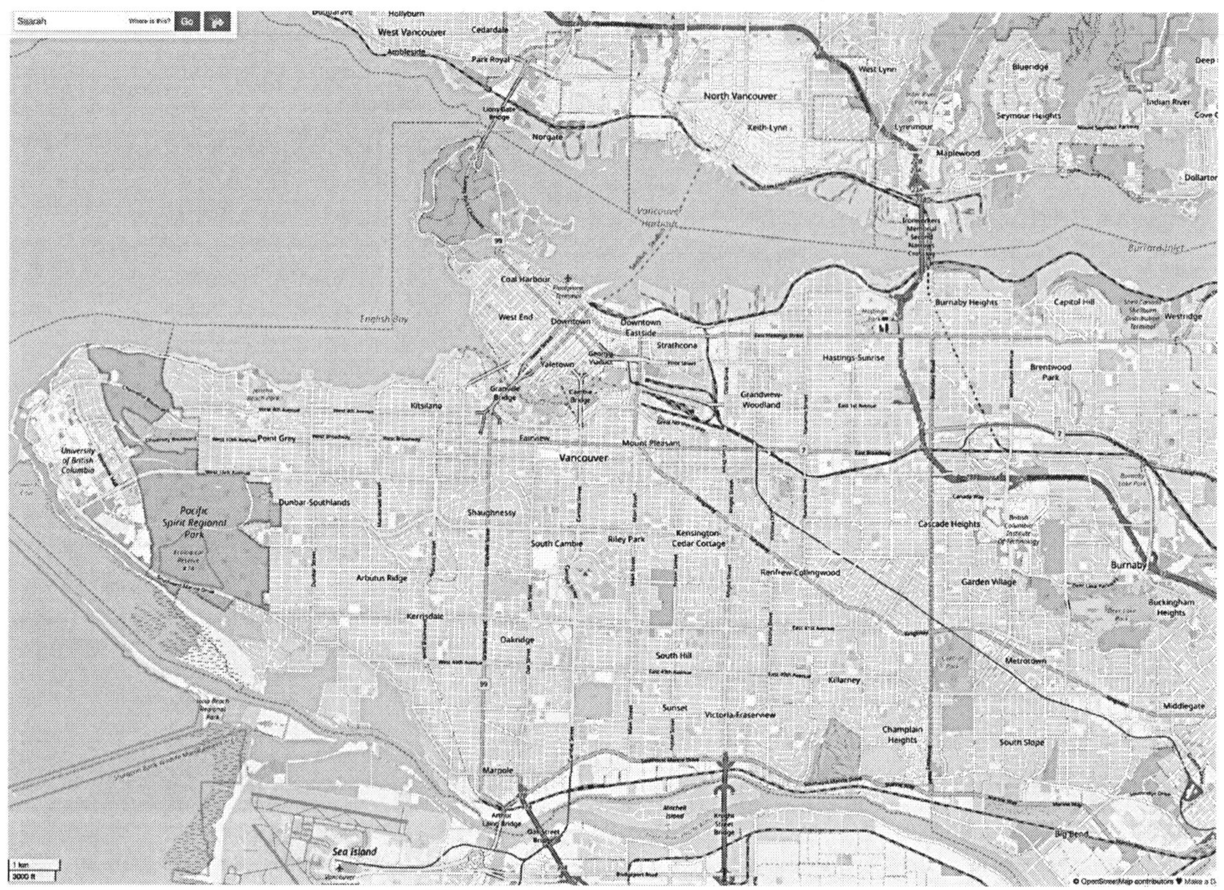

The main city of Vancouver

This map is best viewed directly from OpenStreetMap.com on your personal device where it can be expanded or one specific area can be enlarged. Given the format of this book, it is impossible to display maps with the level of detail you might wish to have while actually out exploring the city. But the OpenStreetMap maps used directly are the tool I always rely upon.

THE DOWNTOWN OF VANCOUVER

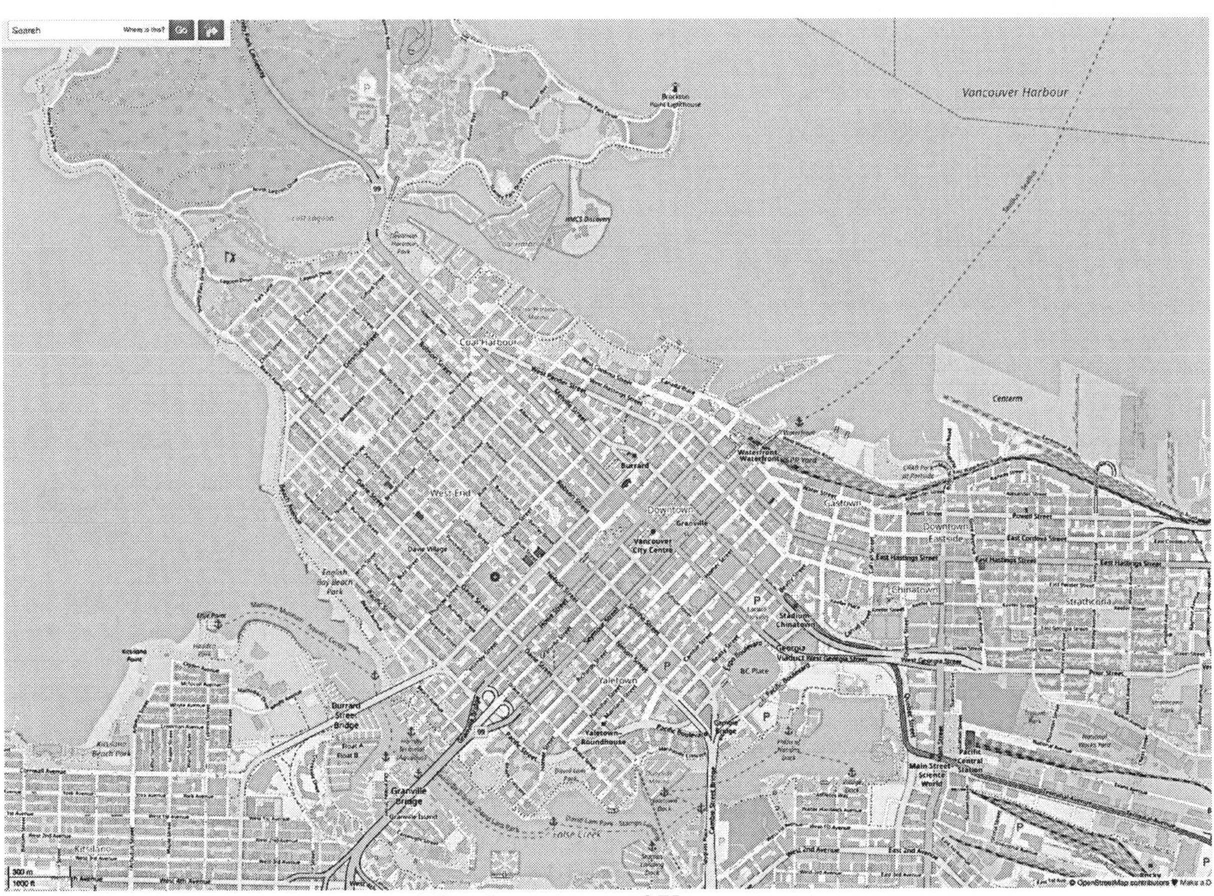

The downtown of Vancouver

This map is best viewed directly from OpenStreetMap.com on your personal device where it can be expanded or one specific area can be enlarged. Given the format of this book, it is impossible to display maps with the level of detail you might wish to have while actually out exploring the city. But the OpenStreetMap maps used directly are the tool I always rely upon.

An aerial of the downtown peninsula. (Work of Shawn, CC BY SA 2.0 Wikimedia.org)

Richmond, typical of the rapidly developing suburban communities around Vancouver

Part of the dynamic West End skyline

A part of the downtown Vancouver skyline.

Downtown Vancouver shows a mix of high-rise office blocks and residential units.

High rise towers crowd downtown Vancouver streets

Georgia Street is considered to be the main street of downtown Vancouver.

The large Hudson's Bay Company department store in downtown Vancouver.

The Sky Train is underground in downtown Vancouver

The Sky Train as it passes through downtown New Westminster now elevated.

Stanley Park brings wilderness into the edge of the West End

English Bay borders the West End.

New apartment blocks east of False Creek

Yaletown is a rapidly growing area along False Creek.

New multi-million dollar condos in Kitsilano Beach

Point Grey in the far west of the peninsula is ultra-expensive today

Beautiful Queen Elizabeth Gardens

Queen Elizabeth Gardens overlooks the city center for a high hilltop

The Hotel Vancouver originally built by Canadian National Railway, (Work of Ken Walker kgw@lunar.ca, CC BY SA 3.0 Wikimedia.org)

Being in the northern Pacific, fresh fish is found in all Vancouver markets

Being typically Canadian, Vancouver bakeries have incredible pastries

KETCHIKAN - THE GATEWAY

A map of the Ketchikan area (© OpenStreetMap contributors)

On cruises northbound out of Vancouver, Ketchikan is the first Alaskan port of call. On southbound cruises Ketchikan is the last port of call before entering Canadian waters about an hour after sailing. As the most southerly city in Alaska, the Ketchikan borough is called the Gateway Borough. The city also touts itself as being the "Salmon Capital of Alaska." All through the downtown area there are shops in which vacuum packed smoked salmon is offered for sale, one of the most sought after items by cruise ship or ferryboat passengers. And the quality is excellent, though the price for a four or eight ounce package is expensive.

With a population of just over 8,000, Ketchikan is the sixth most populous city in Alaska. The entire borough has a metropolitan population of just fewer than 14,000. Despite its small population, the downtown along the Ketchikan waterfront is very lively and offers shops for both locals and visitors alike. Apart from the sale of smoked salmon, there are several art galleries featuring local indigenous artists who produce very fine quality graphic and sculpted art. The economy of Ketchikan is heavily influenced by tourism, especially the summertime cruise season. In addition, the fishing fleet still plays an important role, especially the salmon fisheries. The city is also a center for both local and federal government offices serving the southern panhandle of Alaska. At one time the city was heavily dependent

upon a major pulp mill for the paper industry, but the mill closed in 1997 because of more stringent harvesting of trees in the surrounding national forest lands. Today the Ketchikan Ship Yard is a major employer, producing a variety of ferryboats for use along the inside passage.

THE SETTING: The city is actually located on one of the massive offshore islands within the Inside Passage, the result of past glacial action that fragmented the land through the creation of fjords and islands. There is a small fresh water creek flowing through the city from which it derives its name. Once the Tlingit peoples made this a summer fishing camp.

Most of the land surrounding Ketchikan is part of the Tongass National Forest. This is a thick maritime rainforest in which Douglas fir, cedar and hemlock along with an understory of herbaceous plants and ferns make up one of the richest forest environments outside of the tropics. The climate of this region is especially wet, as moist air comes off the Pacific and is forced to rise over the coastal mountains. There are more rainy days in Ketchikan than there are sunny days, and visitors should be aware that gray skies tend to predominate. The highlight of the area is the magnificent landscape of Misty Fjords National Monument, a preserve that can only be accessed by either boat or plane. The low clouds producing heavy amount of rain often create a misty or foggy environment, thus giving this national monument an appropriate name.

SIGHTS TO SEE: As a cruise visitor, you will have one day in Ketchikan, and the question arises as to what there is to do and see. You can simply walk around the city on your own and visit the various shops. Or you can take either a motor coach or walking tour offered by your cruise line.

The cruise line will offer tours into the backcountry, and the number one trip is a visit to Misty Fjords National Monument. Depending upon your cruise line, a visit to Misty Fjords can be made by small boat, and this is generally an all day tour with lunch included. The shorter, but far more spectacular way to visit the park is to travel by floatplane. This is a more expensive tour, but if the weather is decent, you will get a fantastic overview of the fjords, and it will be a memorable experience. Either way, if seeing a breathtaking landscape is what appeals to you, then by all means this is how your day should be spent. The actual city of Ketchikan is duplicated in many ways by what you will see in Juneau or Skagway, so take in the fjords because they are memorable. If you want to have the ultimate experience, Misty Fjords National Monument is the number one attraction. This is truly an exceptional tour, but of course weather dependent. On some occasions the weather is so bad that the tour can be cancelled.

*** To tour around Ketchikan on your own, it is very easy to see all the major highlights while on foot. There is absolutely no need for a car and driver/guide unless you have a physical disability that precludes walking. There are so few cars and drivers available because of the lack of too many places to visit by automobile. But if this is your wish or need and the ship's price is too expensive, you can contact** *www.BestLimoDB.com* **for rates and booking information.**

*** Ketchikan does have local taxi services that can be pre booked for sightseeing. To obtain further information, visit on line at *www.alaska.org* for information regarding the city's two taxi services.**

Here are the few important local highlights (shown alphabetically):

*** Creek Street - This is the old Ketchikan built along both sides of Ketchikan Creek and offers the flavor of what the old town would have been like during the 19th century. The buildings are either genuine from the gold rush era, or faithful reproductions. But the shops are definitely oriented toward selling the visitor souvenirs or vacuum packed salmon. It is still, however, a scenic attraction.**

*** Great Alaska Lumberjack Show and the Wild Alaska Stunt Show are special attractions for visitors. These are specially staged performances that glorify and exaggerate what life was like in the early years of Ketchikan, but great fun especially for children. The performance center is walking distance from the cruise dock and is open from 7 AM to 5 PM with numerous shows running throughout the day.**

*** Potlatch Park at 9809 Totem Bight Road is another park where you will see authentic Pacific Northwest totem poles. The park does not post specific hours, but is open on days when cruise ships are in port.**

*** Saxman Totem Park and Native Village is three miles south of the town center and is open daily, but does not currently post specific hours. It offers beautiful replica examples of the totem poles that were once so important to the history of the fishing tribes of the region. There are local taxi services on the pier that you can hire for one or more hours to take you to any or all of the totem parks. Or you can have an entire day package tour of the city and its surroundings, which will include this or one of the other totem pole sites.**

*** Southeast Alaska Discovery Center - Located a very short walk from the dock, this center offers exhibits and films about the Tongass National Forest and its incredible landscapes. It is located at 50 Main Street in downtown and is open from 8 AM to 4 PM daily.**

*** Totem Bight State Park covers 33 acres and does contain many genuine totem poles. It is north of the city center at 9883 N. Tongass Highway and will require a taxi to reach unless it is on one of your ship tours. It is open daily from 7 AM to 6 PM.**

*** Totem Heritage Center is located at 601 Deermount Street, a short walk from the dock, and it has several genuine 19th century totem poles from once occupied tribal villages rather than the reproductions generally seen. It is open daily from 1 to 5 PM.**

DINING OUT: As a small city, Ketchikan does not have a great selection of restaurants. Given that this is the salmon capital of Alaska, naturally salmon will figure prominently on most restaurant menus. Here are my recommendations for lunch in Ketchikan, especially for fresh salmon, which the city is so noted for:

*** Alaska Fish House - At 3 Salmon Landing in the center of town, they are famous for their seafood chowders, fresh salmon and crab dishes. It is a feast for the senses. Open daily from 10 AM to 6 PM Sunday thru Wednesday and then to 9 PM Thursday thru Saturday.**
*** Alva's Fish n Chowder - In the heart of town at 420 Water Street, this small red building may not look like much, but the seafood is fresh and delicious. Salmon and halibut are specialties. They are open from 11 AM to 6 PM daily.**

*** Alva's Fish & Chowder – 420 Water Street alongside the tunnel in the heart of town, this is a very popular fresh seafood restaurant for locals and visitors alike. This is a very small restaurant that at first makes many people turn around because it does not have any atmosphere. But it is superb. Their specialty is fresh Alaska cod that is batter dipped and fried. It is absolutely delicious. They also serve fresh halibut and salmon. They are open daily from 11 AM to 6 PM.**

*** Dwyers Crab and Fish Company Restaurant - In the heart of town at 76 Front Street, this is another fantastic restaurant in which to gorge on crab, salmon, halibut and great chowders. Open Sunday thru Thursday from 10 AM to 9 PM and staying open Friday and Saturday until 10 PM.**

*** George Inlet Crab Feast - Located on the south side of town at 11728 S. Tongass Highway, this restaurant is famous for its crab dishes, and many consider it to be a must for lunch. If you like fresh crab. They are open daily for lunch, but specific hours are not given.**

*** Wilderness Exploration and Crab Feed – Located at 11728 Tongass Highway, which is a short distance out of Ketchikan around the southern tip and then up the east side of the island. A taxi is required. Dining is often part of any excursion around the waters of Ketchikan, which perhaps may be on one of the ship bus or boat tours. The reviews are nearly 100 percent perfect. The quality of the fresh crab and the accompaniments are superb, as is the service. If for any reason crab is not a favorite, I would recommend against this experience. If you wish to book the excursion and crab feast on your own, check on line at** *www.ketchikanshoretours.com* **for information and booking. The tour will begin at or near where your ship docks.**

SHOPPING: Apart from souvenirs, T shirts and post cards of which you will find plenty in the downtown area, the main item to buy is the vacuum sealed salmon or smoked salmon. It is expensive, but a wonderful gift item to bring back for anyone or even for yourself. This is sold on every block in the town center, so there is no need to recommend any special store.

FINAL WORDS: Ketchikan is actually a pleasant stop, and it typifies the ports of call in the Alaska Panhandle in that they all have this strong emphasis upon attempting to lure the shipboard visitor into purchasing something, be it salmon, jewelry, fur or other expensive items. But step away from the main shopping streets and you can catch a glimpse at the way Alaskans live in these coastal towns. The tours are of course tailored for the visitor, but the majesty of the scenery is hard to escape.

The north shore residential area of Ketchikan

The downtown skyline of Ketchikan

Cruise ships dock in the very heart of downtown Ketchikan

The famous pioneer sculpture in the heart of town

Downtown is very much tourist oriented

Colorful Ketchikan Creek

Saxman Totem Pole Park

The Great Alaska Lumberjack Show, (Work of Knight 94, CC BY Sa 3.0, Wikimedia.org)

A bit of springtime snow at Misty Fjords National Monument

The Alaska Ferry links Ketchikan with points north in Alaska

JUNEAU - THE CAPITAL

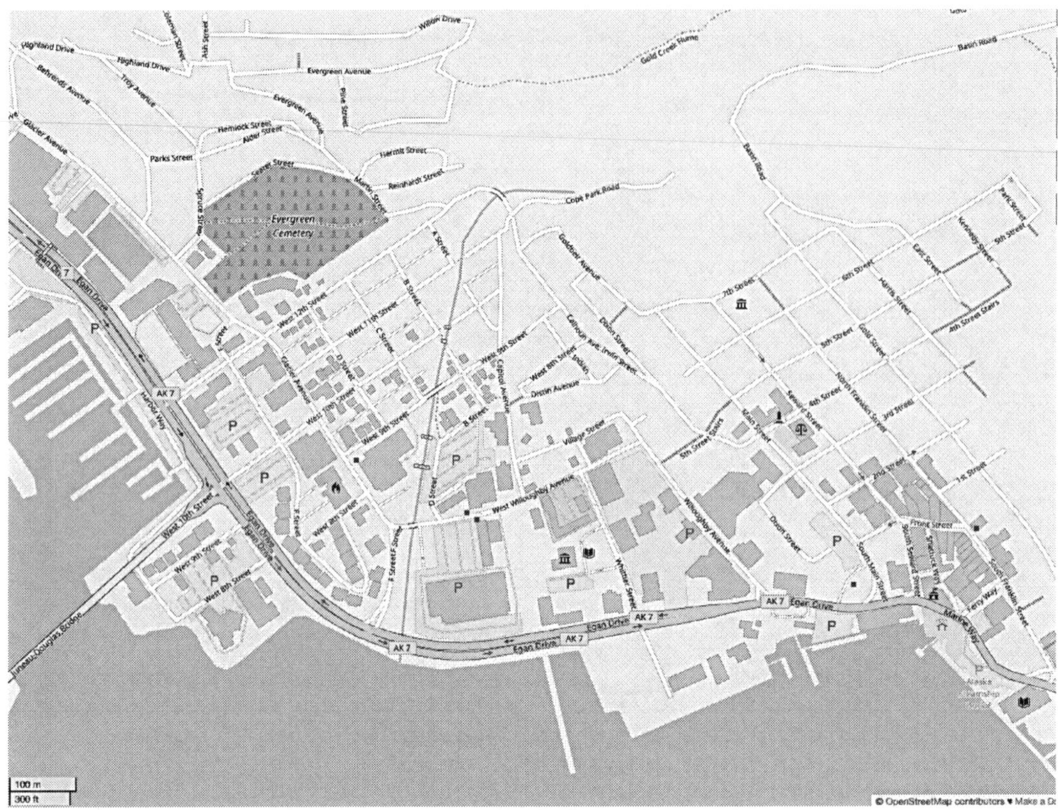

A map showing central Juneau (© OpenStreetMap contributors)

Juneau is the capital city of Alaska and its third largest urban center with just over 32,100 residents. Juneau is, however, the most isolated state capital in the entire nation. No other capital city lacks a highway connection to the outside world. Juneau can only be reached by air or sea. It is also the only capital city in the nation that borders another country, as the city and borough limits reach the crest of the mountains to the east that constitute the international boundary with Canada. But there is no physical connection with Canada, as no roads or trails traverse these rugged mountains. The city and borough also constitute the second largest corporate city in the nation, the largest being Sitka. Juneau is approximately 2.5 times larger in land area than the state of Rhode Island.

NATURAL SETTING: Juneau occupies the eastern shore of the Gastineau Channel, which narrows and becomes shallow to the north of the city center, making it impossible for ships to continue onward. Thus all sea traffic must depart to the south and sail around Douglas Island, which blocks the city from the main Inside Passage. The city is actually composed of three distinct segments. The former city of Douglas, located across the channel from central Juneau is now a residential suburb. The central city, which is quite small in land area, is tucked up against the steep slopes that during winter months can pose an avalanche threat to the downtown and government center. One lone road continues north hugging the shoreline to connect central Juneau with Mendenhall Valley, which is home to the majority of Juneau residents. Thus there is no continuity to the city of Juneau. Each of the three

segments is separated from the other, Douglas by water and Mendenhall Valley by several kilometers or miles of steep mountain slopes.

Mendenhall Valley is the result of the retreating Mendenhall Glacier having carved its channel to the Inside Passage. The front face of the glacier is just a few miles north of the residential area and is a major tourist attraction. This is just one of many outflows from the massive Juneau ice field, one of the largest glacial fields in Alaska. The ice field appears to be relatively stable, but the Mendenhall and Lemon Creek Glaciers have shown retreat since the early 1900's, part of the overall warming of the planet that has been ongoing for 10,000 years since the end of the last Ice Age. Today's addition of carbon dioxide and other pollutants to the atmosphere are simply hastening a process that has its origins in the ebb and flow of temperature on earth for millions of years. But there is no doubt that human contributions to the atmosphere are definitely harmful.

The main core of Juneau is very cosmopolitan in its overall flavor, yet it bears the strong architectural mark of the late 19th century gold rush era with its many Victorian buildings that reflected the wealth of the time. Cruise ships dock in great numbers during summer, the wharves running parallel to the city's main street. There can be as many as five large ships in port on a given day, adding thousands of visitors to mingle with the local populace. Downtown Juneau has many shops strictly catering to visitors. In recent years many of the jewelry stores and fur shops that are so dominant in Caribbean ports of call are now found in the Alaskan ports. I often wonder why a tourist would book an Alaska cruise and then spend time shopping for watches or diamonds when there is so much to see in each port.

HISTORIC JUNEAU: Juneau is a relatively young city, having been developed during the 1880's, when gold was discovered. The territorial capital was moved here in 1906 from Sitka, which had been the prior Russian capital since it was first founded. Before Juneau existed, the Tlingit tribe would fish for salmon in the waters of the Gastineau Channel and make camp along its shores. The first European to see the Gastineau Channel was Joseph Whidbey who was master of one of the ships in the expedition of George Vancouver in 1794. But it was not until 1880, that Europeans showed any interest in the area, and that was only to prospect for gold, which was found at the head of what is now known as Gold Creek.

Today state and federal government payrolls are the largest sources of income in Juneau year around. But during summer over a quarter million cruise ship passengers visit, spending money in the shops and restaurants, as well as purchasing tours. Add to this the docking fees, and tourism is a major addition to the city's economy. Juneau will no doubt remain as the state capital because of the high cost to build a new infrastructure in the event voters chose to relocate the capital. The measure has failed to pass on several occasions mainly because of the high cost of relocation combined with a sentimentality regarding Alaska's history.

One may think of Juneau as strictly a small city catering to the needs of tourists. But Juneau has its cultural side, which is more visible during the long cold, rainy days of winter. Numerous artists live in the city and there is a small arts center. Several galleries do offer local art works for sale. The city also has small theater groups and is not lacking in its

cultural venues. But visitors stay for only a few hours and never really have a chance to get to know this small capital city.

SIGHTSEEING: When visiting Juneau for the day, you can spend your time walking through the downtown area, looking at the shops, but also taking in the Victorian architecture that so characterizes the city center.

Cruise lines all offer a variety of tours outside of the small central core. And, as noted below, they also offer a variety of tours outside of the small city core. Apart from walking the city core or going on a ship sponsored tour, your other options are:

*** You can have the cruise line arrange a private car and driver/guide, which is relative expensive. If you wish to hire a car and driver on your own, I suggest checking on line with Juneau Limousine Service at** *www.juneaulimousineservices.com* **or Best Limo at** *www.BestLimoDB.com* **for further information and booking.**

*** Juneau does not have a hop on hop off bus because the city is too small and does not have that many specific sights to warrant such a service. There is M&M Tours Glacier Express Blue Bus that for $14.00 will take passengers from the cruise ship docks to the Mendenhall Glacier Visitor's Center. The same company does operate a variety of air water and land tours each day during the summer season. For further information, check on line at** *www.mmtoursofjuneau.com* **for itineraries, prices and booking information.**

The main highlights outside of the central city that you are most likely to want to visit either by taxi, private car or on a tour bus are:

*** Mendenhall Glacier - The number one attraction in Juneau, this is the only urban glacier in America. There is a visitor's center that overlooks the face of the glacier, and there is a hiking trail that brings you close to the front edge. The visitor center is open from 8 AM to 7:30 PM daily during summer, and you may see the calving, that is the dropping off of large chunks of ice that splash into the melt water lake at the glacier's edge. Your ship may also offer helicopter tours to the top of the glacier, or dog sled runs farther onto the glacier, as well as tours just to the visitor center. You can also reach the glacier by local taxi or with a car and driver/guide.**

*** Nugget Falls - Located near the Mendenhall Glacier, this powerful waterfall is very prominent. The walk from the parking area is relatively level and gives you a chance to enjoy the fresh air and scent of the trees. The falls can be done on your own with a taxi or car and driver, taking about two hours or less.**

*** Perseverance National Recreation Trail - Leading out from central Juneau this trail takes you into the mountains and forests where you forget that the city center is a short distance away. This is a favored local hiking trail, easy to access from the cruise ship dock.**

*** Tracy Arm Fjord - Two active glaciers are still carving the fjord, but a boat tour will bring you face to face with this spectacular sight located southeast of Juneau. The overall scenery is quite breathtaking. Many cruise lines do offer this as one tour option.**

*** Whale Watching Tours - There are several boat operators that will take you out into the main Inside Passage for a few hours of whale watching. Orca and Humpback whales are often sighted. There are eagles, seals and dolphins to see as well, and this is also a very scenic adventure. This is a very popular option with most cruise lines, but the guarantee of a whale sighting is impossible.**

There are a few important landmarks worthy of note within central Juneau if this is what you are planning to do, or if you go on the three to four hour city tours that most cruise lines offer. These include:

*** AJ Mine Gastineau Mill and Gold Mine Tour - Although oriented to the visitor, this tour does help you gain an understanding of the gold mines that put Juneau on the map. It is at 500 Sheep Creek Mine Road and offers great underground tours all day. Check their web page at** *www.ajgastineauminetour.com* **for further information.**

*** Alaska Governor's Mansion - Built in the early years of Juneau, this beautiful colonial building is home to the governor and a venue for state functions. It is not open to the public, but you can photograph it from the outside, and the view from the street over the Gastineau Channel makes the walk worthwhile.**

*** Alaska State Capitol - Located atop the downtown, this imposing building was built in 1931, but it looks more like a bank building than a capitol. It is relatively small and unimpressive, but the tour does give you an understanding of how the state is run and why the capitol has remained in Juneau, isolated from the rest of the populace. Self-guided tours are available from 7 AM to 5 PM weekdays.**

*** Juneau-Douglas City Museum - It is located opposite the State Capitol at the corner of Fourth and Main Streets. A small collection on the local history and geography makes this a worthy stop to learn more about the area. Open weekdays from 9 AM to 6 PM and Saturday from 10 AM to 4:30 PM. Closed Sunday.**

*** Juneau Public Library - This new building overlooking the cruise docks has a modern vibe and some beautifully designed stained glass windows. It is at 292 Marine Way and open Monday thru Thursday 11 AM to 4 PM, Friday from 1 to 5 PM and weekends Noon to 5 PM.**

*** Macaulay Salmon Hatchery - Located at 2697 Channel Drive. Here you have a chance to learn about the life cycle of salmon and see fry and young salmon being raised for later release. The hatchery is located a short distance from the city center, but a bit too far for many people to walk. Visitors are welcome weekdays between 10 AM and 6 PM and weekends between 10 AM and 5 PM.**

*** Mount Roberts Tramway - Only if the air is clear and visibility is good should you take the tramway from just off the cruise dock to the top of Mount Roberts. The view over Juneau, Douglas Island and the Gastineau Channel is absolutely spectacular when visibility is good. The tramway operates all day when ships are in port, but they do not post their hours of operation. The tramway ticket booth and boarding area are located right in the middle of the long cruise ship docking zone.**

*** Red Dog Saloon - Very touristy, but it does somehow capture some of the feeling of old Juneau back in the gold rush days. This is one of the most popular so called "watering holes" in all of Alaska, and visitors love it. They are at 278 Franklin Street and open from 11 AM to 10 PM Sunday thru Thursday and until 12 AM on Friday and Saturday.**

*** Saint Nicholas Church - Located at 326 Fifth Street, welcoming visitors during daylight hours when services are not being held. A small Russian Orthodox Church constructed out of wood and serving the small native community.**

DINING OUT: Having lunch in Juneau generally revolves around fresh halibut or salmon, which during summer is an Alaskan specialty. The fish is often either grilled on a cedar wood plank or directly on the grate. Smoked salmon is also a popular delicacy. The sides are typical of what you would have in any American seafood house – coleslaw and baked or fried potatoes. But the flavor of the fish is so special since it is fresher than what can be had in the rest of the United States. Fish soups or chowders are also popular, as is fresh Alaskan king crab.

Surprisingly as the state capitol city you would expect to find many great restaurants. But the vast majority of Juneau's restaurants cater to the masses of people coming off the cruise ships. The quality of the food and the service are unpredictable and for the most part not that great. I have selected the few that I have found to be overall consistent and fairly good. Here are my few recommendations for great seafood in Juneau, as your ship will be there only during the day, so lunch should be a must:

*** Island Pub – Located across the water in Douglas at 1102 Second Street, this fine restaurant does not cater to tourists, so the level of quality is quite good. Their menu is quite extensive and consists of soups, sandwiches, pizza and main entrees with a definite American twist. I have put this restaurant on my listing because its quality is well above those Juneau restaurants catering to the tourist crowd, but it is not a seafood restaurant. They are open between 11:30 AM and 10 PM daily.**

*** The Rookery Café – In downtown Juneau at 111 Seward Street, this is a typical American restaurant with a diverse lunch menu that is not seafood oriented. This is more of a local restaurant that is not attempting to capture the ship passenger market. The quality of their salads, soups panini, pizza and sandwiches is very good. They are open weekdays from 7 AM to 3:30 PM and Saturday from 9 AM to 3:30 PM and Sunday from 9 AM to 2 PM.**

*** The Salmon Spot - At 210 Admiral Way in the downtown area, this is a superb restaurant for great salmon among other types of seafood as well. It is not fancy decor wise, but oh so good taste wise. They are open daily from 11 AM to 6 PM.**

*** Tracy's King Crab Shack - Located at 406 S. Franklin St. right downtown, this is one of the best places for fresh crab, but also well respected for their fine salmon and halibut. Also their chowders are excellent. They are open daily from 10:30 AM to 8:30 PM daily.**

*** Twisted Fish Company Alaskan Grill - In the center of town at 550 S. Franklin St., this is one of the very good places in all of Alaska for excellent fresh fish. They specialize in salmon, halibut, crab and oysters to name just the prime items. And they make great seafood chowder. Hours are from 11 AM to 9:30 PM daily.**

SHOPPING: For many people Juneau is a shopping paradise, but I personally found the emphasis upon "so called" bargains to be exactly like the Caribbean islands. In fact many of the merchants are branch stores from the Caribbean, selling diamonds, gems, watches, furs and other luxury goods at what they call bargain prices. In many ways this seems so out of character for the capital city of Alaska, yet people spend their money as if it was the last day on earth to shop. All I can say if you become mesmerized by all the "glitzy" shopping in Juneau is, "Buyer beware." As for the usual tourist kitsch you will find plenty of it available.

FINAL WORDS: As with all the ports of the Alaska Panhandle, there is this strong emphasis upon attempting to entice shipboard guests to shop. But as the capital city of Alaska, the central portion of Juneau does have the state capitol building, governor's mansion and many beautiful old Victorian homes on the streets beyond the shopping district. And even though the tours are packaged for the cruise passenger, they do take you into the immediate surroundings where you see active glaciers, wildlife and the majesty of the coastal mountains.

JUNEAU MAPS

THE DOWNTOWN OF JUNEAU

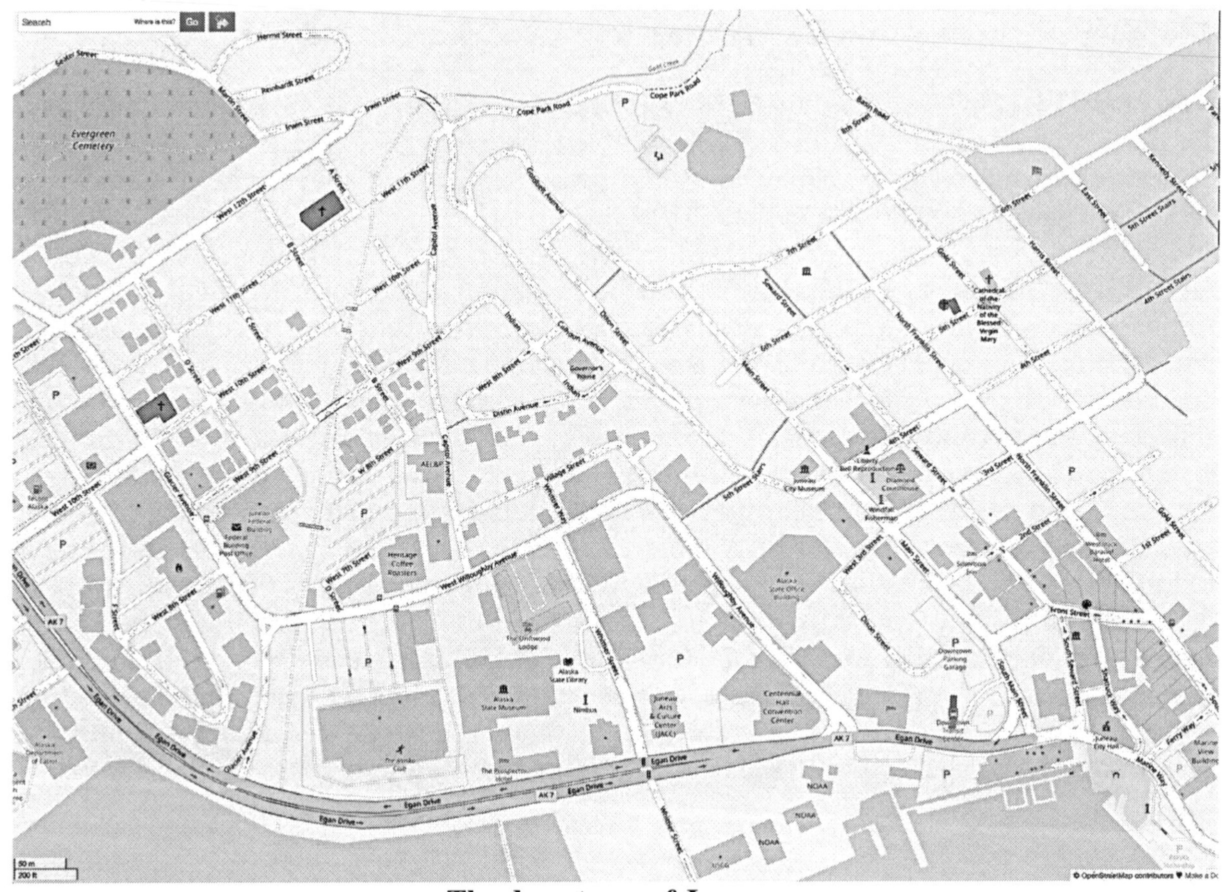

The downtown of Juneau

This map is best viewed directly from OpenStreetMap.com on your personal device where it can be expanded or one specific area can be enlarged. Given the format of this book, it is impossible to display maps with the level of detail you might wish to have while actually out exploring the city. But the OpenStreetMap maps used directly are the tool I always rely upon.

MENDENHALL VALLEY

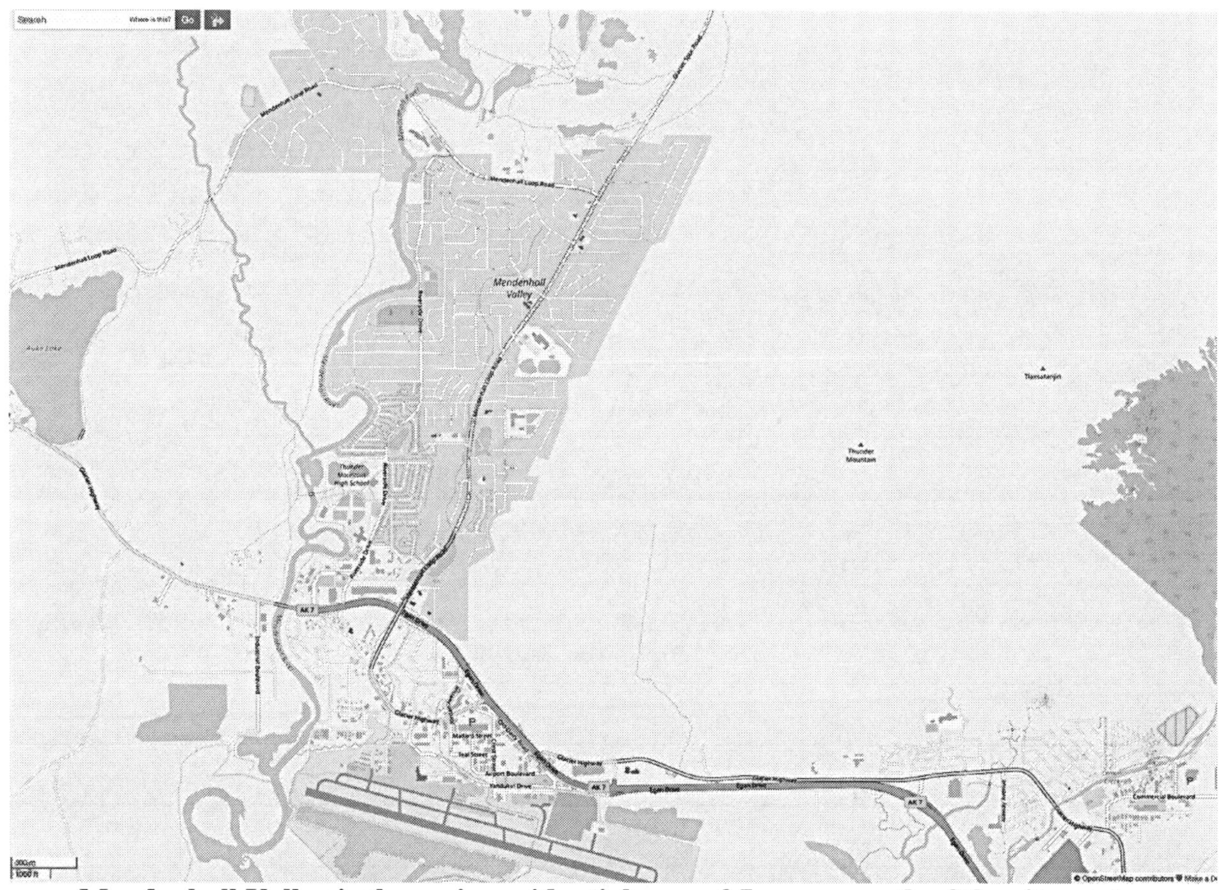

Mendenhall Valley is the main residential core of Juneau, north of the city center

This map is best viewed directly from OpenStreetMap.com on your personal device where it can be expanded or one specific area can be enlarged. Given the format of this book, it is impossible to display maps with the level of detail you might wish to have while actually out exploring the city. But the OpenStreetMap maps used directly are the tool I always rely upon.

Central Juneau tucked under the shadow of Mount Roberts

The mountains rise precipitously behind central Juneau

Crowds of ship tourists along downtown's Franklin Street

The Red Dog Saloon at Front and Franklin Streets

Juneau's downtown is right up against the mountain slopes

There are a few moderate high rise buildings in downtown Juneau

The Alaska State Capitol Building

The Alaska Governor's Mansion

The extreme tidal range shows up along the waterfront at low tide

The front edge of the Mendenhall Glacier

The Mendenhall Glacier up close

Whale watching often does not produce any whales, but the scenery is beautiful

SITKA
THE OLD RUSSIAN CAPITAL

A map of the city of Sitka (© OpenStreetMap contributors)

Sitka is the most historic city in all of Alaska, as it was the focus of Russian Alaska until the United States purchased the territory. Its original name was New Archangel. Most cruise itineraries do not include Sitka because of its location. It is located on the west coast of Baranof Island, one of the largest islands of the Inside Passage, but this means that the city faces the open sea and it requires leaving the calm waters of the passage to navigate into the harbor. Depending upon weather conditions, it can be a bit rough navigating out to Sitka. Also the harbor is very small so the cruise terminal is about eight kilometers or five miles from the town center. However, shuttle service is provided. Some cruise lines, especially the more up market companies, prefer to anchor off the shore adjacent to the city center and then tender their guests ashore using the lifeboats.

NATURAL SETTING: The city and borough includes the entire Baranof Island with 7,433 square kilometers or 2,870 square miles of land, making Sitka the largest city in the United States in area. Yet the population stands at just under 9,000. There is a peaceful charm to Sitka because it is not on the main tour route for cruise ships. This is the one port in which the large jewelry chain stores found in the other major ports are absent. Numerous excellent galleries that feature both Russian and native art, with many of the artists having their

studios right in town, replace the chain stores found in Juneau and Ketchikan. There is a definite emphasis upon quality and not mass production. Anyone interested in fine quality works of art by Alaskan or Russian artists will find the main street of Sitka quite enjoyable. And yes of course there are a few of the usual souvenir shops.

The site of Sitka is that of an expansive bay on the west coast of Baranof Island, and the bay is dotted with small, thickly forested islands, making it quite beautiful. The mountains rising up behind Sitka are snowcapped much of the year and rich evergreen forests totally engulf the city. Across the bay is the 975-meter or 3,200-foot volcanic cone called Mount Edgecumbe. This beautiful snow covered volcanic cone dominates the harbor, but its last known eruption was around 4,200 years ago. Geologists say it is dormant and not extinct, which means that it could possibly erupt. Decades back, the thinking among volcanologists was that if a volcano had not erupted in over 1,000 years it was potentially extinct, but today that is no longer the belief, as there have been eruptions after 1,000 years of dormancy. On the morning of April 1, 1974, black smoke was seen billowing out of the crater of Mount Edgecube, and this caused near panic in Sitka. With the mountain so close to the town, many residents were ready to flee. The Coast Guard sent up a helicopter to assess whether the city should be evacuated. But to their surprise they found a mound of burning rubber tires. This was the prank of a local resident known as Oliver "Porky" Bickar. He had been planning this for quite some time and a friend of his who had a helicopter helped him place the tires atop the mountain and set them alight. Rubber tires emit a dark, oily smoke when they burn and it did simulate a possible awakening of the volcano. His prank garnered worldwide attention and thus local law enforcement decided not to charge him. Why was he able to get away with creating panic? Remember the date, April 1, which is "April fool's day" and he certainly did fool everyone. His stunt was so clever and the press so enjoyed it that the local officials did not have the heart to charge him for creating panic.

Sitka has a marine west coast climate, but its rainfall total is higher than either Juneau or Ketchikan because of its direct exposure to the Gulf of Alaska where the warm North Pacific Drift first strikes the mountains and rise abruptly causing heavy precipitation. Temperatures are cool year around and during winter it is often cold enough right at sea level for snow to accumulate. Summer weather is very mild, and often it is cloudy and rainy. Thus a visit to Sitka is most likely to not be sunny even in summer.

SITKA HISTORY: The history of Sitka dates back to the early Russian attempt to establish a fort in 1799. This was to become the home base for the Governor of Alaska appointed by the Russian Tsar. He also commissioned the Russian America Company to establish trade with the native Tlingit as well as to trap for furs. The Tlingit, however, were not pleased with these invaders and in 1802 they attacked the fort, overwhelming its defenses. They killed many of the Russians and 200 of the Aleuts who the Russians had brought from the Aleutian Islands to help with the work of running the fort and trading outpost. The governor then had to ransom the remaining survivors. Back in Saint Petersburg the authorities were outraged at such an incident. Thus Governor Baranov was returned to Sitka in 1804 with a Russian naval vessel, which bombarded the fort that the Tlingit now occupied. The bombardments did little to damage the stockade, so the Russians launched a full-scale attack that also proved unsuccessful. Fortunately the Tlingit ran out of gunpowder from the reserves within the fort

and then abandoned their position, enabling the Russians to claim victory. It was only after this so called victory that the Russians actually established the settlement of Sitka, originally calling it New Archangel. The Tlingit built their own fort across the Chatham Strait and kept the Russians from trading or trapping in their territory.

In 1808, Sitka became the capital of Russian America and remained so until the Americans moved the territorial capital to Juneau. During the Russian period, several important structures were built such as the bishop's palace and the Cathedral of Saint Michael, both of which still stand today. By 1840, the Russian Orthodox Bishop for Alaska and the Kamchatka Peninsula (Russia) was based in Sitka. The town became the most important trade center for the entire Russian colony and it did offer many of the comforts to be found in Saint Petersburg so many thousands of kilometers or miles away.

There were many workers in Sitka from the Baltic Sea region, and being protestant they were allowed to build the Sitka Lutheran Church, and after the American purchase in 1867, other denominations came. But Saint Michael's still dominates the town center and gives Sitka that special Russian historical flavor. Once the Americans purchased Alaska, attention was turned toward the Inside Passage, and with gold discovered in Juneau and then later the Klondike Gold Rush occurring, Sitka became almost forgotten, especially once the capital was moved to Juneau in 1906.

Sitka continued to serve as a fishing port for the salmon and crab fleets, and some fish canning was done. And on Baranof Island there was some gold mined. But what brought Sitka back to life was World War II. During the war, the U. S. Navy developed an air station on Japonski Island adjacent to Sitka, and this helped swell the population for the duration of the war. Today the island is home to the U. S. Coast Guard Air Station and port facility, and it along with the base at Kodiak serve to protect the entire Alaska coast. But today, salmon and crab fishing are still the major employers for the city, although governmental and health services combined provide more jobs. Tourism is still not as major as in Juneau and Ketchikan because of the more isolated location of Sitka, which in the end gives this small port a greater degree of authenticity.

WHAT TO SEE AND DO: Once again you will only have a day in Sitka if your cruise itinerary includes this port. There is very little for the majority of visitors in the town itself, so I highly recommend one of the many tours out into the wilds of Baranof Island or its offshore waters so that you can enjoy the beauty of raw nature.

*** If you wish to tour around Sitka on your own with a car and driver/guide, your cruise line most likely can arrange it for you, but at a premium cost since availability is limited. If you wish to try on your own, you can look into Best Limo at *www.BestLimoDB.com* for availability and rates.**

*** Local taxi service is provided by Baranof Taxi & Tour. Their web page is *www.baranoftaxi.com.* They do offer tours around Sitka on an hourly basis, which is less costly than a private limousine. Another provider is Hank's Taxi whose web page is *www.hankscab.com* and they do offer tour services.**

*** There is no hop on hop off bus in Sitka. But there is a public bus service. For information on their routes and service check their web page at *www.ridesitka.com.***

*** If you plan on just staying in town, it is quite easy to walk to many of the interesting venues once you have arrived in the small downtown.**

Your cruise line may have several motor coach tours available for the Sitka area, but if you are not one who enjoys being on a bus with many other people, I am offering what I feel are the important attractions. Here are the major highlights of Sitka (listed alphabetically):

*** Alaska Raptor Center - This is a sanctuary that cares for birds of prey, especially bald eagles. At the center you can see many of Alaska's great hunting and fishing birds up close. The sanctuary is located just east of the town center, but it is a bit of a walk unless you are visiting on a tour. The center is open from 8 AM to 4 PM on weekdays only.**

*** Baranof Castle Hill State Historic Site - This hilltop viewpoint is the spot where the Russian government handed over control of Alaska to the United States. There is little here except a good view of the Sitka region. A taxi can take you there in a few minutes unless it is already on the itinerary of a regular tour that you book. The site is open daily, but actual hours are not posted.**

*** Fortress of the Bear - Located a few miles out of the city at 4639 Sawmill Creek, this sanctuary raises young grizzly bears and offers a chance to see these still wild animals, especially at feeding time. This sanctuary rescues young wayward bears and keeps them from being culled or shot often out of necessity. It is open daily from 9 AM to 5 PM.**

*** Russian Bishop's House - Located right in the heart of Sitka at 501 Lincoln St., this old building dating to Tsarist Russia is now a museum of Russian culture. It once was the home to the bishop who ministered to all of Alaska and Kamchatka on the far eastern coast of Russia, The house is open daily from 9 AM to 5 PM.**

*** Saint Michael's Cathedral - Right in the heart of Sitka, this small Russian Orthodox Cathedral once served as the home for the Bishop of all Alaska and Kamchatka. It offers a look at the Russian Orthodox faith, as practiced on the remote frontier. No specific hours are posted, but it is open every day except when services are being held.**

*** Sitka National Historic Park/Totem Park - Located a short distance south of the city center, this federally operated national park combines a series of nature trails through the beautiful maritime rainforest with a collection of traditional totem poles. The park offers both the natural and the historic aspects of Baranof Island and it is a very beautiful experience. If you are not visiting the park as part of a tour, you can take one of the limited local taxis to the park visitor's center at 103 Monastery St. It is open daily from 9AM to 9 PM during the summer months.**

*** Sheldon Jackson Museum - This small museum features excellent arts and crafts representing native tribes for all parts of Alaska. It is located at 104 College Street in the heart of Sitka. The museum is open Monday thru Saturday from 10 AM to 4 PM.**

OTHER OPTIONS: There are a great variety of options that include kayaking, river rafting, nature hiking, whale watching or fishing. Your cruise line will offer many package tours that you would be hard pressed to try and arrange on your own after arrival. If you are seeking some adventure and a chance to savor more of the wild side of Sitka, there are plenty of opportunities too numerous to mention, as each cruise line will have its own special packages. But since the options vary so much by cruise line, it is impossible for me to make note of each and provide accurate information.

If the ship's outdoor activities are not to your liking, you may wish to check out Sitka Wildlife Tours at *www.sitkawildlifetours.com* to see what they offer for people who just have a limited timeframe.

DINING OUT: Sitka is a smaller port of call and not as frequently visited, especially by the large mega cruise ships because of its more isolated location. This cuts down on the number of visitors and also on that frenetic dining and shopping experience you will find in the Ketchikan, Juneau and Skagway.

There are far fewer good restaurants, but I have found a handful that I find meet my personal standards that I recommend them here:

*** Beak Restaurant - Located at 2 Lincoln Street A, and offering a more relaxed dining experience. They specialize in superb chowders, fresh fish and shellfish dishes as well as a variety of accompanying items. They do not show their hours on their web page, but they are certain to be open for lunch when a ship is anchored in the bay. They are open Monday thru Saturday from 11 AM to 9 PM and on Sunday from 11 AM to 2 PM.**

*** Halibut Point Crab and Chowder - Located on the north edge of town at 4513 Halibut Point Road, this fine establishment features crab, but also halibut, salmon and whatever else is fresh, as the fishermen bring in their catch daily. The meals are well prepared and served in a somewhat rustic atmosphere. They are open for lunch and dinner, but do not post their hours of service.**

*** Ludvig's Bistro – Located at 256 Katlian Street in the heart of Sitka, this restaurant is quite unpretentious, but does serve very good seafood and chowders, which is fresh and well prepared. Their menu also carries a bit of a Mediterranean touch with regard to some of its offerings such as seafood pastas and calamari. Their service is also very attentive. They are open Monday thru Saturday from 4 to 9 PM for dinner only. A few cruise ships do stay in port into the evening hours, and if yours is one that does, this is a good place for dinner.**

SHOPPING: Unlike Juneau, shopping in Sitka is totally different. This small city is home to many fine artists and craftsmen. Thus the main shopping area has numerous genuine

galleries featuring local artists and artisans. If you like fine quality art, then Sitka is a city in which it is a pleasure to shop. Here are my recommendations for fine gift shopping in Sitka:

*** Raindance Gallery - At 205 Monastery Street, this gallery is known for its fine quality hand crafted arts with a strong local native tradition. Their masks and other traditional carved items give you a wide array of tempting treasures. They are open from 10 AM to 4 PM daily.**
*** Artist Cove Gallery - At 241 Lincoln Street, this gallery offers a beautiful selection of hand crafted objects d'art, traditional native art as well as mineral pieces. They do feature many local artists. They are open from 10 AM to 5 Pm weekdays.**

*** Russian American Company - At 134 Lincoln Street, this gallery features art from art works imported from Russia. Remember that Sitka has a strong Russian heritage. I have traveled extensively in Russia and I am pleased to say that their Russian arts are of fine quality with many hand signed pieces, especially the matrushka dolls and lacquered boxes. They are open from 10 AM to 5:30 PM Monday thru Saturday but only until 4 PM on Sunday.**

*** Sitka Rose Gallery - Located at 419 Lincoln Street in a quaint Victorian house with beautiful flowers growing outside, this gallery is packed with a variety of paintings, woodcarvings, glass and jewelry by both native and non-native artisans. The collection is very tasteful and I would defy any fine art critic not to find something that they would add to their collection. They are open daily from 8:30 AM to 5:30 PM.**

FINAL WORDS: I find Sitka to be the most charming and genuine of the Alaska Panhandle ports because the mass market merchants who have taken over Ketchikan, Juneau and Skagway have not invaded Sitka. This small city still enjoys the peace and quiet and genuine flavor that has been lost in the other three primary ports of call. And the natural setting is far more beautiful than the other panhandle ports. Also Sitka has become home to a small artist colony and it is the one place in the panhandle that offers a nice selection of native and Russian arts and crafts.

The tours offered outside of Sitka have a more genuine feel than those catering to thousands of visitors. The natural landscape is more accessible because the land is not as rugged and difficult to approach, therefore, you can enjoy some of the natural beauty with far less difficulty.

DOWNTOWN SITKA

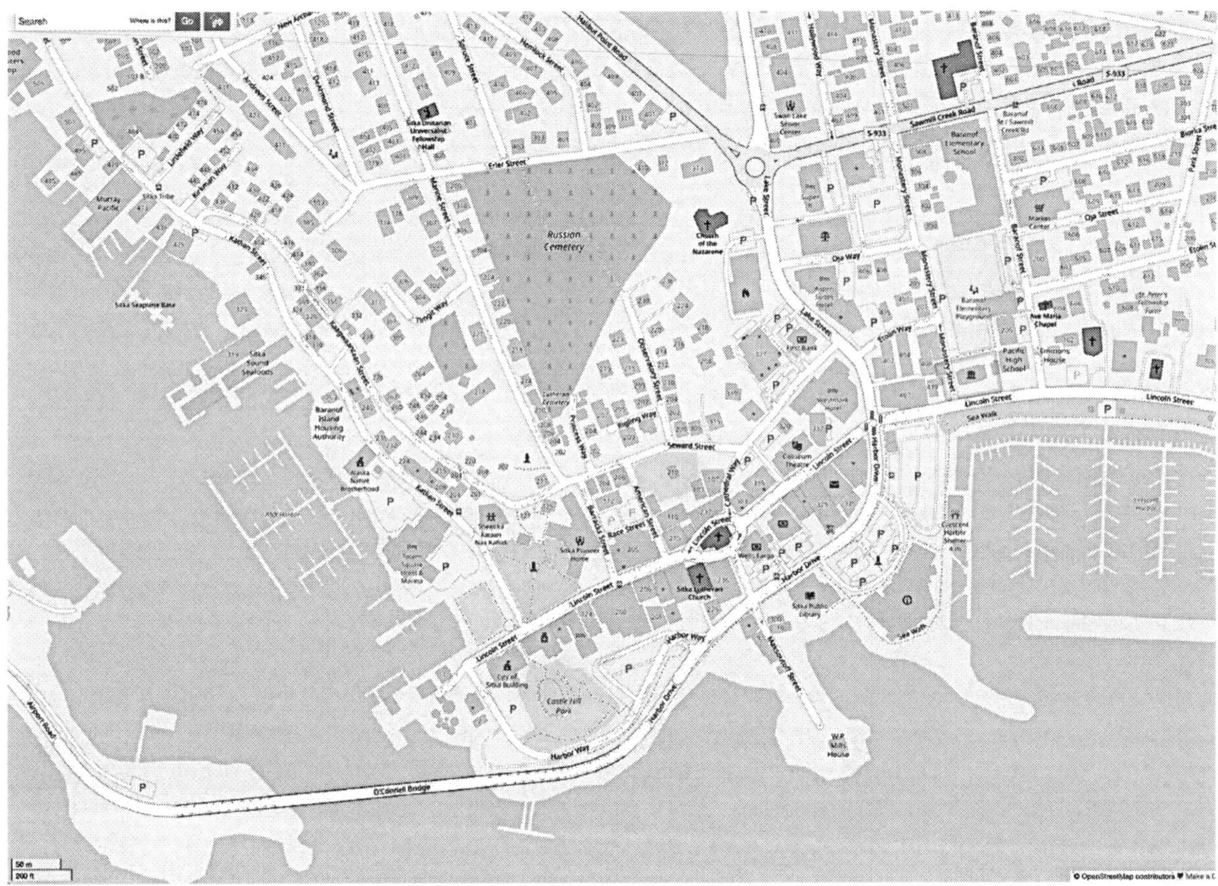

Sitka's small but unique downtown core

This map is best viewed directly from OpenStreetMap.com on your personal device where it can be expanded or one specific area can be enlarged. Given the format of this book, it is impossible to display maps with the level of detail you might wish to have while actually out exploring the city. But the OpenStreetMap maps used directly are the tool I always rely upon.

Mt. Edgcumbe is a dormant volcano overlooking Sitka

Early morning mist burns off the mountains behind Sitka

The islands of Sitka Harbor

Sitka Harbor under the shadow of Mount Edgecombe

A portion of the Sitka salmon fishing fleet

The surviving watchtower of the old Russian Fort

The historic Russian Bishop's House

Saint Michael's Russian Orthodox Cathedral in downtown Sitka

The Fisherman's Eye Gallery - one of many in Sitka

The Sitka Rose Gallery, one featuring Russian and local art

Inside the Sitka Rose Gallery filled with local art

Elegant handmade glass art found in Sitka Wild Arts Gallery

Tulips grace the streets of Sitka in early spring

The Sitka Pioneer's Home

SKAGWAY
YUKON GATEWAY

Map of the Skagway and White Pass region (© OpenStreetMap contributors)

There are two small towns at the upper end of the Inside Passage, Haines and Skagway. Both are served by the Alaska State Ferry, bringing cars north to then travel overland through the Yukon Territory of Canada to make the link to the interior of Alaska. From either port, you can travel onward to Anchorage or Fairbanks since there are no coastal road links given the rugged nature of the landscape, the numerous fjords that would need to be crossed and the vast distance. From Haines to Anchorage via Canada the distance is 756 miles or 1,217 kilometers. Cruise Ships call in at Skagway because of its famous narrow gauge rail link with Canada that was built during the end of the Klondike Gold Rush. The White Pass Railroad is one of the highlights for cruise passengers, as it gives you a chance to see some magnificent wild country, as you climb the mountains to cross the divide into the interior. Some choose to remain in Skagway and walk around the town, but frankly I think they do themselves a great disservice because the rail journey is one of those memorable experiences you will later cherish.

Skagway is a very small community of just under 1,000 residents, but it plays host to tens of thousands of cruise ship visitors during the summer season. During the summer cruise season the resident population can more than double with the availability of part-time jobs

in the tourist services sector, especially young college age workers who combine a job with adventure. Apart from cruise passengers, there are a few tourists who arrive with their car by ferryboat and then continue on into to the Yukon and the core area of Alaska. This is why Skagway is also one of the two land gateways to Alaska.

WHITE PASS RAILROAD: The White Pass and Yukon Railroad is the cornerstone of Skagway's tourism, and with nearly a million summer visitors, the train ride is greatly anticipated. Prior to gold being discovered in the Klondike of the Yukon and Alaska, the area was home to bands of Tlingit, as is true of much of the Alaska panhandle region. What brought American settlers was the discovery of White Pass, the only significant route through the rugged, steep and glacier filled Coast Mountains leading to the Yukon River that could be navigated to the interior of Alaska during summer months. William Moore, who helped survey the boundary with Canada in 1887, believed that these mountains and the lands beyond contained gold bearing strata. He staked a claim and built a cabin so he and his son could prospect the surrounding region. Up until the survey of 1887, the border between the two countries was ill defined because the Russians and British had never agreed upon a demarcation of their respective territory. Although Moore did not find gold in the immediate area, it was discovered in large quantity in the Klondike along the Yukon River to the north, and Skagway would become the port of embarkation for the dangerous land journey through the mountains to the goldfields.

Eager prospectors arrived in great numbers, ultimate swelling Skagway into a major town of tens of thousands. Those not prepared for the arduous journey into the Yukon found that there was money to be made in opening shops to supply the would be prospectors with needed supplies. The Canadian authorities set up strict rules as to the amount and type of supplies people had to carry over the pass to be allowed to cross the border. And Skagway merchants became prosperous. In addition, the lure of riches attracted gamblers, prostitutes and many shady types bent upon crime rather than legitimate enterprise. By 1900, Skagway was a boom town, but one with a wild and unsavory flavor. For the first few years of its existence it was rife with thieves, card sharks, gunslingers and unscrupulous businessmen that preyed upon the would be miners and town folk alike.

There were two routes to the upper reaches of the Yukon River, one being White Pass and the other was Chilkoot Pass. From over the border it was then possible to travel by barge or small boat down the Yukon River to Dawson City, which became the hub of the goldfield region known as the Klondike. During winter the snow made travel exceptionally difficult, but then during summer the soggy ground and mosquitos made the journey equally as uncomfortable. The Chilkoot Pass route lost favor because the landing at a place called Dyea was too shallow for larger boats. They began to service the top end of the Inside Passage by calling in at Skagway where the water is deep and not affected by tidal ranges.

With the strict Canadian rule requiring prospectors to carry heavy loads of supplies, there was need for a railroad, and construction began in 1898, utilizing narrow gauge (three foot six inch) tracks, a more sensible gauge for steep mountain terrain. Unfortunately the gold fever of the Klondike began to wane at the time the railroad was completed in 1900. But the commercial mining of copper, lead-zinc and silver along with routine passenger traffic kept

the railroad in business.

The railroad continued to make a small profit, but the depression years of the 1930's almost brought its demise. The World War II construction of the Alcan Highway saved the railroad from collapse, as Skagway became an important supply port to ferry men and equipment into the interior for the highway's construction. But it was the U. S. Army that actually ran the railroad so as to maximize its use for wartime purposes. For the American army to operate in Canada required the Canadian Parliament to authorize a foreign military unit to function within its territory, including the actual construction of the Alcan Highway, which was done by the U. S. Army Corps of Engineers. More traffic was transported over the White Pass and Yukon Railroad during the building of the Alcan Highway than in any time in its history, taking a heavy toll on the rolling stock and rails.

After World War II, the railroad continued operation, switching over to diesel locomotives in the late 1950's, and hauling specialized smaller size containers for freight because of the smaller gauge. When a major lead-zinc mine was opened in 1969, the railroad upgraded its rolling stock, dug a tunnel to bypass a bridge too light for the greater load. The White Pass and Yukon ultimately became the continent's only narrow gauge line to continue operating as a working railroad when others either were abandoned or became tourist oriented.

Being heavily dependent upon hauling ore as its major cargo left the railroad vulnerable and in 1982, a severe drop in lead-zinc prices spelled disaster. The mine shut down and the bulk of the rail traffic ceased. Much of the rolling stock and many of the diesel locomotives were sold and the line ceased to operate. What is ironic is that this happened just when cruise passenger traffic on the Inside Passage was starting to develop into a major potential. Like the Durango Silverton Railroad in Colorado, the White Pass and Yukon also became tourist oriented, as the cruise lines pressured for the creation of a scenic and historic service, guaranteeing great numbers of passengers given the love people have for unique railway journeys that can be made in a few hours. It did not take long to have the line up and running in 1988 and today it is the life-blood of Skagway. Few cruise passengers do not ride the rails during their one-day visit, as this is the great highlight of a visit to Skagway.

Today most passengers ride the train across the Canadian border to Fraser or Bennett, but the line has not been certified as totally safe for passenger service beyond into Whitehorse, the capital and only true city in the Yukon Territory. In 2006, it was certified to Carcross on the banks of the Yukon River and there are excursions with one way by motor coach now offered through some cruise lines. There are various options depending upon what the cruise lines offer. Some journeys include one way by motor coach from Bennett, which affords an opportunity to see the railway line from the highway and to watch the train on its route. There are various local excursions on the Canadian side of the border such as visiting a dog sled facility that can also be incorporated into the train trip. These excursions require that passengers carry their passports and immigration inspection takes place at the border. Some cruise lines offer a round trip that just reaches the summit at the Canadian border and then returns without actually allowing passengers off the train in Canada, thus avoiding immigration formalities.

For a select few charter services mainly for the upmarket cruise lines the railroad does use a steam locomotive during the summer months, but diesel locomotives are used on most trains. Given the vast crowds that visit Skagway, it is impossible to plan to ride the White Pass Railroad on your own, so if this is an activity you are looking forward to, definitely book it through your cruise line as early as possible, especially if your cruise line has booked the steam train.

A DAY IN SKAGWAY: For those who spend the day in Skagway and those taking the shorter half-day rail journey, there is plenty of time to walk around the town and enjoy the 100 old Victorian buildings that date back to the days of the Klondike Gold Rush. And Skagway residents have provided a variety of entertainments in the local pubs and restaurants as well as the shops with many dressed in traditional 19th century garb.

Skagway is so small that there is no need for hiring a private car and driver/guide or even taking advantage of the local taxi. If you wish to drive into Canada on your own, there is an Avis car rental office on Third Avenue between Spring Street and Broadway. You can pre book at *www.avis.com.* The only road leading out of Skagway follows the route to the White Pass and the Canadian border, which is just a few kilometers or miles out of town. Taxis cannot take guests into Canada.

* Skagway Tours does offer private coach tours inside and around Skagway, including the White Pass route into Canada. For more information, check their web page at *www.skagway.tours.com.* Alaska Travel Adventures offers a variety of outdoor activities for those who wish to experience a more rugged day. Their web page is *www.alaskatraveladventures.com.*

There is a quaint shuttle bus that takes guests from the cruise dock to the town center on a frequency of every twenty minutes at a cost of $2.00 each way or on an all-day ticket of $5.00

Here are a few of the venues in and around Skagway that can help keep you busy and entertained (listed alphabetically):

* Klondike Gold Rush National Historic Park - Operated by the National Park Service there are hikes, float tours and an excellent visitors center that provides the history of Skagway and the gold rush era. The park visitor center is at 291 Broadway and is open daily from 8:30 AM to 5:30 PM.

* Red Onion Saloon Brothel Museum - A colorful part of Skagway kept alive, but only in spirit, as there is no working brothel. It is located in the heart of town at 305 Broadway and is open daily from 10 AM to 10 PM.

* Skagway Museum - A small venue that has many of the artifacts of the past to help bring the gold rush days to life. The museum is at 700 Spring Street and is open weekdays from 8 AM to 5 PM. Closed Saturday and Sunday.

* State Street and Broadway - Walk the few blocks of the historic district and simply soak in

the architectural flavor of old Skagway.

I personally recommend the rail journey because the scenery is spectacular and the train has a very nostalgic flavor. This is one of the few international scenic trains in the world. And for some cruise lines that pay extra, the steam locomotive is used, making this an even more memorable journey.

The train in many ways takes you through a time warp, back around a century. The passenger carriages are original and the only heat provided comes from a wood burning stove at one end of each car. You get the feeling of what it would have been like to travel across the country before modern conveniences. Yes there are bathrooms in each car, so do not be alarmed about this being an old train. The cars all have front and rear porches, and the coupling between cars is very narrow, so guests are asked to remain in the car where you are seated, however, for those who are not afraid of heights, the best vantage points are on those two porches in each car. As the train climbs into White Pass, there are spectacular drop offs of over 300 meters or 1,000 feet and if the weather is clear, the views are amazing. Even if it is cloudy and raining a bit, you will still enjoy the rushing waters of the Skagway River, which is crossed numerous times. And you will feel a sense of awe or wonder at the magnitude of the broad canyon or valley along whose slopes you travel.

Most round trip journeys have a turnaround at the Canada border, and you cross about two kilometers or just over a mile into British Columbia. The steam train continues on for about 10 kilometers or six miles to the small town of Bennett where there is both a broad turnaround, but also a water tank for the locomotive to refill. But again, you do not leave the train. In both instances passports are not required.

But again depending upon the cruise line, there are some one-way excursions where you visit a sled dog kennel and training facility or simply leave the train and then travel back by motor coach. In these instances you will need to take your passport because both Canadian and American immigration stations will be passed.

Without question, I highly recommend the journey for both the spectacular scenery and the nostalgia of an old fashioned train. I have made the trip numerous times and will do so again in the future. Even if the weather is poor in Skagway, when you cross through White Pass and emerge onto the high plateau of northern British Columbia you often come out into brilliant sunlight. And if your cruise is in May or June there will still be deep snow at the summit where you cross the border. This is an excellent journey for those who love to take photographs.

DINING OUT: Many people enjoy having a chance to dine in each port of call. In Skagway it is possible to have lunch, as most train journeys last only half a day while the majority of cruise ships do stop for the entire day. Of the restaurants in Skagway, I am only comfortable recommending the few that are listed below in alphabetical order:

*** BBQ Shack – Located on Broadway between Fifth and Sixth Streets, this typical American restaurant with a Gold Rush atmosphere is well known for its barbecue, but it also does offer**

vegetarian dishes as well. They have a reputation for large and delicious iced cinnamon buns served mainly in the morning for breakfast. They are open daily from 8 AM to 5 PM.

*** Bites on Broadway – Located at 648 Broadway, this combination bakery and café serves typical American sandwiches, cakes, brownies and breakfast items in a quaint atmosphere. They are open from 6 AM to 6 PM daily during the busy summer season.**

*** Skagway Fish Company – At 201 Congress Avenue, this restaurant offers fresh local seafood served in a variety of ways. Their cold fish or shellfish salads are quite well presented as is their batter dipped fish and chips. They also offer chowders and sandwiches along with a very good salmon burger. Their hours are from 11 AM to 9 PM daily.**

*** Woadie's South End Seafood – At Fourth Avenue and State Street, this seafood restaurant is not much on atmosphere, but they do serve fresh fish and shellfish . They make a good crab bisque, and they also have excellent fish and chips. Their hours are Monday thru Thursday from 11:30 AM to 7 PM, Friday and Sunday Noon to 6 PM.**

SHOPPING: Skagway is a town that lives for tourists. There are many shops that sell the usual souvenirs and tourist kitsch, but none that I feel comfortable recommending as having anything special.

FINAL WORDS: Apart from its historic Victorian architecture, Skagway is not what one could call a real town. It lives only for tourism and most of its 1,000 residents are here just to service the summer cruise passenger traffic. What makes Skagway a major port of call is the incredible White Pass Railroad journey up over the mountains, tracing the route of the Klondike Gold Rush Era. It is a memorable rail journey and one of the most famous in the world when it comes to scenic routes.

DOWNTOWN SKAGWAY

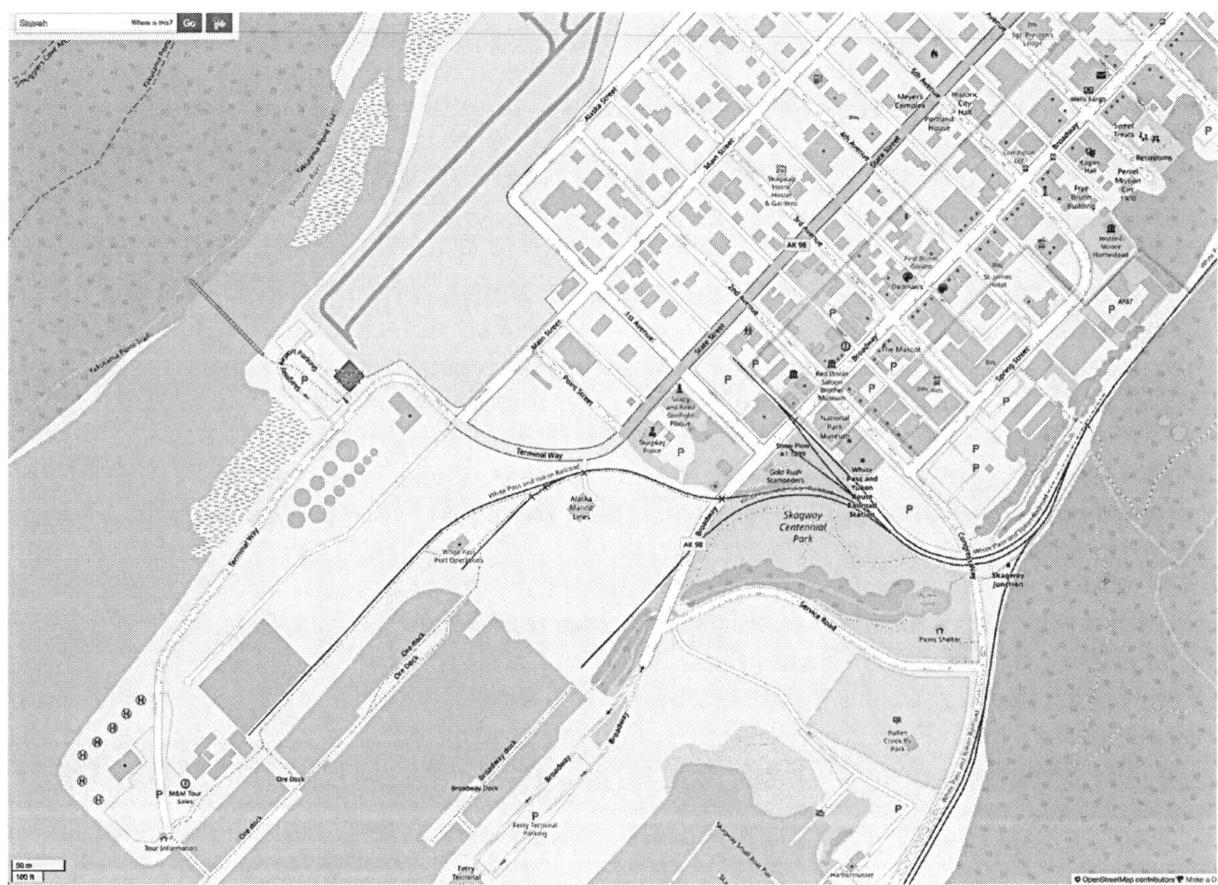

Skagway's small but unique downtown core

This map is best viewed directly from OpenStreetMap.com on your personal device where it can be expanded or one specific area can be enlarged. Given the format of this book, it is impossible to display maps with the level of detail you might wish to have while actually out exploring the city. But the OpenStreetMap maps used directly are the tool I always rely upon.

Skagway on a bright, sunny day, (Work of Wknight 94, CC BY SA 3.0, Wikimedia.org)

Downtown Skagway on a rainy afternoon

If you are fortunate you will have steam locomotive 73 pull your train

Diesel locomotives pull most trains

If you are lucky enough to have the steam locomotive it adds to the journey

These are the typical old fashioned carriages for passengers

Following the Skagway River up to the Canadian border

The Skagway River carries quite a volume of water for its width

Approaching White Pass in June still has brutal conditions at the top

Crossing the Canadian border high up in snow country

The old Northwest Mounted Police border checkpoint from the gold rush days

The high country landscape of northern British Columbia once over the pass

The U. S. Immigration Building along the main highway seen from the train

Crossing the upper reaches of the Skagway River on the return journey

The train winds its way down from White Pass to Skagway

Even with the diesel locomotive the journey is spectacular

Crossing the lower portion of Skagway Creek on the return

End of the line back in Skagway

GLACIER BAY

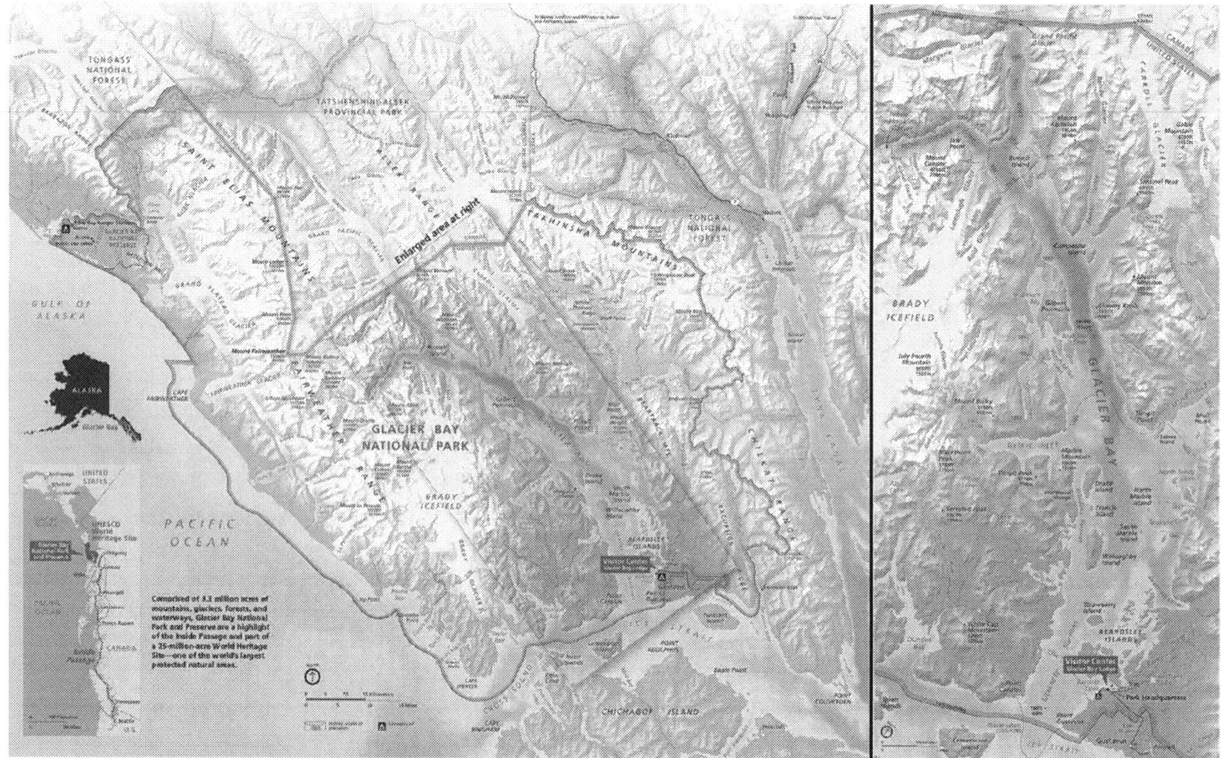

A map of Glacier Bay National Park

The glaciers of Alaska are one of the primary highlights of any Alaska cruise. And one of the most spectacular venues is Glacier Bay National Park and Preserve at the top end of the Alaska Panhandle. Glacier Bay is part of a UNESCO World Heritage Site that also includes adjacent Klulane National Park and Tatshenshini-Alsek Provincial Park on the Canadian side of the border. The bay is located at the narrowest part of the Alaska Panhandle where at one point the Canadian border is only 15 miles from the Gulf of Alaska, almost severing the panhandle from the main body of the state. The total land area of the park extends over 13,286 square kilometers or 5,130 square miles making it larger than the entire state of Connecticut.

What provides the glacial ice that extends down to the bay through all of the tributary coves is the height of the St. Elias Mountains and Fairweather Range, part of the greater Coast Ranges of the United States and Canada. Mt. Fairweather in Alaska is 4,663 meters or 15,300 feet high and just across the border Mt. Logan in Canada is 6,050 meters or 19,849 feet high, the tallest peak in the country. The height of these mountains intercepting the moist air off the Gulf of Alaska means that snowfall is almost continual throughout the year with no melting at such altitudes. As snow continues to fall, it compresses the lower layers into ice that ultimately accumulates to thousands of feet in thickness, and then it flows down every valley or canyon toward the sea.

The Brady Ice Field in the Fairweather Range on a peninsula that extends southeast between the Gulf of Alaska and Glacier Bay creates numerous glacial outflows. East of Glacier Bay,

the Takishna and Chilkat Ranges form a second peninsula that is bordered by Lynn Channel, an inlet from the Inside Passage. It is here that the Brady Ice Field totally eliminates the possibility of ever developing a land route between Haines and the main core of Alaska without the need to cross over into Canada.

Glacier Bay is totally isolated from any land contact with the rest of Alaska, accessible only by air on a year around basis and by ferryboats and cruise ships during the summer months. The popularity of Glacier Bay has led to an estimated 400,000 visitors each summer, but the majority of guests never leave their ships, simply cruising the waters and marveling at the glaciers from on board. Some of the smaller cruise lines, however, do send select groups on shore in small zodiacs for brief forays.

The national park also includes the offshore waters, thus providing protection for the multitude of whales, dolphins, seals and other marine wildlife that add to the overall spectacle of this truly wild environment. The government also allows the Tlingit people access to two areas that were once part of their homeland, and they are allowed to fish and hunt to a limited degree. Archaeological fieldwork has been difficult in this region because of glacial advances and retreats, rising sea levels since the end of the last major glacial advance and tectonic uplift. But it is understood that the Tlingit and other tribes have been utilizing these lands and fishing grounds for thousands of years.

The glaciers of the park have a long documented history that dates back to the 1780's, and it can be seen that many glaciers have experienced periods of advancement and recession. However, today there is a high degree of recession and some glaciers that were once right at sea level have retreated back from the water's edge, now requiring a short hike to reach their face. By matching the logs of early explorers it is possible to see how some glaciers have retreated while others have advanced. From 1791 to 1879, Glacier Bay has seen its water surface extend inland 48 miles where once glacial ice blocked the way. The Grand Pacific Glacier coming out of the Fairweather Ice Field has retreated 65 miles from where it was at the mouth of Glacier Bay. All of these retreats occurred well before our awareness of global warming, proof that the phenomenon has its roots back to the end of the last great glacial advance that began to reverse itself over 10,000 years ago. Scientists are today studying why some glaciers in the park are still advancing while most are continuing their retreat. Yes there is no question that on a global scale human pollution of the atmosphere especially carbon dioxide is having an impact. But even if we were to discontinue all of our gas and particulate emissions, which of course we cannot do, it is believed that there would still be a degree of warming. The question now is to determine to what degree our actions are exacerbating the condition. In any event, we need to become better stewards of our environment and curb our pollution of air, water and land for the long-term health of our planet. It is pretty clear that despite the rapid warming and retreat of many glaciers in the park, the heavy snowfall at the higher elevations on the mountains will provide sufficient snowpack to compress into glacial ice and keep some of the glaciers from disappearing.

In addition to being subjected to changing climate, this is a region of strong tectonic activity. The mountains are essentially still rising. Periodic earthquakes, landslides and mini tsunami within confined narrow fjords all play a role in molding the changing landscape. Fortunately

there is no active volcanic activity in this part of Alaska. Volcanic activity is confined to the Alaska Peninsula and the Aleutian Islands far to the west.

The climatic conditions are typical of the marine conditions found in the Alaska Panhandle. But elevation plays a major role in altering the temperature, with averages of .5 degree Celsius drop for every 100 meter rise or 3.3 to 5.5 degree Fahrenheit drops for every thousand-foot rise in elevation. Thus it can be raining at sea level and a few thousand feet above the temperature can be well below freezing with falling snow.

Depending upon the weather conditions on the day your cruise ship visits Glacier Bay, you may see orcas, humpback whales, grizzly bear, moose, deer, mountain goats, wolves, bald eagles, ducks and even salmon. This is a very active wildlife zone, but of course from one of the upper decks of the ship it is often difficult to get a close up view of the animal life. And unfortunately there are days when visibility is reduced to near zero by heavy fog or pouring rain. Thus the quality of the weather during a visit to Glacier Bay can never be guaranteed.

When you visit Glacier Bay on board a modern cruise ship, sailing into its frigid waters, watching the primal forces of glacial calving during summer and feeling the chill of the air, you feel like you have made a great discovery of nature at her best. But Glacier Bay has seen many before you. The first European to explore the bay was a French captain in 1786, followed by a Russian vessel in 1788. British explorer George Vancouver visited in 1794. During the period of Russian occupation of Alaska, the bay was nothing more than a curiosity, as it was deemed uninhabitable. The great naturalist John Muir visited the bay in 1879 as part of his studies of glaciers, which ultimately helped him to understand the geological creation of his beloved Yosemite National Park. Likewise during the Klondike Gold Rush, the area was considered too formidable to attempt to utilize other than for a bit of offshore salmon fishing. But tourism on a very limited basis began during the gold rush era, as the bay is not far from Skagway. John Muir made successive return visits during the 1890's and was instrumental in helping to promote tourism to Glacier Bay and Alaska's Inside Passage by publishing articles in a San Francisco paper. Ultimately a glacier was named after him, but a severe earthquake in 1899 damaged that glacier.

During the 1920's, studies of the ecology and unique landscape were submitted to the Department of the Interior in an attempt to gain protection for Glacier Bay, but the Geological Survey opposed the idea believing that there was a great mineral potential that could be exploited. In 1925, President Calvin Coolidge signed the bill creating the first Glacier Bay National Monument, which was much smaller in land area than today's park. In 1939, President Franklin Roosevelt expanded the size of the monument to include lands that would protect the ecology.

Glacier Bay Lodge was opened in 1966, providing the first accommodation for those who braved the arduous journey, flying into the park on small aircraft from Juneau. This paved the way for more public awareness of the beauty and majesty of the landscape. And by the early 1970's, many cruise ships were making the bay a part of their Alaska itinerary. President Carter added to the land area of the monument and in 1980, he elevated the status to that of national park and preserve.

UNESCO had designated the Canadian parks adjacent to Glacier Bay as a World Heritage Site in 1979, recognizing their spectacular scenery and wildlife. Glacier Bay was added to the Heritage Site in 1992, thus making this a trans-border collection of parks and preserves. The lack of easy access is what will help to keep most of the land pristine, this in contrast to many American and Canadian national parks that are literally overrun by tens of thousands of visitors mainly coming by car, truck or recreational vehicle. It is easy to simply love an environment to the point of detriment. Fortunately Glacier Bay will not suffer this fate. Even the number of cruise ships allowed to enter the waters of the park at a given time is controlled. And simple activities such as having loud speakers broadcasting live narration of the landscape are no longer allowed. In this way the peace and tranquility are maintained.

A Landsat enhanced satellite view of Glacier Bay

At the front edge of a still active glacier, (Work of gailhampshire, CC BY SA 2.0, Wikimedia.org)

Glacial calving in the John Hopkins Inlet

The Margerie Glacier

Up close to the Margerie Glacier

The calm waters filled with small ice chunks, (Work of David Levine, CC BY SA 2.0, Wikimedia.org)

Cruise ships are dwarfed by Glacier Bay's mountains and glaciers

HUBBARD GLACIER

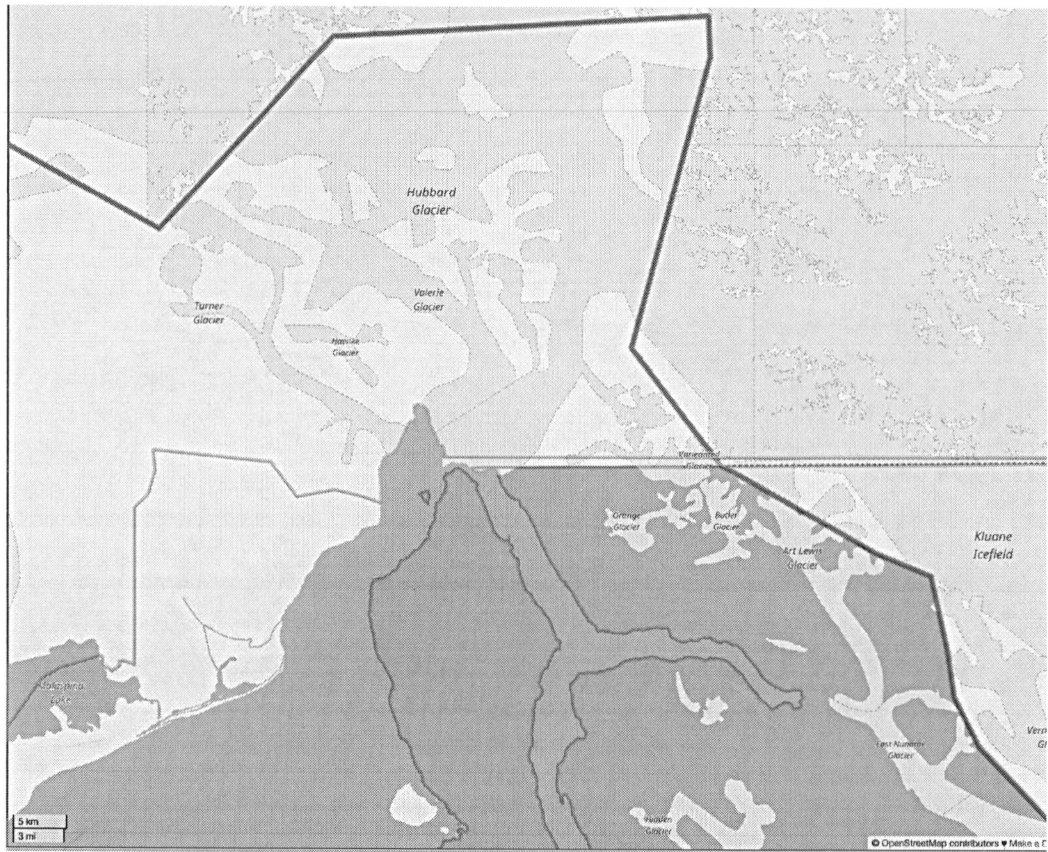

The extent of the Hubbard Glacier (© OpenStreetMap contributors)

The smaller five-star cruise lines will often visit the Hubbard Glacier either in addition to Glacier Bay or in lieu of it, depending upon the length of the itinerary. But most of the major cruise lines concentrate upon Glacier Bay, as this is often the turnaround point on seven-day cruises that start and end in Vancouver. On cruises that traverse the entire distance between Seward or Whittier (ports for Anchorage) and Vancouver, the options for scenic cruising are Glacier Bay, Hubbard Glacier or Prince William Sound.

Hubbard Glacier is one of the longest of Alaskan/Canadian glaciers, its origin being high up in the Alaska Range at over 3,350 meter or 11,000 foot altitude at a distance of over 120 kilometers or 75 miles from its terminus in Yakutat Bay. Several smaller glaciers are tributary to the main Hubbard Glacier channel, creating a massive total ice flow.

In the 12th century, the front of the glacier was at the present opening of Yakutat Bay, about 40 kilometers or 25 miles from its present terminus. Yet despite the apparent retreat of the ice in 900 years, at present the glacier appears to be relatively stable, advancing in some years and retreating in others, but within a relatively narrow window. In spring 1986, the glacier surged forward and blocked the adjacent Russell Fjord, which caused the melt from the upper end of the fjord to back up behind the glacier, forming a massive lake that rose to over 24 meters or 80 feet in height. That fall, the front of the glacier gave way and a massive

flood surged down through the narrower Disenchantment Bay into Yakutat Bay and out to sea. This flood saved many of the marine creatures living in Russell Fjord from extinction because of the decrease in salinity that was occurring. In 2002, the advance of the Hubbard Glacier created a low dam of rubble and debris, what is called a terminal moraine, in front of Russell Fjord, but it did not stay for too long before being swept away.

The ebb and flow of the Hubbard Glacier fascinates scientists because of the rapidity with which it occurs. It will in all likelihood dam Russell Fjord in the near future. If the glacial advance were to continue and remain intact for a few years, Russell Fjord could reach the point where the southern arm could break through directly to the Gulf of Alaska, re drawing the map of the region.

Because of its activity during the summer with massive blocks of ice calving off the front end of the Hubbard Glacier, cruise ships maintain an average distance from the terminus of at least a mile or more. You must remember that when you see a large iceberg floating in the bay in front of any glacier that approximately 90 percent of its mass is hidden from view. Ice has more buoyancy than water because of the air trapped inside. Just drop an ice cube into a glass a water to see how much actually floats above the surface. One of the lessons learned by the Titanic disaster was that of keeping a safe distance from what even appear to be small icebergs.

When ships cruise Disenchantment Bay to view the Hubbard Glacier the total time spent from the entry into Yakutat Bay until departure back into the Gulf of Alaska is around three hours. But the scenery is memorable, and by late summer with the warmer temperatures there is generally quite a bit of calving that is spectacular to watch. At that point, cruise ships must stay well back from the glacier's front. But in May when the temperatures are still hovering near freezing, it is possible for ships to approach the front edge of the glacier. This gives guests a chance to hear the cracking sounds made by the softening ice, and then the large crack that heralds a major piece dropping into the bay.

The massive front edge of Hubbard Glacier seen from three kilometers or 1.6 miles

Small icebergs floating in Disenchantment Bay in mid spring

Numerous small icebergs out in Yakutat Bay near its mouth

Approaching close to the front of Hubbard Glacier

Up against the front edge of the Hubbard Glacier

Approaching to within 50 feet of the glacier

So close as to hear the glacier cracking and groaning as it calves

The narrow opening to Russell Fjord that is sometimes blocked

Passing the smaller Valerie Glacier

PRINCE WILLIAM SOUND

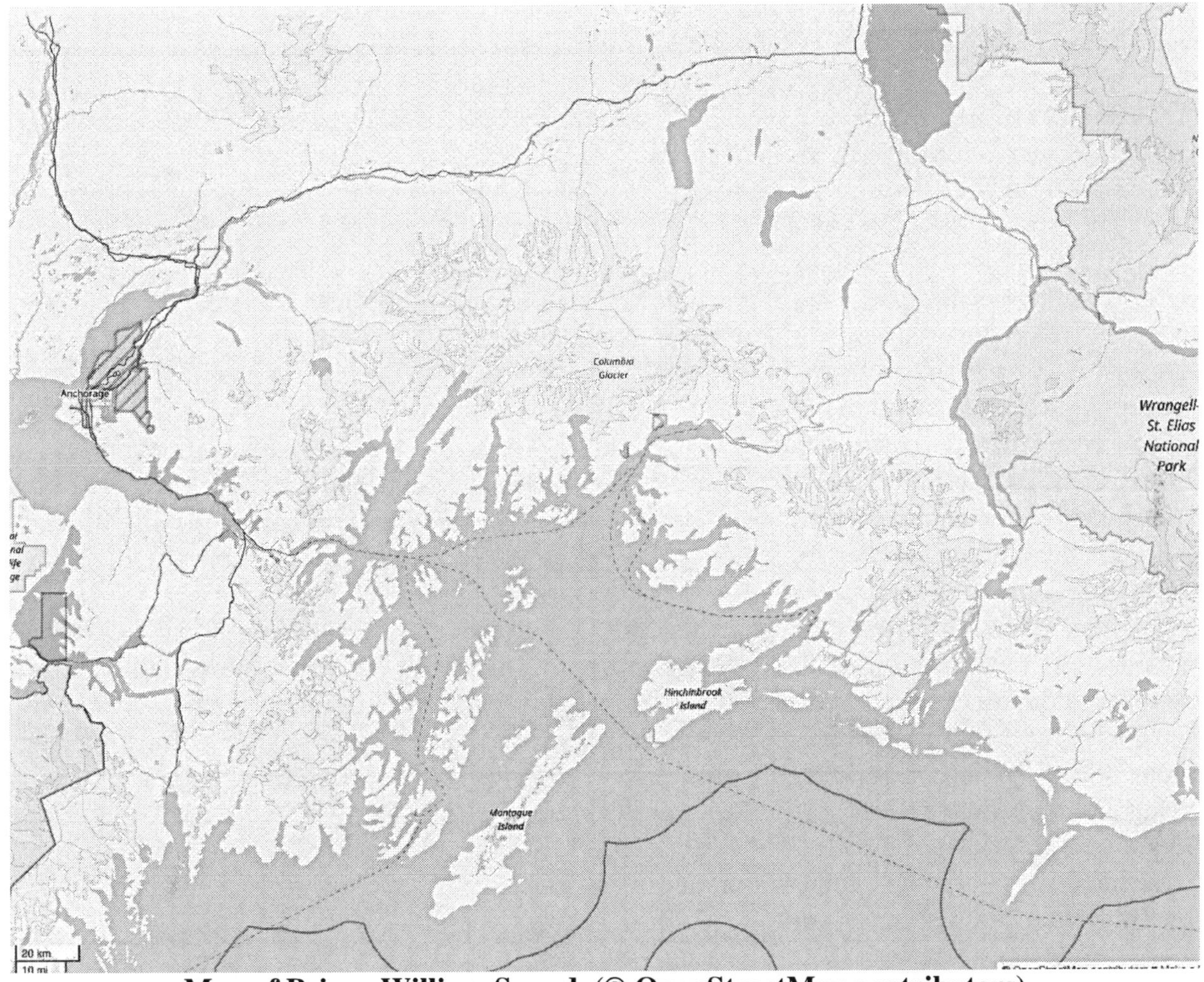

Map of Prince William Sound (© OpenStreetMap contributors)

Prince William Sound is a large arm of the Gulf of Alaska that is protected by a series of major islands, creating a very sheltered bay with numerous small and fjords. The port town of Whittier is located at the southwestern end of the sound, and this is the location for docking facilities servicing the large cruise ships of the major lines that have Alaskan itineraries. Many of the medium-size and smaller cruise ships; especially the high-end luxury lines use the port of Seward on the Kenai Peninsula as their turnaround port. Both Whittier and Seward are connected to Anchorage by means of the Alaska Railroad. The rail journey from Whittier is about 90 minutes whereas from Seward it takes nearly four hours to reach the Anchorage airport. However, that rail journey is quite spectacular.

British Captain James Cook first explored the sound in 1778, but he named it Sandwich Sound after the Earl of Sandwich. This is the same name he also gave to the Hawaiian Islands. But it was Captain George Vancouver who renamed it Prince William Sound in honor of the Prince of Wales who would become King William IV, uncle of Queen Victoria from whom she inherited the throne since she was the only surviving heir.

The sound is surrounded by the massive arc of the Alaska Range that contains some of the highest and most spectacular peaks on the continent. Numerous fjords extending back into the mountains are the result of past glacial action and at their upper ends of many of these channels there are still major glaciers that are the outflow of the large ice field in the mountain mass.

Prince William Sound has seen two major disasters during the 20th century, one natural and the second man-made. On Good Friday 1964, a massive 9.2 magnitude earthquake offshore created a tsunami that destroyed the town of Valdez and one of the native villages with significant loss of life and property. This was the second most powerful earthquake ever recorded since the creation of the Richter Scale. And in 1989, the Exxon Valdez oil tanker ran aground on its way out of Valdez and created one of the most devastating oil spills to damage any part of the United States. Valdez is the terminus of the Alaska Oil Pipeline that brings crude oil south from the Arctic Slope of Northern Alaska. The spill was deemed ultimately the result of officer carelessness, and its impact upon marine life was devastating. Today there are much more stringent requirements for oil tankers, especially the demand that they have double walled hulls to cut down on the danger of a spill.

The vast majority of cruise itineraries will not actually do any sightseeing in Prince William Sound or its tributary fjords. They will simply sail in during the early morning hours and disembark passengers at Whittier where most will take the train or motor coach into Anchorage and end their cruise. Most guests are either still asleep or are busy finishing their preparations for disembarking the ship. Some itineraries include a charter land option by rail or motor coach to visit Denali National Park north of Anchorage. And the reverse is true for those whose cruise begins out of Whittier. In southbound voyages the ships will sail in the evening, but at least passengers can be out on deck to enjoy the vistas while the ship is heading into the sea. During summer there is nearly perpetual daylight.

Small cruise ships only visit Valdez on rare occasions. The town is primarily a fishing port, center for sportsmen setting off into the interior and since 1977 terminus of the Trans Alaska Pipeline where huge tankers take on oil for distribution to the lower 48 states and beyond. There is paved highway leading into the interior with connections to both Anchorage and Fairbanks. Valdez is also connected to other ports along the Alaska coast by what is called the Marine Highway, a ferryboat route that links the coastal communities.

The town owes its founding to what was essentially a swindle. A few unscrupulous steam ship companies promoted Valdez as an easier gateway to the Klondike Gold Rush, which of course was not true, as the distance is far greater and the interior terrain equally challenging. The name dates to a 1790 Spanish exploration of the sound.

The town of Whittier is located on a narrow arm of Prince William Sound known as Passage Canal. Its harbor provides deep-water access to large cruise ships and is linked to Anchorage by means of both a paved highway and the Alaska Railroad. Whittier owes its existence to the U. S. Army, which built the original port facility to provide the quickest access to the interior of Alaska by way of Anchorage. The city of Anchorage is located on Cook Inlet, but

despite its width and direct access to the open sea, this body of water is quite shallow and has a great tidal range making the maintenance of a port exceptionally difficult and requiring continual dredging well out into the inlet to keep a channel at sufficient depth during low tides.

Whittier has an impressive initial appearance because of being in possession of a 14-story apartment block that was built by the Army for its personnel following World War II when there was still a strong Cold War concern for the safety of Alaska. The army maintained facilities in Whittier until 1960.

Like Valdez, Whittier also suffered severe damage from the Good Friday Earthquake in 1964. When traveling by either motor coach or train from Whittier to Anchorage the route passes Turnagain Arm of the Cook Inlet. And there are many dead tree trunks standing ghost like along the edge of the water, reminders of the subsiding of parts of the coastline combined with seawater invasion that killed the trees during the tsunami. And it is bound to happen again someday in the future, as this is the nature of living adjacent to such a volatile plate boundary.

The Alaska Railroad offers special summer rail service direct to Denali National Park for passengers traveling on Princess Cruise Lines ships. Most passengers disembarking in Whittier will travel to Anchorage, either to spend a few days or transferring to outbound flights later in the day. Your cruise line may offer rail transfer as part of the cruise package, but many lines offer motor coach service. The travel time into Anchorage is approximately 90-minutes.

Prince William Sound does offer beautiful scenery, but to enjoy the sights you must plan activities on your own. At the moment, none of the major cruise lines serving Whittier are offering any excursions in the sound except for passengers who have booked a back-to-back return cruise and have the full day in Whittier. Often the number of such passengers is so small that it does not pay for the ship to offer any special tours.

The tranquil natural beauty of mid-summer in Prince William Sound

Entering Prince William Sound filled with tiny bergy bits

The often calm waters of Prince William Sound near Valdez

Numerous small coves tucked into the mountains

Numerous large glaciers descend into the various bays of the sound

The front edge of one of the many small glaciers

In beautiful College Fjord there are numerous glaciers

Sailing into Whittier on a windy day with choppy water, (Work of Barbara Ann Spengler, CC BY SA 2.0, Wikimedia.org)

A Princess Cruise ship docking in Whittier

SEWARD

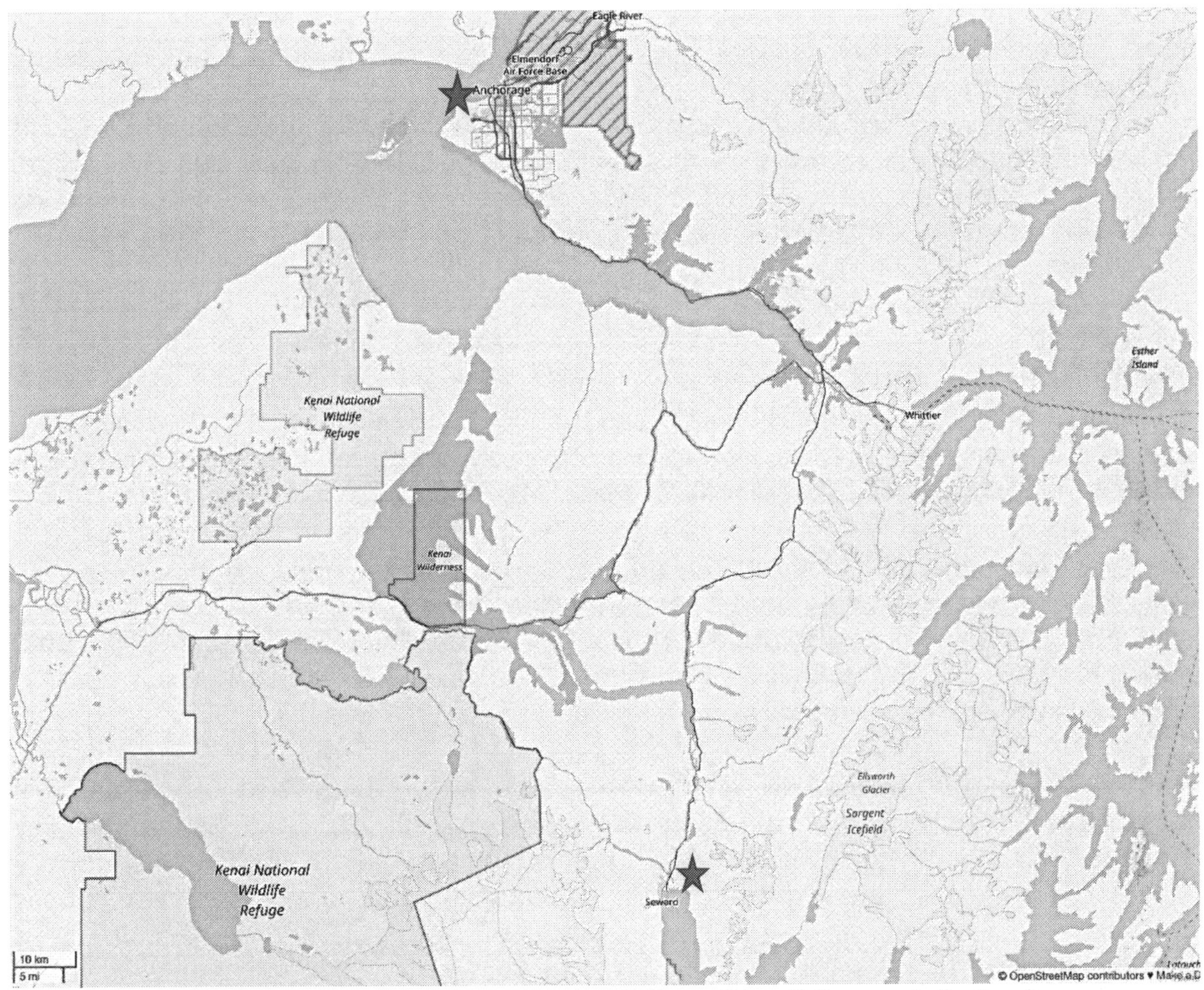

The Seward to Anchorage route (© OpenStreetMap contributors)

There are many cruise itineraries, especially those of the smaller more upmarket cruise lines, that begin or end their voyage in Seward on the Kenai Peninsula, south of Anchorage. Seward is 204 kilometers or 127 miles to Anchorage whereas Whittier is only 98 kilometers or 51 miles. The journey by either rail or motor coach is highly memorable, but it does take three to four hours depending upon conditions. I would only choose to begin or end an Alaska Panhandle cruise in Seward rather than in Whittier simply to take advantage of the magnificent landscapes of the Kenai Peninsula. Normally the high end cruise lines provide charter rail service between Seward and the Anchorage International Airport, a journey that I have taken several times and have always been captivated by the strikingly beautiful scenery.

NATURAL SETTING: The Kenai Peninsula is quite large, extending over 255 kilometers or 150 miles to the southwest from the high Chugach Mountains that are part of the greater Alaska Range. The peninsula is separated from the greater Alaska Peninsula to the west by Cook Inlet and its eastern shore fronts on the Gulf of Alaska. The heart of the peninsula is

occupied by the Kenai Mountains with peaks rising up to 2,134 meter or 7,000 feet in elevation, and the major part of the range is protected land known as Kenai Fjords National Park. The mountains front on the Gulf of Alaska where the majority of the fjords are to be found, as the western side along Cook Inlet is rather low lying marsh and woodland. Within the Kenai Mountains there are two major ice fields, with glacial outflows that are very dramatic. The many rivers that flow outward from the glacial lakes amid high peaks are fast flowing and home to large numbers of salmon. The surrounding forests are thick with spruce, Douglas fir, hemlock and cedar. And these forests are home to large numbers of grizzly bear and moose. Often from the train's large picture windows you will be treated to a number of bear or moose plus deer.

The earliest European history of the peninsula is Russian, with the first exploration made in 1789. The native population inhabited the peninsula for many centuries prior to the coming of Europeans. They are Athabaskan speakers, related to tribes in the interior Yukon. And their most distant relatives, migrated to the American Southwest during the 11th and 12th centuries and today are the Navajo and Apache of Arizona and New Mexico.

The port of Seward is located at the top end of Resurrection Bay, a fjord that joins the Gulf of Alaska. Seward is a small community of only 3,000 residents, named in honor of Secretary of State William Seward who negotiated the purchase of Alaska from Russia in 1867. But it was the Russians who first settled the bay in 1793. The Russian settlement was a fur-trading outpost located where the modern town is today.

The Seward Highway connects the port to Anchorage, a three-hour drive by car, and a bit slower by motor coach. It is one of the most scenic highways in Alaska because of the many glacial lakes, the high snow covered peaks and the many views of glaciers. The town of Seward is also the southern terminus for the Alaska Railroad and a major trans shipping port for goods in and out of Anchorage. For cruise ships docking in Seward, many of the high end lines offer charter train service to Anchorage, a scenic four-hour journey in carriages replete with glass domes and offering food and beverage service. The trains taking guests to the Anchorage International Airport or bringing guests to the ship for the southbound cruise have their Anchorage rail terminal right in the airport with trains arriving and departing at an elevated platform. And for cruise lines that have land packages inland to Denali National Park, there is direct train service that can be included. These trains simply pass through Anchorage on their journey north to the park.

Fishing helps to augment the Seward economy. It is one of the ten most important fishing ports in the nation with regard to the dollar value of its catch. Salmon, halibut and crab account for much of the catch.

Cruise passengers rarely even see the town of Seward, as their motor coach or train brings them directly to the dock where they board the ship on arrival. Departing passengers leave the ship and immediately board the train to Anchorage. Thus their only exposure to this magnificent landscape is seen through the train windows.

The Kenai Peninsula looking southeast on a flight Vancouver to Hong Kong

Early morning view of the town of Seward

Boarding an Alaska Railroad charter train in Seward

A standard rail carriage on a charter Alaska Railroad train to Anchorage

Beautiful lakeside views from the train an hour north of Seward

One of the many rivers coming out of the high Kenai Mountains

Approaching the highest point on the rail journey between Anchorage and Seward

At the high point of the line between Anchorage and Seward

Low tide along Turnagain Arm outside of Anchorage

Arriving at Anchorage International Airport on departure

ANCHORAGE

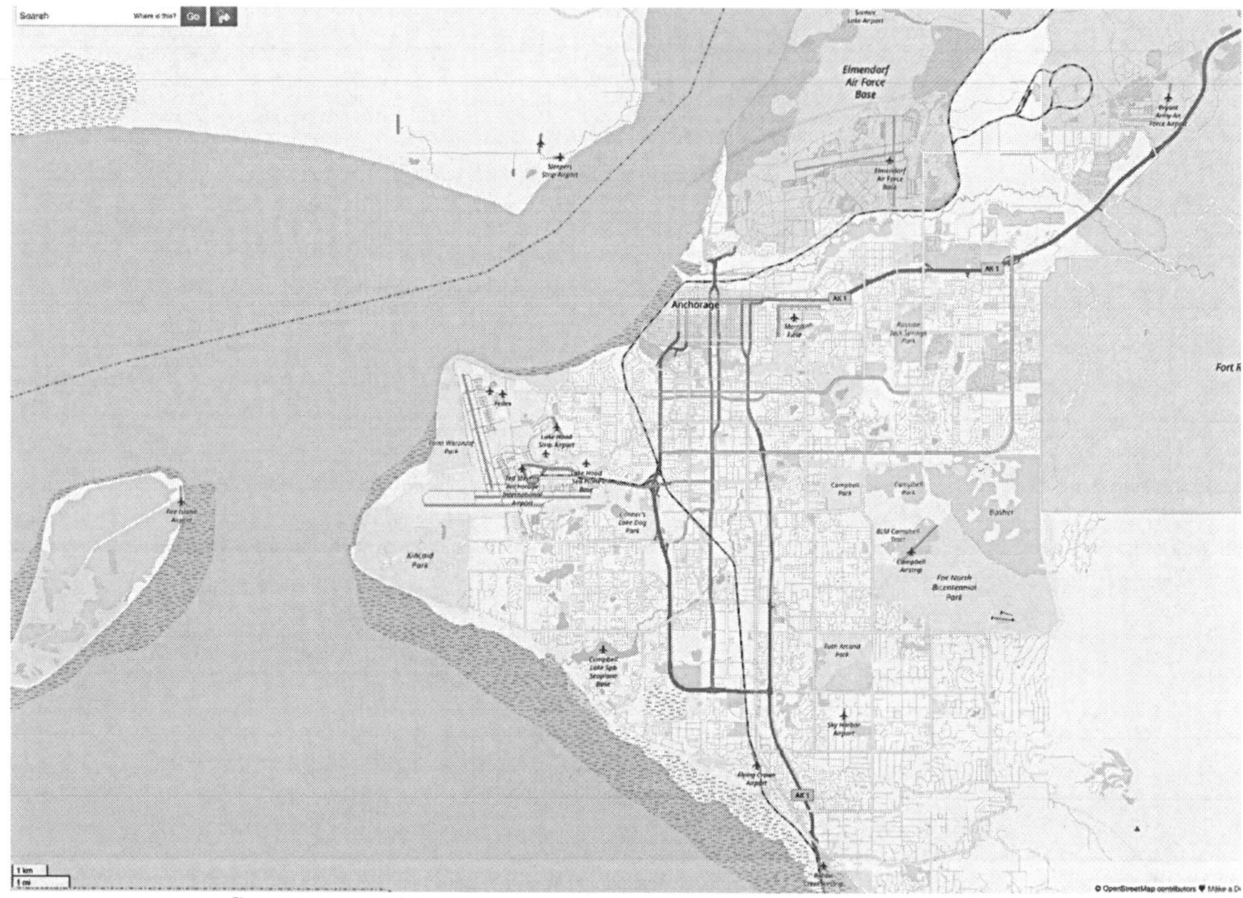

Street map of Anchorage (© OpenStreetMap contributors)

Most cruise passengers spend very little time, if any, in Anchorage, which is a shame. This is a very picturesque city because of its natural setting and it is the cultural heart of Alaska, a state not recognized by outsiders as having much in the way of urban sophistication. This is the largest city in the state with a metropolitan population of 301,000, which is 41 percent of the state's total. The vast majority of cruise passengers who are starting their cruise in Seward or Whittier will simply fly into Anchorage and stay overnight to be ready for the trip to their cruise ship the next day. Guests who are arriving via Seward or Whittier either book a land excursion onward to Denali National Park or travel direct to the airport for a flight out later in the day. Thus they never see much of the city apart from the view from the train or their motor coach. In this chapter you will become acquainted with the city and its surroundings as well as learning about its short history. And if you have not booked your flights, you may be convinced to spend two nights so as to have one day in Anchorage.

NATURAL SETTING: The geographic setting of Anchorage is one of the most beautiful of any American city. The Cook Inlet stretches northeastward between the highly volcanic Alaska Peninsula to the west and the Kenai Peninsula to the East. When it reaches Anchorage, the inlet splits into the Knick Arm that continues the northeast route and the

Turnagain Arm that branches to the east. The split occurs right at the Anchorage International Airport. Despite being on the shores of these three bodies of water, Anchorage is not a significant port. The tidal ranges of the Cook Inlet are extremely high, going from deep water to mud flats every 6 hours and 15 minutes. Thus the costs of attempting to maintain a dredged harbor are too great to warrant making Anchorage a seaport.

This is the most northerly city of over 100,000 in population on the North American continent, and it is the only major city in the nation that is surrounded by such a vast amount of mountainous wilderness, yet offering its residents all of the amenities of a major American city. The latitude of 61 degrees north places Anchorage just a bit farther north than Helsinki, which is the most northerly capital city on mainland Europe. The only other city of over 250,000 located in the far north is Murmansk, Russia, which is actually above the Arctic Circle. With great circle aviation routes, Anchorage is a major air crossroads for flights between Europe and eastern Asia or the east coast of North America and eastern Asia. Thus the airport serves as a major refueling center on these long trans global routes. This factor has diminished slightly because of the greater range of modern commercial jets. It also handles a lot of cargo, especially for FedEx, making it the world's third busiest apart from Memphis and Hong Kong.

Anchorage is surrounded on the east, north and west by the great peaks of the Alaska Range, including the Chugach Mountains to the east and two major active volcanic peaks at the northern end of the Alaska Peninsula. Denali Peak, also known as Mt. McKinley, is due north of the city. It is the tallest mountain on the continent.

Given its northerly latitude and the height of its surrounding mountains, Anchorage has what is called a continental cold winter climate, but one modified by the influence of the sea. Summer rains give way to winter snows, but there are periods during winter when the temperature hovers just above freezing giving the city rain instead of snow. Summer temperatures are mild and rarely go above 80 degrees Fahrenheit. And because of the sea's influence, winter temperatures rarely drop below zero Fahrenheit. The lands around the city are rich in timber, primarily Douglas fir, cedar and willow. And wildlife often strays into the suburban neighborhoods where spotting a moose, deer or bear is not uncommon. As noted before, this is a major city with a wilderness hinterland.

Anchorage, like all Gulf of Alaska coastal regions, sits atop a major active plate boundary. This subduction zone has produced a string of volcanoes stretching along the Alaska Peninsula and out across the Aleutian Islands. Earthquakes are a common occurrence and every two hundred years a catastrophic event takes place. On Good Friday, March 27, 1964 at around 5:30 in the afternoon a 9.2 magnitude earthquake tore through the region, causing massive physical damage to the city of Anchorage and surrounding towns. This was the second strongest earthquake every recorded on the Richter scale since its creation. The loss of life was 113, and property damage over $300 million, which today would equate to over 2.5 billion. There were large shifts in the crust, and in downtown Anchorage a portion of Fourth Avenue sunk several feet. The earthquake also touched off a major tsunami that devastated towns like Homer, Seward, Whittier and Valdez along with places as far away as northern California. Today Anchorage is eight times larger than in 1964, and the ever-

present danger still lurks. It is only a matter of time before another catastrophic quake will occur.

HISTORIC SKETCH: The city lacks a Russian heritage and it was also not a gold rush town. It developed because of its location as a transit point between the far north reached through low passes east of Denali Peak, and the coastal communities of the Gulf of Alaska and the Alaska Peninsula. When the decision was made to build a railroad to connect the deep interior with Seward, Anchorage was chosen as a rail construction site. Despite the tidal ranges of the Cook Inlet, barges with construction supplies could still be shipped into this camp during the high tide cycles. The town site was chosen on slightly elevated ground overlooking Knick Arm and it quickly grew into a small service center, incorporating as a city in 1920.

Initially it was essentially a railroad town, and the Alaska Railroad controlled most aspects of life in Anchorage. But by the late 1930's with the potential threat of war on a global scale, and with the growing importance of aviation, Anchorage became an important commercial and military air center. Fort Richardson Army Base and what would become Elmendorf Air Force Base developed north of the city and are today important to the overall economy. Today the two bases serve as a joint military command, and their total area and staff have been lessened from the Cold War Era. However, their combined personnel and families still account for roughly ten percent of the greater Anchorage population.

But since 1968 with the discovery of oil at Prudhoe Bay, Anchorage has become the nerve center for the state's oil industry. It is the financial hub of the state along with also being the wholesale and retail center for all of Alaska. State and federal government offices also add greatly to the overall payroll of Anchorage despite the capital still being located in Juneau. There are nearly twice as many state government employees working out of Anchorage as out of Juneau because of the city's greater centrality and the fact that it is the heart of the state's most populated belt. But all attempts at moving the capital to Anchorage or one of the towns to its north in the Matanuska Valley have failed partly because of costs and also fear that Anchorage will gain even more power over the state. And surprisingly there is a degree of nostalgia for Juneau because of its early mining history.

Anchorage has matured to where it has become an important regional cultural center. There are theater companies that play the Alaska Center for the Performing Arts. There is an annual Fur rendezvous festival, a winter ice festival and the start of the Iditarod dog sled race held each year. The city also has a convention center and several sports facilities, though it does not have any major league teams.

SEEING THE SIGHTS: What is there for the visitor to see and do in Anchorage if you choose to stay a day or two before either traveling into the interior or flying home? There is not a lot to do in Anchorage. The city does not have a long history, and it has always been primarily a railroad and military center, but it also has become the state's financial hub since it is the urban gateway to Alaska. Getting around the city can be accomplished in the following ways:

*** Private car and driver/guide service is available from three limousine companies. All three offer good service with competent and friendly drivers. You can check out the following companies on their web pages at:**
**** Limo Service Anchorage at *www.limoserviceanchorage.com***
**** BAC Transportation at *www.bactrans.com***
*** * Orion Limousine Service at *www.orionlimousineservice.com***

*** Private touring is offered by Tours by Locals, a company capable of arranging any type of tour activity a guest might wish. Check their web page at *www.toursbylocals.com***

*** Trolley tours of Anchorage are offered by through Viatour. Check their web page at *www.viatour.com* and put in Anchorage as your destination. There is no hop on hop off touring in Anchorage at this time.**

*** Walking limits you to the city's downtown area where most will stay, as this is the hub of the major hotels. By walking you will see very little of the urban area.**

Here are my recommendations for what to see in Anchorage (shown alphabetically):

*** Alaska Aviation Heritage Museum - Located adjacent to the Lake Hood Seaplane Base, this museum exhibits a variety of aircraft that have played a major role in servicing Alaska. Without so called "bush" pilots many parts of the state would be inaccessible, and this museum does honor their role. The museum is located at 4721 Aircraft Drive and is open from 9 AM to 5 Pm daily.**

*** Alaska Botanical Garden - If you have an interest in the types of flowers and shrubs that are capable of surviving in this northern latitude, this is the place to visit, as it is dedicated to the state's beautiful flora. The gardens are at 4601 Campbell Airstrip Road and are open daily from 9 AM to 6 PM.**

*** Alaska Native Heritage Center - Located on the northeast edge of the city on the Glenn Highway, it can be accessed by taxi, public bus or private car. The center has recreated mock villages that represent the five native cultural regions of the state. There are dances, demonstrations of arts and crafts and storytelling to recreate the native history of Alaska for the visitor. The center is located at 8800 Heritage Center. Hours are from 9 AM to 5 PM daily.**

*** Anchorage Museum at Rasmuson Center - This is the most important museum in the state. It features exhibits on local history and culture as well as the arts and sciences. It is located downtown in a very modern building and easily accessible from all major hotels. The address is 625 C St. and the museum is open from 10 AM to 6 PM Tuesday thru Saturday and from Noon to 6 PM Sunday, closed on Monday.**

*** Earthquake Park - On the site of one area that was heavily damaged during the 1964 Good Friday quake, this park helps you to visualize what it was like being here on that fateful day. The park is at 4601 W. Northern Lights Blvd. and it is open daily from 6 AM to 11 PM. For**

anyone who recalls that fateful afternoon hearing the news about the devastating earthquake, this is probably the most important site in the city to visit even though little evidence of the disaster is visible today.

*** Potter Marsh Bird Sanctuary - Located at the southern edge of the city, this sanctuary is a good place to view the summer migratory waterfowl that come to the Anchorage area. The sanctuary has a series of walkways elevated above the marsh to allow for comfortable viewing. The sanctuary is south of the city on 154th Avenue and is open daily but does not post hours on their web page.**

*** Tony Knowles Coastal Trail - This is a walking and bicycling trail that runs around the outer edge of the city center starting at Knick Arm and extending along the shore down to Turnagain Arm. The trail is free of automotive traffic and is easy to either walk or bicycle, affording great views of the skyline, the water and the distant mountains. When the weather is nice this is one of the best ways to enjoy both the urban and wilderness aspects of the city.**

*** Kincaid Park - This natural parkland is located at the point where the Knick and Turnagain Arms split off from Cook Inlet. It is a large natural reserve that offers an opportunity for long nature walks or bicycle rides during which you will have an opportunity to see moose and quite often bear even though you are on the edge of the urban area. When the weather is good, you can look across the inlet and see two of the major volcanic peaks on the Alaska Peninsula and on very clear days you can see Denali Peak to the north. The park entrance is at 9401 Raspberry Road and it is open daily from 10 AM to 10 PM.**

*** Wells Fargo History Museum - A smaller, but equally as interesting collection of artifacts and memorabilia on the history of Alaska. It is located at 301 Northern Lights Blvd. and it is open from Noon to 4 PM weekdays only.**

There are many natural wonders to be seen in the mountains surrounding Anchorage, many preserved as state parks where access is relatively easy. But in order to get out into the surrounding wilderness you need to rent a car or have your hotel hire a car and driver. There are several small tour operators that also offer wilderness adventures for the day.

VISITING DENALI NATIONAL PARK: If you have at least two to three days to spare, a visit to Denali National Park is one way to truly enjoy the wilds of Alaska. Mt. McKinley, locally known by its native name of Denali, is the tallest mountain in North America. It is dramatic when the weather is clear, as it towers well into the clouds much of the time. The surrounding landscape grades from forest to tundra depending upon the elevation, and the wildlife is spectacular. In the event you choose to visit the park, you should book one of the before or post cruise land packages with your cruise line, as that would be easier than attempting to visit the park on your own. Renting a car and driving to Denali is not difficult, but often it is seen as a bit daunting to drive on your own by a large number of people. And it is a long drive of 381 kilometers or 237 miles. If you are one who enjoys self-drive tours, be certain that you have advanced hotel reservations in Denali before making such a trip, as accommodation is very limited and people often book up to a year in advance.

The trip to Fairbanks is another possibility, but it is a full day's drive just to get there, or you can travel by train. The train schedule does provide through service to Fairbanks, but then you would need a car upon arrival. Fairbanks is the major inland city of the state, but its population is still under 50,000. It is home to the University of Alaska. It is also quite close to the Arctic Circle and thus presents a different landscape than the coastal region. I will not present any further descriptions of Fairbanks because this book is meant to discuss cruising along the Alaska coast.

RECOMMENDED HOTELS: Anchorage will be either the starting point for your cruise or the terminal city depending upon whether you are traveling southbound or northbound. I would recommend spending at least one full day in Anchorage, as it is a rather enjoyable city given that it is the most northerly major urban center on the continent. Many cruise passengers will continue on to Denali National Park or Fairbanks either on a pre or post cruise land package offered by the cruise line. Others may make private arrangements to travel on their own, but in either case it is a good idea to spend at least two nights in Anchorage to rest up and also check out this Alaskan metropolis. Here are my recommendations for the best four-star hotels in the city, as there are no five-star hotels (listed alphabetically):

*** Anchorage Marriott Downtown - Located at 830 West 7th Avenue, this high-rise hotel is a typical four-star Marriott. It offers all the basic services such as a restaurant, room service, bar and lounge, fitness center, indoor pool, business center and meeting rooms. Its color scheme uses warm tones and the rooms are very bright.**

*** Hilton Anchorage - Downtown at 500 West 3rd Avenue, this high-rise hotel is the largest of the major hotels, having an older main building and taller new tower. It is a full service hotel with a restaurant, room service, bar and lounge, fitness center, indoor pool, banquet and meeting rooms and it offers a very nice breakfast buffet.**

*** Hotel Alyeska - Outside of Anchorage in the small city of Girdwood, this is the only resort style hotel in the greater urban region. It has a restaurant, room service, bar and lounge, fitness center, pool, spa and a shuttle bus into the city. Situated at the base of the mountains in a wooded environment with beautiful grounds, this hotel does offer a peaceful and spectacular setting that no other Anchorage hotel can match. You must weight its overall amenities and setting against the distance of 64 kilometers or 40 miles from the city. But The Alaska Railroad services the hotel through Girdwood, the same railroad that services the cruise ships in Whittier or Seward. If your cruise line has chartered a train, you need to check if it will stop for cruise guests in Girdwood.**

*** Hotel Captain Cook - At 939 West 5th Avenue in downtown, a well-known known hotel with a good four-star reputation. It is a traditional high-rise property that offers all the basic services such as a restaurant, room service, bar and lounge, pool, workout room, business center and meeting rooms. Its rooms are well appointed with a deep tone brown and beige color scheme.**

*** Sheraton Anchorage - Downtown at 401 East 6th Avenue, the Sheraton also offers all of the same four-star amenities such as a restaurant, room service, bar and lounge, fitness center, indoor pool, meeting facilities and concierge service.**

DINING OUT: Anchorage does have a fair number of good restaurants. Normally my recommendations are based upon lunch since most ports of call are part of the actual cruise and you will only be able to dine out at lunchtime. However, Anchorage is the embarkation or terminal port on the vast majority of Alaska cruises. Therefore most people will stay over a minimum of one night while others may stay a couple of days to take in the local sights. Thus my restaurant recommendations for Anchorage include restaurants serving lunch and dinner, with one that does feature breakfast. Normally I assume most guest will choose to have breakfast in their hotel. Here are my Anchorage recommendations (listed alphabetically):

*** F Street Station - At 325 F Street in downtown, this is another one of those local restaurants that residents of Anchorage enjoy. The atmosphere is casual, but has a definite local flavor. They serve up superb seafood dishes along with a good selection of other typically American dishes. They are open daily from 9 AM to 11 PM.**

*** Glacier Brewhouse - At 737 West 5th Avenue in downtown, this is a very popular seafood and vegetarian restaurant with a wide selection of dishes to please those who are not looking for meat. All of their seafood is the freshest available and prepared in a both healthy and tasty manner. They do accept reservations for dinner on line through Open Table. Their hours are from 11 AM to Midnight daily.**

*** Haute Quarter Grill – In the downtown at 525 West 4th Street, this is a very good restaurant featuring fresh seafood, but it also offers vegetarian dishes as well. The menu is small, but seafood, pasta and three meat entrees do offer tempting selections. Dinner is served Tuesday thru Thursday from 5 to 9 PM, and Friday and Saturday from 5 to 10 PM.**

*** Jen's Restaurant – South of downtown at 701 West 36th Avenue, this is another local restaurant with a very good set of reviews. Seafood is the main specialty but there is a wide selection of beef, pork, poultry and numerous pasta dishes. The cuisine, service and atmosphere are all quite good, considered among the city's best. Serving hours are Monday thru Friday from 11 AM to 2 PM for lunch and Tuesday thru Saturday from 6 to 10 PM for dinner.**

*** Kincaid Grill and Wine Bar – Located at 6700 Jewel Lake Road, south of the Anchorage International Airport, you will need a taxi unless you have a rental car, as it is a bit far from downtown. This restaurant is popular with locals for its fresh seafood menu. There are a few meat and poultry items among the main courses, but fresh fish and shellfish dominate. It offers an upscale atmosphere and is locally considered to be a fine dining establishment. The restaurant is open Tuesday thru Saturday from 6 to 10 PM.**

*** Marx Brothers Café – Located downtown at 627 West 3rd Street, this restaurant has a very fine reputation for quality. The menu is small, but it does offer a good variety of appetizers,**

salads and mains, with seafood figuring prominently. They are open Tuesday thru Saturday for dinner from 5:30 to 10 PM.

* Moose's Tooth Pub and Pizzeria - Located out of the downtown at 3300 Old Seward Highway, this restaurant is exactly what the name implies. They combine a lively pub with a restaurant where pizza is a specialty. At times the entire restaurant can become rather frenetic, but most people love the atmosphere. I only note it in my recommendations, as so many people do love the typical pizzeria atmosphere even though I personally do not. But in all fairness to my readers, if you want a good pizza in Anchorage, this is the place. Their hours are from 11 AM to 11 PM daily with hours extended to Midnight on Friday and Saturday.

* Seven Glaciers - In Girdwood at Arlberg Road, located in the Alyeska Prince Hotel, this is one of the finest dining establishments in the greater Anchorage area and many locals will drive here for dinner. The view is absolutely incredible, looking out over Turnagain Arm, and the dining is considered to be very good by Anchorage standards. It is not haute cuisine, but their menu is quite good and the service is what one would expect in a fine dining establishment. They are open daily for dinner only from 5 to 10 PM and reservations are advised.

* Simon & Seaforth's Saloon and Grill - In downtown Anchorage at 420 L Street, Suite 200, this restaurant is known for its good quality seafood and typical American fare. The atmosphere is rustic, but the food and service are both excellent. Reservations are always recommended at dinner. Their hours are from 11 AM to 2:30 PM weekdays, 10 AM to 3 PM weekends and dinner is served on weekends from 4:30 to 10 PM.

* Snow City Cafe - Located at 1034 West 4th Avenue in downtown Anchorage, this restaurant is open for breakfast and lunch. It is one of the city center's most popular and well-patronized restaurants. They serve absolutely awesome omelets, salmon cakes, sandwiches, smoothies and other dishes to be considered as "comfort food." This is not fine, elegant dining, but rather the type of food most people crave when traveling. They are open from 7 AM to 3 PM weekdays and until 4 PM on weekends.

SHOPPING: Anchorage does not offer any special shopping advantage such as Vancouver. It has several shopping malls and if you are in need of any last minute items you may have forgotten, you will be able to get them in Anchorage. Downtown, especially along 4th Avenue you will find many shops catering to visitors, offering a wide array of souvenirs along with some native craft items.

* For everyday shopping, there is a J. C. Penney store in the 5th Avenue Mall at 406 West 5th Avenue that is open Monday thru Saturday from 10 AM to 9 PM and Sunday from 11AM to 6 PM.

* For more upscale shopping, there is a Nordstrom store located in the 5th Avenue Mall at 603 D Street that is open from 10 AM to 9 PM Monday thru Saturday and 11 AM to 6 PM Sunday.

There are two somewhat unique galleries I do recommend:

*** Alaska Mint - At 429 West 4th Avenue is a very high end shop that fine jewelry, gold, jade, amber, other gemstones and expensive gift items. The staff is very friendly and you need not feel intimidated in that you need to buy anything. Browsing is welcomed. They are open from 10 AM to 5 PM Tuesday thru Saturday.**

*** Sevigny Studio Alaskan Art - At 608 West 4th Avenue, suite 101, this is a very eclectic gallery featuring a variety of art items including paintings, jewelry, carved bowls, scarves and distinctive clothing items. It has much to tempt the buyer. They are open from 10 AM to 7 PM daily.**

FINAL WORDS: When you consider that there are no other cities with a population of over250,000 located this far north anywhere else in North America, it gives Anchorage a degree of uniqueness. As the nerve center for Alaska, the city is worthy of a visit if even just for one day. It is typically American, but its setting is totally unique in that no other city in the nation has such dramatic mountain backdrops. And despite its major size, there are only really two main roads connecting it to the rest of the state.

ANCHORAGE MAPS

THE MAIN CITY OF ANCHORAGE

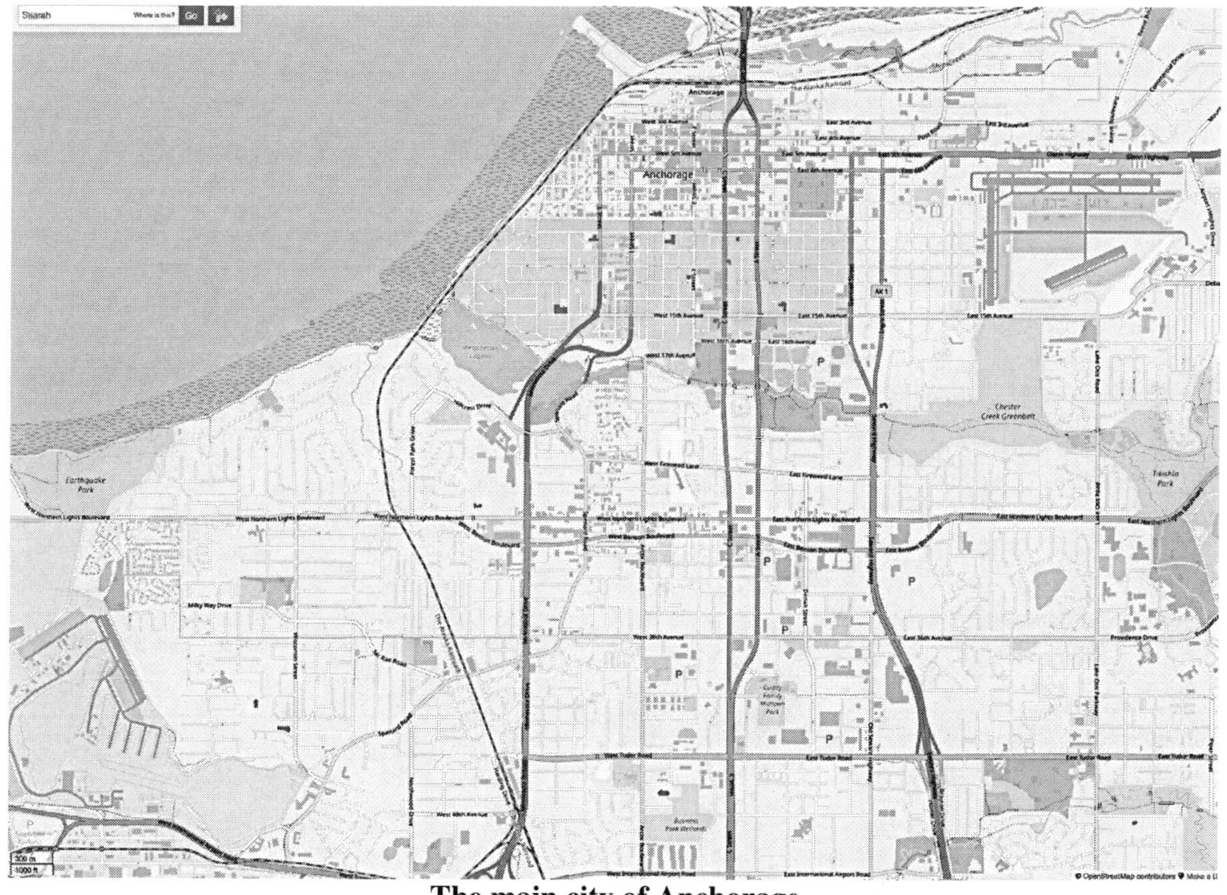

The main city of Anchorage

This map is best viewed directly from OpenStreetMap.com on your personal device where it can be expanded or one specific area can be enlarged. Given the format of this book, it is impossible to display maps with the level of detail you might wish to have while actually out exploring the city. But the OpenStreetMap maps used directly are the tool I always rely upon.

THE MAIN CITY CENTER OF ANCHORAGE

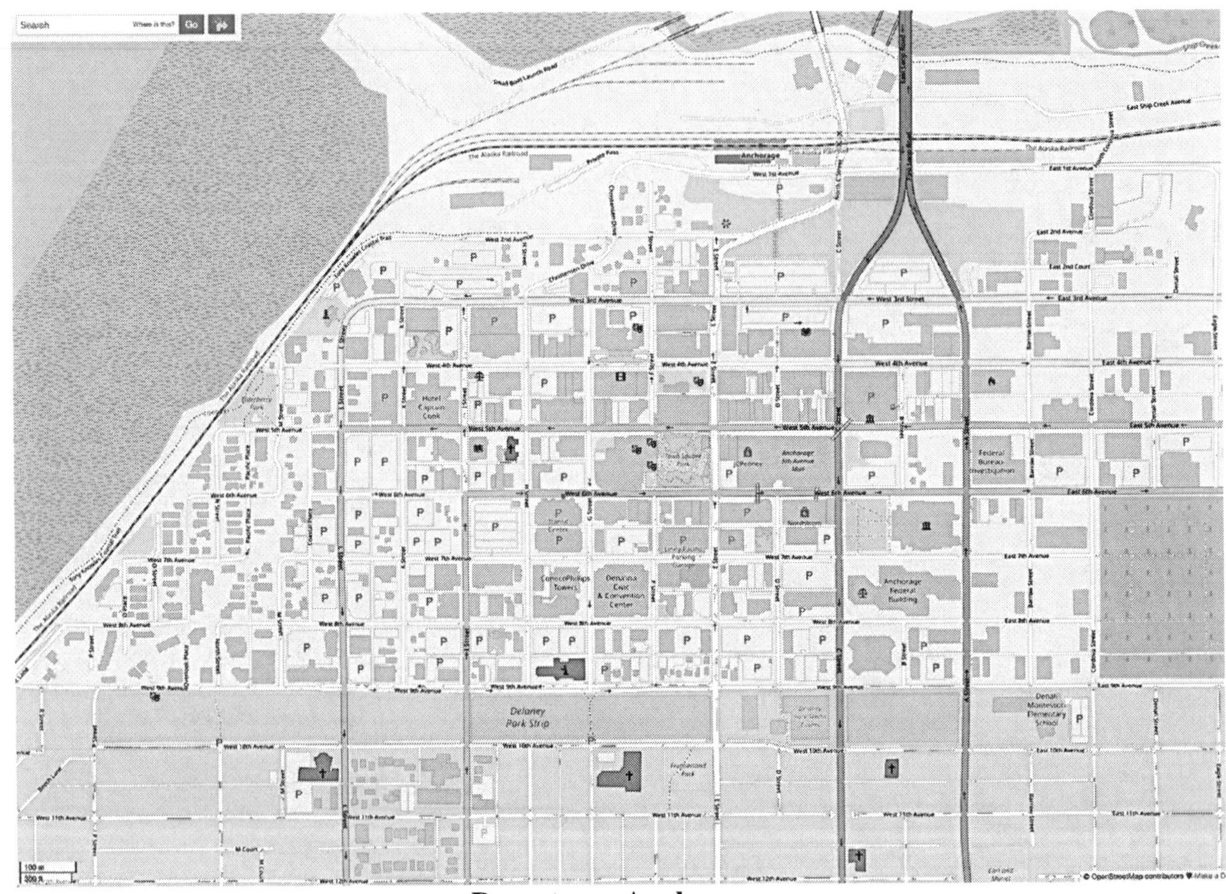

Downtown Anchorage

This map is best viewed directly from OpenStreetMap.com on your personal device where it can be expanded or one specific area can be enlarged. Given the format of this book, it is impossible to display maps with the level of detail you might wish to have while actually out exploring the city. But the OpenStreetMap maps used directly are the tool I always rely upon.

The limited Anchorage harbor seen from the air at low tide

A skyline view of downtown Anchorage from the Cook Inlet shoreline

In the heart of downtown Anchorage

Fourth Avenue once devastated by the 1964 earthquake

A view of suburban Anchorage to the east looking at the Chugach Mountains

Winter chill in Anchorage, (Work of Wonderlane, CC BY SA 2.0, Wikimedia.org)

PORTS BEYOND ANCHORAGE

Seward and Whittier are the farthest destinations for the vast majority of Alaska coastal cruises. The lands beyond are considered rather remote and the small towns do not offer the necessary airport or hotel facilities to enable cruises to either begin or terminate. However, there are adventure cruises on very small ships that do proceed beyond Anchorage, offering a different type of travel experience. These ships are oriented toward visiting remote coves and bays, seeking out wildlife with passengers often going ashore in zodiacs and having a chance to hike and observe nature. This is a totally different type of cruising, and I do comment on it at the end of the book. However, the focus of this book is upon the more traditional luxury cruising that the vast majority of guests are seeking.

There are, however, two times a year when major cruise ships do visit such ports as Homer, Kodiak and Dutch Harbor. During the spring, usually in early May, many cruise lines relocate ships from Hong Kong that have been cruising southeastern Asia to the Vancouver-Alaska market for the upcoming summer. And again in late September those ships are relocated from the Vancouver-Alaska itinerary back to Hong Kong to begin the autumn and winter southeastern Asia itineraries. These are called repositioning cruises, and they are very popular with guests to are looking for a longer itinerary and are ready to combine the voyage with sightseeing in Japan, China or southeast Asia.

Normally on these itineraries the cruise is broken into three segments. When coming from Hong Kong in May, the first cruise segment is between Hong Kong and Tokyo, the second between Tokyo and Anchorage (via Seward or Whittier) and the third constitutes the first of the season Alaska coastal cruises to Vancouver. Those guests with sufficient time and financial resources will often elect to experience the entire repositioning. Stops are generally made in Shanghai, occasionally in Tianjin for an overland tour of Beijing, one of the southern ports in the Republic of Korea (South Korea), several ports in Japan, Petropavlovsk in Russian Kamchatka and then the three outer ports of Alaska starting with Dutch Harbor on Unalaska Island in the Aleutian chain, then Kodiak and Homer. In the fall, the reverse itinerary is offered.

These are incredibly magnificent cruises. The weather in May and late September is generally quite cool, and in the northern Pacific, this is most often a calm period, especially in the Bering Sea. Jackets and scarves are needed, as it can be rather nippy on deck as well on shore. Generally in May there is still a fair amount of snow on the ground in Petropavlovsk, the Aleutian Islands, Kodiak Island and the Kenai Peninsula. But the snow adds greatly to the scenic qualities of the experience. In late September you will experience the golden hues of willows and the reds of larch, as the autumn progresses. And if you continue on to Hong Kong, you will experience the full magic of autumn colors in Japan, which can rival those of eastern Canada and New England.

This final chapters of the book will introduce you only to the three Alaska ports of call that are part of that repositioning cruise. You will discover what there is to see and do in Homer, Kodiak and Dutch Harbor. Each of the ports will be treated in an independent chapter with photographs following the text material. As this book is about cruising Alaska, there will be

no details on Japan, Korea or China. Perhaps in the future, I may do a small text on cruising the northeastern coast of Asia. But given the long historic connection between Alaska and the Far East of Russia, I am including a chapter on Petropavlovsk. The native peoples of the Aleutian Islands have close ancestral ties to the Kamchatka Peninsula, and the city of Petropavlovsk is either the last port in Asia before the Aleutians traveling eastbound or the first Asian port traveling westbound from Dutch Harbor in the Aleutian Islands. The city was founded by Vitus Bering as a base of operation for his explorations of Alaska. Thus I felt in appropriate to include it in this book.

HOMER

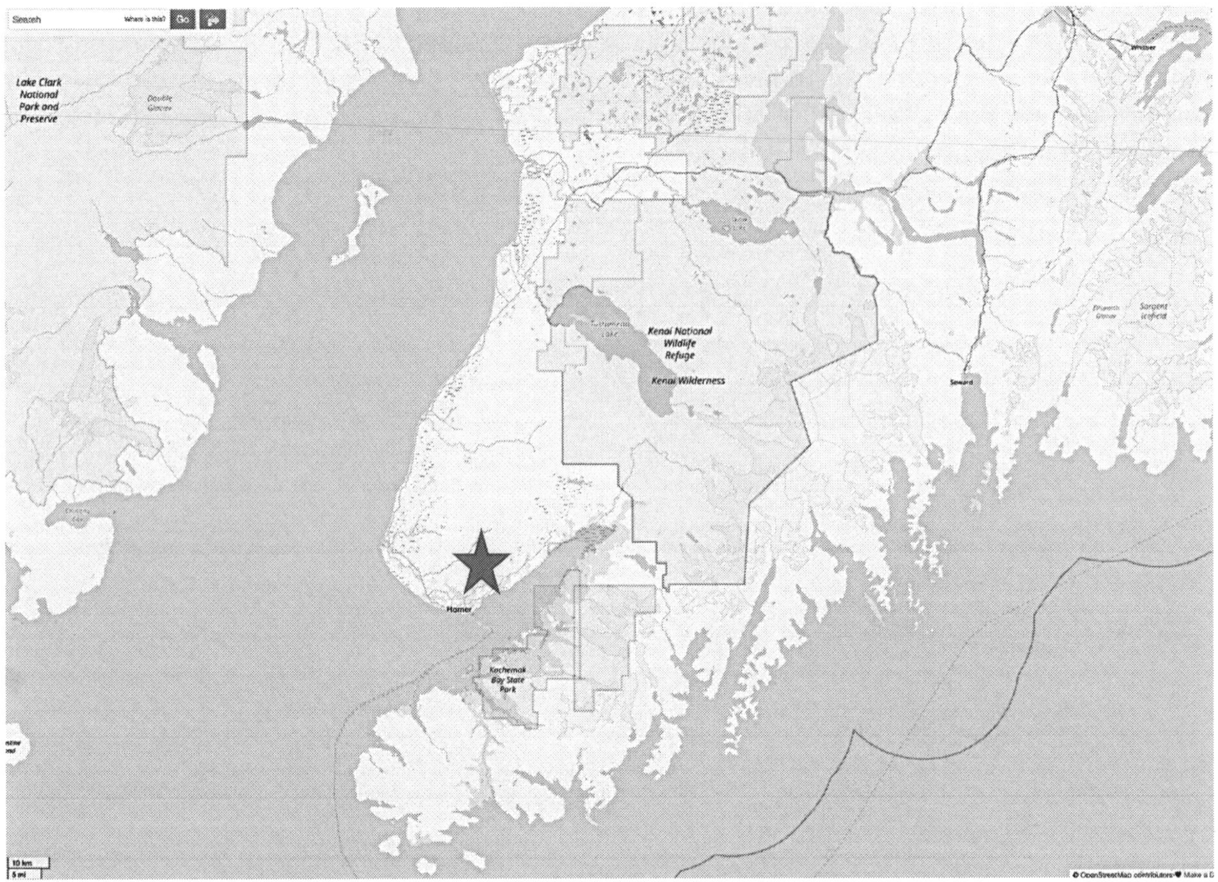

The location of Homer (© OpenStreetMap contributors)

HOMER'S SETTING: Homer is located on the southwestern edge of the Kenai Peninsula, accessible from Anchorage by road, but not by rail. It is an overnight sailing by cruise ship between Homer and Seward, thus normally an entire day is spent docked in the Homer port. The town has a population of just over 5,000, but it is relatively spread out and there is no specific downtown or main street core. It is a dispersed community with its residential areas primarily hidden among the evergreen trees of the forest that engulfs the area. But there is a long sand spit that extends into Kachemak Bay. The spit is very narrow, but extends for over four miles in length. Prior to the Good Friday Earthquake of 1964, the spit was much wider in size, but the landward end of it sunk several feet below the water's surface. If you take a tour of Homer or a shuttle into town, you will notice that as you approach the mainland, the north side of the Spit is submerged, and this is the result of the earthquake. A future major quake could sever this sandy spit and thus isolate the harbor facilities and the numerous seafood restaurants at the tip of this tiny precarious neck of land.

The Port of Homer is located at the far end of the Spit because this is where the water is sufficient in depth to accommodate both cruise ships and the occasional cargo vessel. Most of the port facility is devoted to fishing, and the main catch is halibut. Homer has dubbed

itself "The Halibut Capital of the World." And in many ways that is an apt nickname because of the vast amount of fish caught and processed. And for the visitor there are several small restaurants located at the end of the spit near where the cruise ship docks. Each is noted for its various halibut dishes, and one should not leave Homer without having the mild flavored fish for lunch. Further on in the chapter, I identify the best seafood restaurants in town.

The scenic potential of the Homer area is quite dramatic. Across Kachemak Bay is the southern edge of the Kenai Peninsula's major mountain range. The snow covered peaks rise from the by and present a very dramatic backdrop for Homer. Across the Cook Inlet, which is west of Homer, are the mountains of the Alaska Peninsula, much higher in elevation than those of the Kenai Peninsula and containing several active volcanic peaks. However, these mountains can only be seen from offshore or across Kachemak Bay. There have been eruptions in the past twenty years that have blackened the sky with ash, but Homer itself is in no serious danger from even a catastrophic eruption, but could experience a tsunami in the future from any major earthquakes.

The climate of Homer is considered to be subarctic with very cool summers and snowy winters. However, the sea does provide a moderating influence and long periods of sub-zero weather as found farther inland are rare along the coast.

HISTORIC HOMER: During the 1890's, the town was established primarily as a service center for a mine that operated until World War II, producing large quantities of coal. Gold prospecting in the area never revealed much worth developing. But ultimately halibut and salmon fishing came to dominate and kept the town of Homer viable. Today many residents from Anchorage enjoy camping and fishing in the Homer area and this has become the second major segment of the economic base.

WHAT TO SEE: The town is quite spread out for its small population. There is not a lot to see with regard to the actual town, as it consists of residential areas tucked into the forest and the main highway that is lined with scattered shops. There is no actual downtown, as one would expect even in a small town the size of Homer. But there are the few small museums that enable you to spend some time learning about the local region. Some cruise lines do offer boat trips across Kachemak Bay to either visit one of the nearby glaciers or the small fishing village of Seldovia.

*** Homer is so small and limited in terms of land access that attempting to hire a car and driver are exceptionally difficult. There is a local taxi service that may be able to offer local sightseeing on an hourly basis. Their web page is** *www.homertaxi.com* **for information.**

*** If your ship offers a shuttle into town, the driver will most likely point out the few sights of interest. There are no specific sightseeing busses in Homer.**

Here are the major attractions within Homer if your cruise line offers a shuttle into town and you choose to spend the day on your own:

*** Alaska Islands and Ocean Visitor Center - Located on the Sterling Highway at the north edge of town in the Alaska Maritime Wildlife Refuge, this center offers interpretive exhibits on the natural and cultural life of the Kachemak Bay area and surrounding countryside. If you love birds and their habitats this is worthy of a visit. You can either find a taxi on the dock or at one of the shuttle bus stops in town since most cruise lines do offer a town shuttle. The refuge visitor center is open daily from Noon to 5 PM.**

*** Homer Spit - You can walk the outer end of the spit where there are numerous restaurants and the notable Salty Dawg Saloon. The spit is a good place for fresh seafood and it is within easy walking distance of the ship. There are many small restaurants located along about a one mile stretch of the Spit, all looking rather rustic or ramshackle, but do not let looks fool you. They all serve exceptionally fresh seafood, especially Alaska King Crab and halibut. You will not find it fresher anywhere, so indulge.**

*** Pratt Museum - This small museum at 3773 Bartlett Street in Homer offers exhibits on the cultural and natural history of the area along with works of art. There is also a nature trail and garden on site. It is open daily from Noon to 5 PM.**

*** Seldovia - A local fast ferry will take you to this sleepy town on the opposite of Kachemak Bay for a chance to step back into early Alaskan history. Often the cruise lines will offer a chartered visit to Seldovia, which then makes it easier to visit this charming coastal town.**

Excursions often provided by your cruise line leaving from Homer include a hike to Grewingk Glacial Lake, a helicopter tour that lands on the Grewingk Glacier, halibut fishing experience or a chartered tour to Seldovia. Sea kayaking for the more adventurous is also often provided. Thus apart from spending time in the town where there are limited facilities, a visit to Homer is best enjoyed with an outing into the surrounding wilds.

DINING ON THE SPIT: If you love fish, especially halibut, then lunch at one of the restaurants located on the Spit is a must. Here are my recommendations:

*** Café Cups – In Homer at 162 Pioneer Avenue, this uniquely decorated café offers outstanding seafood dishes, especially halibut and king crab, in a pleasant atmosphere with very good service. Because they are popular, reservations are recommended. If you have a cell phone you can call them at 1-907-235-8330. Their hours of service are Tuesday thru Saturday from 5 to 8:30 PM, which is good if your ship is staying until mid-evening.**

*** Captain Pattie's Fish House - At 4241 Homer Spit Road, a bit of a walk from the deep-water dock, but well worth the effort. Their fresh halibut, crab and mussels are hard to beat. The atmosphere is rustic and the service is basic, but it is the freshness and preparation that count. They are open daily for lunch and dinner from 11 AM to 9 PM daily.**

*** Fresh Catch Cafe - Located at 4025 Homer Spit Road, just opposite where the one road from the deep-water dock emerges on to the Spit. It does not look like much from the outside, and it is very small and crowded inside, but the food is incredible. You could not ask for halibut to be any fresher and the ways they prepare it are all incredibly good. I have never**

eaten such fantastic halibut. And their seafood chowder is also amazingly good. They are open from 5 to 9:30 PM daily. Most cruise ships do stay in Homer until early evening, so you should be able to have dinner here.

*** Little Mermaid Café – Located at 4246 Homer Spit Road, this rather quaint café offers the freshest fish, especially halibut you have ever tasted. And their Alaska king crab is also a specialty. And the do offer a few vegetarian dishes for those who choose not to indulge in seafood. And they also offer a variety of sandwiches and pizza for those not wanting to try their fish. As with other restaurants on the spit, the Little Mermaid is small and sometimes so crowded that there is a long wait to be seated. They are open Thursday thru Tuesday from 11 AM to 9 PM.**

FINAL WORDS: There is little to occupy you in Homer for an entire day. If the weather is good, I suggest taking one of your ship's tours across the bay to explore some of the countryside. If you remain in port, and if your ship offers a shuttle you will find that apart from walking around and visiting the small museum, the day can be relatively dull. But if you plan to have a late lunch and indulge in halibut, crab or other fresh seafood, you will definitely remember the town of Homer.

MAPS OF HOMER

THE TOWN OF HOMER

The main town of Homer

This map is best viewed directly from OpenStreetMap.com on your personal device where it can be expanded or one specific area can be enlarged. Given the format of this book, it is impossible to display maps with the level of detail you might wish to have while actually out exploring the city. But the OpenStreetMap maps used directly are the tool I always rely upon.

THE HEART OF HOMER

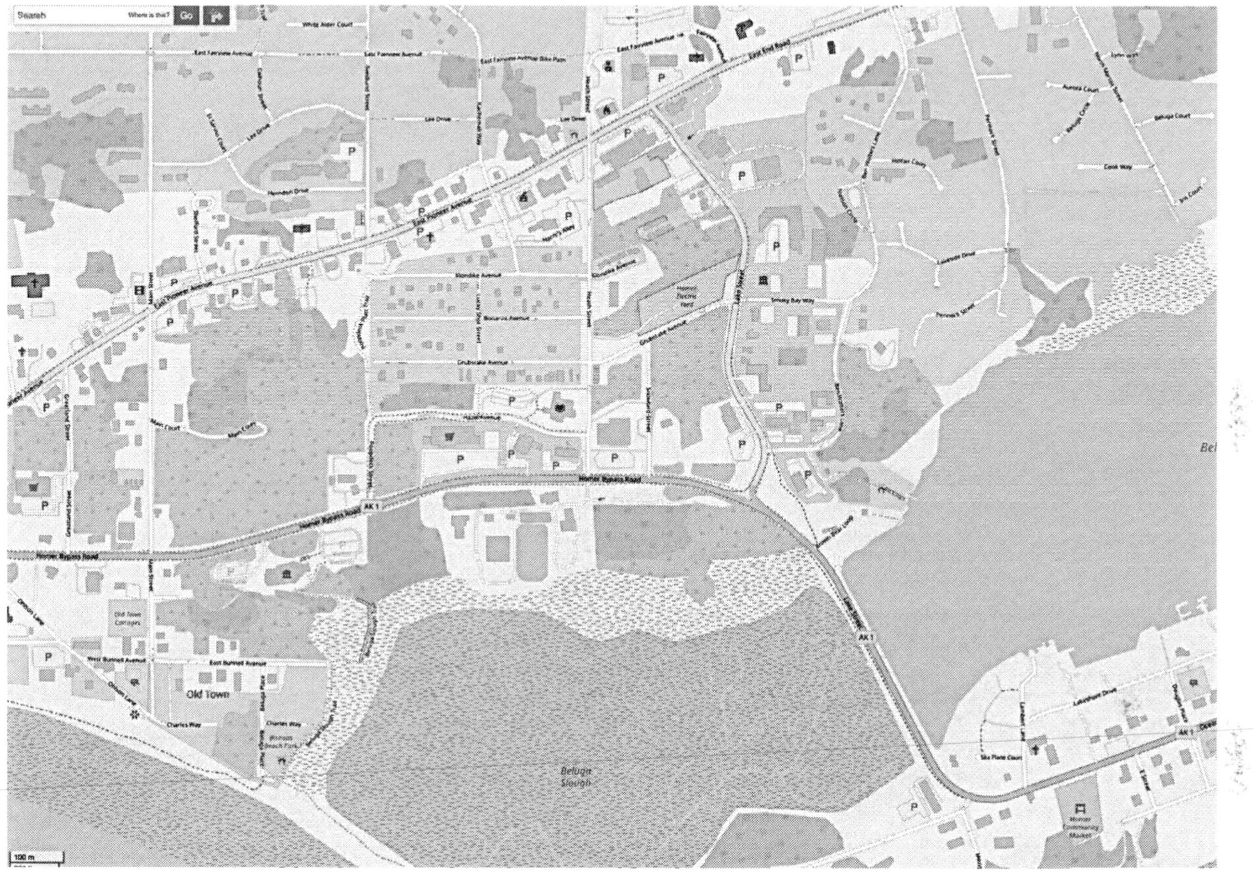

The heart of Homer

This map is best viewed directly from OpenStreetMap.com on your personal device where it can be expanded or one specific area can be enlarged. Given the format of this book, it is impossible to display maps with the level of detail you might wish to have while actually out exploring the city. But the OpenStreetMap maps used directly are the tool I always rely upon.

THE TIP OF THE HOMER SPIT

The tip of the Homer Spit

This map is best viewed directly from OpenStreetMap.com on your personal device where it can be expanded or one specific area can be enlarged. Given the format of this book, it is impossible to display maps with the level of detail you might wish to have while actually out exploring the city. But the OpenStreetMap maps used directly are the tool I always rely upon.

Looking over Homer and out to Kachemak Bay

Aerial view of the Homer Spit (Work of Scott McMurren, CC BY SA 2.0Wikimedia.org)

The ramshackle restaurants along the Spit (Work of Keith Parker, CC BY SA 2.0, Wikimedia.org)

Sea gulls line the piers in Homer waiting for a free meal

The main harbor on the Homer Spit

The setting for Homer is quite spectacular with its snowcapped mountains

Beautiful Kachemak Bay is Homer's back yard

Back yard views are dramatic in Homer

The Homer countryside on the edge of town, (Work of Beeblebrox, CC BY SA 3.0, Wikimedia.org)

KODIAK

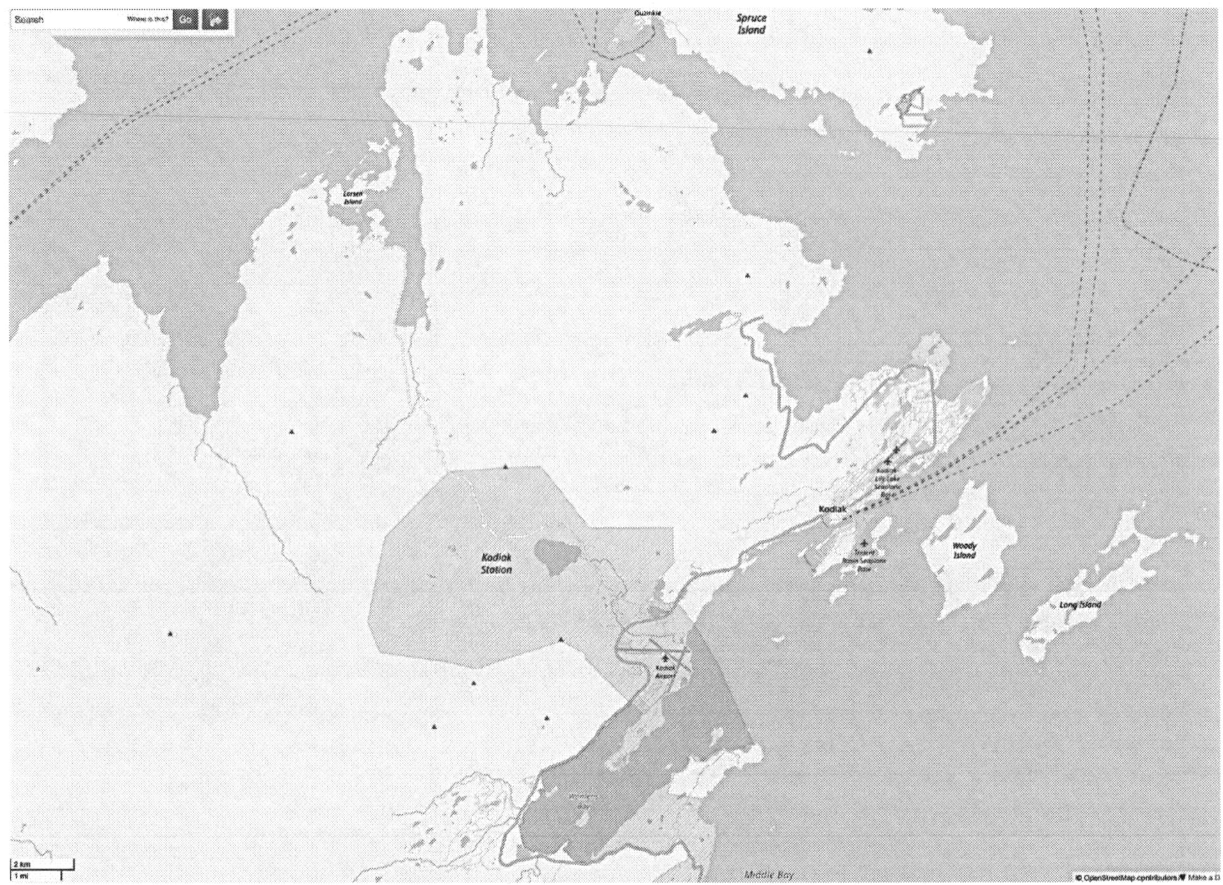

Map of Kodiak Island (© OpenStreetMap contributors)

For most who read this book, your basic Alaska cruise will begin or end in Seward or Whittier. Only expedition cruises or the large cruise ships in transit between eastern Asia and Vancouver stop in Kodiak.

THE SETTING: Kodiak Island is located parallel to the Alaska Peninsula and is just south of the Kenai Peninsula. It is an uplifted island that is part of an ancient seamount along the Aleutian Trench, thus it presents a very rugged, mountainous landscape that has a fjord coastline and numerous glacial lakes in its interior. With 9,311 square kilometers or 3,595 square miles, Kodiak Island is the second largest island within the 50 states, the big island of Hawaii being the largest. Kodiak Island is thickly forested because of its cold, maritime climate. And the island is home to large numbers of Kodiak brown bears, which are actually grizzly bears. The waters around the island are especially rich in salmon, halibut, crab and other commercial species, thus enabling a large fishing industry to have developed, mainly in and around the town of Kodiak.

A popular TV show in the United States on the Weather Network has been "Coast Guard Alaska," most of which is filmed at the U. S. Coast Guard Base on Kodiak Island. This base and the one in Sitka essentially maintain patrols and provide search and rescue missions for

the entire long coastline of Alaska, working under some of the most extreme of weather conditions. From Kodiak the Coast Guard patrols out into the Aleutian Islands where some of the worst gale force winds and fierce seas can occur. When cruising between Petropavlovsk, Russia and Kodiak on the repositioning itineraries there is never any guarantee as to what the weather and sea conditions will be like. During spring or fall, either early or late winter gales can come up quite suddenly and cause incredibly rough seas. I have personally been fortunate in making the crossings during calm weather, and the scenery of the Aleutian Islands is very dramatic.

KODIAK HISTORY: The Russians were the first Europeans to explore Kodiak Island in 1763, and Captain James Cook landed here briefly in 1778. But it was not until 1784 that the Russians established their first fur trapping outpost at Three Saints Bay, later in 1791 moving it to Saint Paul Harbor, which is the present day site of the town of Kodiak. The primary fur was sea otter, which the Russians hunted to near extinction. The native Aleuts opposed the Russian fur trade and were in a constant struggle with the trappers, necessitating some fortification for Pavlovskaya (Kodiak). Ultimately Russian Orthodox priests came to the island and by the early 19th century most of the Aleut had converted to the Orthodox faith and ceased their harassment of the trappers. But disease ultimately took its toll on the Aleut and their numbers rapidly declined.

Once Alaska was sold to the United States in 1867, Kodiak developed as a major fishing center, and today it is still an important industry. Canning is not as major as it once was because of the ability to ship fresh fish out to the lower 48 states by air. Most consumers today demand fresh seafood as opposed to willingly accepting it canned or smoked.

During World War II, Kodiak was heavily fortified with the development of Fort Abercrombie. The Japanese did attack the outer Aleutian Islands and had they penetrated farther east Kodiak would have become a prime target. Today Fort Abercrombie is an historic park, and the only military role on the island is that of the Coast Guard operating from their base south of the town, primarily to protect the fishing boats and commercial cargo traffic that plies between Alaska and eastern Asia.

The Good Friday earthquake of 1964 that touched off a major tsunami brought damage to Kodiak both from the actual quake, but also from the tsunami, waves having been estimated at 10 meters or 33 feet. Much of the coastal fringe of the town was either destroyed or heavily damaged. Although rebuilt, it does face that potential danger in the future, but an early warning system will preclude any great loss of life.

SIGHTSEEING: There are several historic and natural sites in and around Kodiak to enable cruise passengers to have an enjoyable day while visiting. But again like in Homer, Kodiak is not much in the way of an urban center. The downtown consists of about two square blocks with just a handful of stores providing for basic needs. Much of the local shopping is done outside of the town core at the island's Walmart and a neighboring supermarket. The downtown core thus contains a few shops, local banks and government offices and does not offer much for the visitor.

*** The majority of ship sponsored tours will take guests out of the town to various sites where there is a good chance to see the Kodiak bear, moose, otter and at certain times to observe whales from on shore.**

*** If you wish to have a private car and driver/guide, you can ask the cruise concierge to arrange it for you, but the cost will be quite high due to the limited service. The local office of Best Limo may be able to offer you service at a lower cost. Check their web page at** *www.bestlimodb.com* **for information and rates.**

*** Local taxi service exists, but is limited to a handful of vehicles. But if they are not busy with local calls you may be able to arrange for sightseeing on an hourly basis. Their web page is** *www.kodiakcitytaxi.com* **will provide information regarding their service plus both phone and e-mail contact details.**

*** Kodiak is far too small and isolated for any hop on hop off bus service.**

*** Walking will only take you through the downtown area, which does have a few of the local sights worth seeing, as noted below.**

My recommendations as to what to see are as follows (listed alphabetically):

*** Alutiiq Museum and Archaeological Repository - This museum stresses the early native history of Kodiak Island dating back over 7,000 years, and for those who enjoy learning about native cultures, this is a major highlight. It is located in town at 215 Mission Road, Suite 101 and is open from 10 AM to 4 PM daily.**

*** Baranov Museum - An excellent museum displaying much of the early native and Russian history of Kodiak, located right in the heart of the city at 101 West Marine Way. Although small, the museum does offer a nice array of artifacts from the early history of the city. The museum is open daily from 10 AM to 3 PM.**

*** Fort Abercrombie State Historical Park - The remains of old Fort Abercrombie where you will see the bunkers and other works that were created to protect the island in the event of a World War II invasion. The park is just over three miles from the town center at 1400 Abercrombie Drive and can be reached by local taxi in the event your cruise line has not scheduled a visit as part of an excursion. No specific hours are posted, but since they do have a campground, the visitor's center will be open during normal daytime business hours.**

*** Holy Resurrection Orthodox Church - Located on a slight hill above the town center, this church is a strong reminder of the early Russian history of Kodiak. The church is still active, as many of the locals are descendants of those early converts to the Orthodox faith. But today the services are conducted in English, as few locals do speak Russian. Visitors are welcome during the day when there are no services. No specific hours are posted.**

*** Kodiak Military History Museum – Located at Fort Abercrombie, this museum is dedicated to the role of the Military in Alaska, especially featuring exhibits from the World**

War II Era. The museum is small, but the exhibits are a reminder that Alaska was so vulnerable during the Second World War and Cold War periods. They are open from 1 to 4 Pm Friday through Monday during summer.

*** Kodiak National Wildlife Center - Here you will find a very fine assortment of displays on the local wildlife and marine life of Kodiak Island. This small museum at 401 Center Avenue is very well run and its displays are quite meaningful. There is one display called the grizzly bear's supermarket that shows you the diversity of foods that a bear is capable of eating. They are open from 9 AM to 5 PM daily.**

*** Kodiak National Wildlife Refuge - This is a large wilderness park set aside on Kodiak and neighboring islands that protects both land and sea environments. It is only going to be accessible if your cruise line offers a tour to the refuge or if you hire a car and take the drive yourself, but you will then be lacking the services of a competent guide. The refuge is home to a large number of Kodiak brown bear. It is open to the public from 9 AM to 5 PM daily.**

*** U. S. Coast Guard Station Kodiak - There are certain days of the month that the base will host visitors. If your cruise line has not arranged for a visit, you should check on line with the Coast Guard at *www.dcms.uscg.ml* to see if your visit to the island will coincide with a base open house. To arrange for a visit on the day your ship is in port, you need to first send an e-mail to *Thomas.d.dukes@uscg.ml* to request a base visit. If a visit is granted, you and others in your group will need to provide valid identification such as a passport or driver's license.**

I highly recommend that you sign up for one of the ship's excursions in Kodiak, as visiting the local museums, the Orthodox church and just walking around the town center will only occupy at most a couple of hours of your day. And getting away from the town and seeing parts of the island is very worthwhile because of its remoteness and beauty. I cannot comment directly on the nature of the tours, as they would depend upon the cruise line and the itinerary.

DINING OUT: Kodiak is a very small town and there are few restaurants from which to choose, especially for lunch. Most of the reviews show the restaurants to be mediocre at best. Here are my choices:

*** Aquamarine Café – In the heart of town at 508 West Marine Way, this is a very typical American style café. The food is good, but nothing special. The reviews written by ship passengers are mixed, some very good others just average. They have a varied selection of sandwiches, pizza and of course salmon, but their overall seafood selection is small. They are open daily from 10 AM to 10 PM.**

*** Kodiak Hana Restaurant - In town at 516 East Marine Way. This restaurant has a great selection of fresh seafood served in a Japanese and East Asian manner, and if you are en route to or coming from Japan, it should be a great place to enjoy lunch. Locals give it two thumbs up. Open Tuesday thru Thursday from 11:30 AM to 9 PM, Friday and Saturday 11:30 AM to 10 PM and Sunday 5 to 9 PM.**

*** Monk's Rock Coffeehouse and Bookstore - In town at 202 East Rezanof Drive, this rather uniquely decorated cafe has real local color. Their lunch menu is diverse and even includes a few dishes with a Russian flavor, part of the Kodiak heritage. They even have a few handmade Russian gift items available for sale. They are open Tuesday thru Friday from 8:30 AM to 3 PM and Saturday from *9:30 AM to 1 PM.**

*** Rendezvous Bar and Grill – This restaurant is located well south of town, so a taxi is necessary, but worth the effort. The address is 11652 Chiniak Highway. The restaurant and pub is probably the best you will find in Kodiak. However, the menu selections are limited, but do include fresh local seafood. Overall they receive the highest ratings by locals, which should be an indicator that you will get a good meal. And the drive out and back does show you a bit of the island scenery. They are open Tuesday thru Sunday from 11:30 AM to 10 PM.**

FINAL WORDS: **Kodiak is one of the more substantial small towns located in the remote parts of Alaska once you get out into the western reaches of the state. This is a fishing port, and its largest economic component is the U. S. Coast Guard. Thus the town has a strong military flavor, as well as reflecting its historic past in the image of the Russian Orthodox Church.**

If you are visiting Kodiak and do want to really see the island, then I suggest you take one of the tours offered by your ship out of town into the raw wilderness of the island.

THE HEART OF KODIAK

The heart of Kodiak

This map is best viewed directly from OpenStreetMap.com on your personal device where it can be expanded or one specific area can be enlarged. Given the format of this book, it is impossible to display maps with the level of detail you might wish to have while actually out exploring the city. But the OpenStreetMap maps used directly are the tool I always rely upon.

Morning approach to Kodiak Island

Approaching the port for Kodiak

The raw wilderness that is Kodiak Island

Into the depths of this rugged island

Docking in Kodiak Harbor

A panorama over the small town center of Kodiak

Exhibit about what bears eat at the Kodiak National Wildlife Center

A whale skeleton at the Kodiak National Wildlife Center

The Russian Orthodox church in Kodiak

The Baranov Museum in Kodiak

The small park in the center of Kodiak

One of the nice, quiet residential streets of Kodiak

DUTCH HARBOR
UNALASKA ISLAND

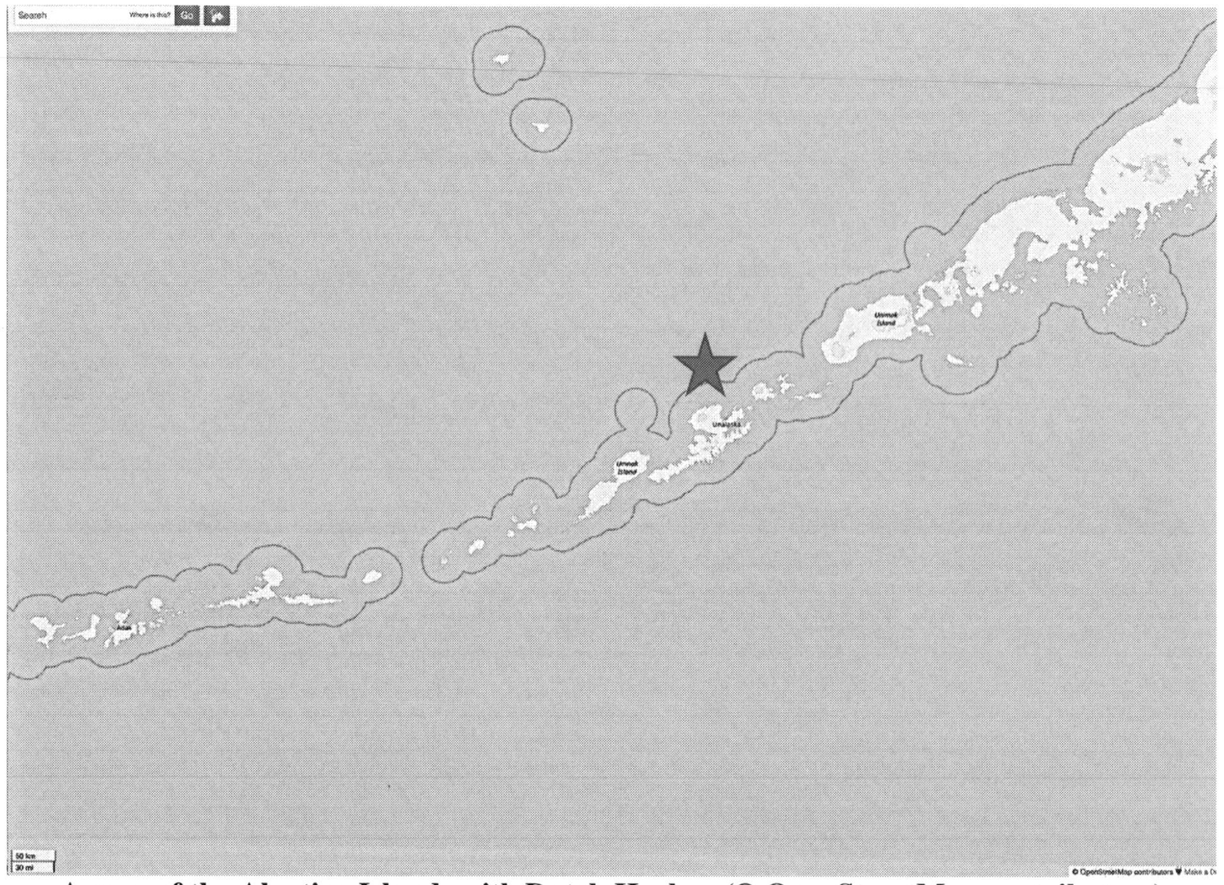

A map of the Aleutian Islands with Dutch Harbor (© OpenStreetMap contributors)

NATURAL SETTING: The Aleutian Islands are the most remote part of the continental United States, even remote with reference to the rest of the state of Alaska of which they are a part. They form an archipelago of 69 islands that stretched from the end of the Alaska Peninsula over 1,930 kilometers or 1,200 miles in a curving arc that first trends to the southwest and then bends slightly northwest toward the Kamchatka Peninsula of Russia. The westernmost portion of the islands is actually across the International Dateline in the Eastern Hemisphere, but for convenience the dateline has been bent around the outermost island to keep the entire chain within the same calendar day. But the outer islands are so far west that an additional time zone had to be created, referred to as Bering Standard Time, which is Greenwich Mean Time minus 10, even though in reality the actual position of these outer islands is Greenwich Mean Time plus 12. It points to the ability that we humans have to alter how we view the natural environment. Remember that if you are ever asked a trivia question that wants you to name the most western state in the United States, it of course is Alaska. Maine is not the eastern most state in the United States. It is also Alaska. This is because the farthest of the Aleutian Islands are actually in the Eastern Hemisphere.

The arc of the Aleutian Islands is the result of a massive subduction zone along which two of the earth's major plates meet and one is being submerged below the other. This causes massive reservoirs of molten magma to be created and pressure ejects the magma in the form of volcanic eruptions that ultimately built up the islands. There are 57 volcanoes within the Aleutian chain; all being potentially active yet some presently sit dormant. Earthquakes frequent the islands on a regular basis, as the plate boundary that has created the islands is still very active. It is the same plate boundary that was responsible for the Good Friday Earthquake of 1964 and the recent 2018 Anchorage earthquake.

The islands all are especially rugged, many rising to elevations of over 1,830 meters or 6,000 feet above sea level. Most of the volcanic cones are quite steep and show the classic shape of tapering cones that represent strato volcanoes, the most explosive type. Yet there are parts of some of the larger islands that are not of volcanic origin, containing rock layers that are sedimentary and reflecting a period of time millions of years ago when these islands were tropical in nature, evidenced by deposits of log grade lignite coal.

The climate of these islands is especially blustery. During winter, the Arctic storms that are swept across Canada and the United States form in the Bering Sea, making this region stormy to the point of the sea being one of the most difficult to navigate in the world. The popular TV show called "Deadliest Catch," all about the crab fishermen of the Bering Sea is actually based upon the fishing fleet whose home port is Dutch Harbor. Summer is very cool, and can also be fraught with high winds and angry seas. Rainy days outnumber days without precipitation. Sunny days with nice blue skies are rare in the Aleutian Islands. Fog is often more prevalent during summer. And add to this the fact that the islands have exceptionally rugged shorelines and you can see the potential for maritime disasters. So when doing a repositioning cruise, you never know if your crossing along the Aleutian Islands will be calm or rough. But normally May and September are among the calmer times of year to cross. In the last three years I have made two crossings and both times the Bering Sea was as calm as a lake. And fortunately for my photographic efforts, the sky was blue yet the air was quite cold.

Because of the very cool to cold temperatures and the high impact of wind most days of the year, little substantial vegetation grows on the Aleutian Islands. Grasses, low willows and other herbaceous shrubs dominate the vegetation, as trees have a difficult time withstanding the elements. A few tenacious conifers grow in sheltered areas. The Aleutian Islands are also devoid of most land animals other than the few cattle or caribou that have been introduced. But the shorelines are home to many seabird species and eagles because of the abundance of fish in these waters.

For people living on the few inhabited islands, fishing is the mainstay of the economy. Many of the fishing fleets hire on temporary workers for the few weeks of the crab-fishing season, and the money is good. In addition to crab, large quantities of Pollock and black cod are caught, primarily sent out as frozen fish, best known in fish sticks. Thus in Dutch Harbor you will see dormitory facilities for the workers who come for the season. It is expensive to reach Dutch Harbor, and if a temporary fisherman does not fulfill his contract, the fare off the island can be as high as an overseas fare to Europe or Asia from the heartland of the

United States. Among the locals, they augment their involvement with fishing by raising a few vegetables to add to their diet and cut down on the need to import fresh foods, which are very expensive in the supermarket of Dutch Harbor.

The only port capable of hosting a cruise ship is Dutch Harbor on Amaknak Island, which is a small island, tucked up alongside the much larger Unalaska Island and geologically a part of it. The bay is highly protected by the fluted shores of Unalaska Island and a sand spit that protrudes from Amaknak Island, making this an ideal port.

BRIEF HISTORY: The native peoples of the Aleutian Islands are known as Aleut, and they were adept at hunting seals, whales and fishing the near coastal waters. When the Russians settled what is now Dutch Harbor in 1799, it was otter pelts they were after. The Aleut did help them in their exploits, and surprisingly in return they embraced the Russian Orthodox faith knowing that their children would receive the educational benefits of these newcomers to their land.

When Alaska was sold to the United States in 1867, Dutch Harbor became an important exporter of seal and otter fur to San Francisco. But by 1900, the populations of fur seals and otter had declined and thus the market began to collapse. And by 1897, interest had shifted to the Alaska Panhandle and the Canadian Yukon with the Klondike Gold Rush. Dutch Harbor languished as a distant outpost with some trapping and fishing for domestic and export markets. But with the winds of war brewing in both Europe and eastern Asia, the Navy developed a significant base at Dutch Harbor. The Japanese navy bombed Dutch Harbor on two major raids starting in June 1942. By the time of the first Japanese attack, Dutch Harbor had also become a secondary submarine base. The base did serve as a staging area for the retaking of Attu Island in the far western Aleutians, which Japan had actually occupied.

During the height of the war, nearly 20,000 sailors and soldiers occupied Dutch Harbor, and it remained viable until 1947 when it was no longer deemed necessary. Ultimately in the 1980's, the Army burned and buried the World War II barracks and today there are few traces of either the naval or army base. In their place are canneries and processing plants to handle the large summer tonnage of fish and crab harvested offshore.

Today Dutch Harbor is essentially a processing center with an adjacent residential community called Unalaska. It is an expensive place to live and has few diversions. But of course the wages on the fishing boats and in the processing plants are quite high. All there is to do is drink, and there are a couple of very wild "watering holes" that have notorious reputations.

SIGHTSEEING: When your ship docks there is not a lot to do in Dutch Harbor or Unalaska. A few miles separate Dutch Harbor, which is the port facility and former military base from the main town referred to as Unalaska, the same name as the island. There is no actual town, but rather just a village that consists of small houses and the old, historic Russian Orthodox Church.

In Dutch Harbor there is a bank and a large Safeway store along with a hotel because of the number of visiting executives and officials with regard to the important fishing trade. With very little to see or do, here are my few recommendations, which are easily reached utilizing the locally provided shuttle. There are no private cars available quite simply because there is no place to go other than the stops made by the local shuttle. The main sights are:

*** Aleutian World War II Visitor Center - Located in Dutch Harbor, this museum tells the story of the impact of the military and the raids by Japanese forces, a story lesser known than that of Pearl Harbor. Open Wednesday thru Saturday from 10 AM to 6 PM.**

*** Holy Ascension Cathedral - Not open to visitors during services, this old wood church was built at the end of the 18th century and is still ministering to the needs of the community. It is a traditional Russian Orthodox Church in design and its interior trappings. If services are in progress, you may not enter the church.**

*** Museum of the Aleutians - Located in Dutch Harbor near the main hotel, this small museum tells the story of the Aleut people and is an excellent place to gain an understanding of Aleutian life. The exhibits are very well presented. The museum is open Tuesday thru Saturday 10 AM to 4 PM.**

*** Whale watching - There are whale-watching boat expeditions offered during the summer season for visitors, however, cruise ships only come as part of their repositioning in the spring or fall. It is possible that on the fall repositioning itinerary your ship may arrive when whale watching is close to its finish for the season. Thus the only activities are those listed above. But just to be on this remote Aleutian island is a unique experience that in itself is memorable. The majority of the island is actually inaccessible since there are no roads, and the remoteness makes organizing any type of hiking activity during the few hours the ship is in port next to impossible.**

DINING OUT; In this small community the only restaurant that offers nice meals is the one located in the main hotel.

*** Grand Aleutian Hotel - The only first class hotel in Dutch Harbor, its gift shop does feature many local crafts. And its restaurant offers very fresh and well-prepared local seafood, and they are open for lunch when ships are in port.**

IMMIGRATION NOTE: If you are coming in May, you are eastbound with your last stop having been in Petropavlovsk on Russia's Kamchatka Peninsula. Therefore you will have a full United States Immigration Service clearance conducted on board ship. You will need to show your passport and non-American or Canadian guests will need to have necessary visas, if required depending upon the home country.

For those of you taking the cruise westbound in September, Dutch Harbor will be your last stop in the United States. You will sail for three days across the lower Bering Sea and your next port of call will be Petropavlovsk, Russia. Keep in mind that when Vitus Bering made his historic voyage to claim Alaska for the Russian Tsar, he established Petropavlovsk and

named it in honor of his two ships St. Peter and St. Paul, which contracted in Russian is Petropavlovsk. There is an historic connection between this Russian port and the state of Alaska, making it an appropriate port of call in conjunction with visiting the far-flung Aleutian Islands. Fortunately the Russian government does not require visas to visit Petropavlovsk, so you will be able to get around this small outpost city on your own. But keep in mind that few people speak English and signs are written in Cyrillic, so this will be quite an exotic port of call even though the natural landscape is so reminiscent of Alaska.

DUTCH HARBOR AREA

DUTCH HARBOR AND UNALASKA

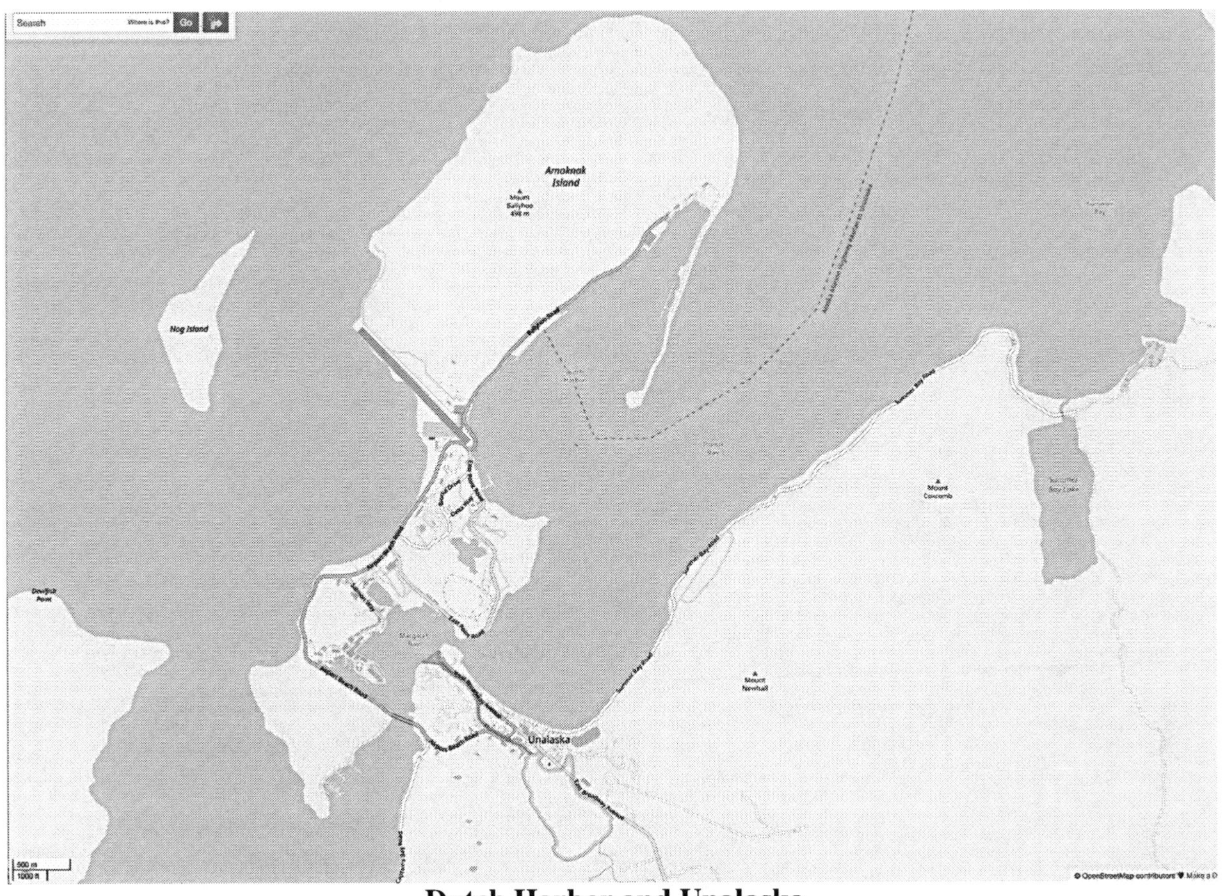

Dutch Harbor and Unalaska

This map is best viewed directly from OpenStreetMap.com on your personal device where it can be expanded or one specific area can be enlarged. Given the format of this book, it is impossible to display maps with the level of detail you might wish to have while actually out exploring the city. But the OpenStreetMap maps used directly are the tool I always rely upon.

THE HEART OF DUTCH HARBOR

Dutch Harbor and Unalaska close up

This map is best viewed directly from OpenStreetMap.com on your personal device where it can be expanded or one specific area can be enlarged. Given the format of this book, it is impossible to display maps with the level of detail you might wish to have while actually out exploring the city. But the OpenStreetMap maps used directly are the tool I always rely upon.

The southern tip of the Alaska Peninsula

The many volcanic cones of the inner Aleutian Islands

Unimak Volcano emits small puffs of sulfuric steam

Another one of the many volcanic islands in the Aleutian Archipelago

The docks of Dutch Harbor in spring before the fishermen arrive

The bleak tundra like landscape of Unalaska Island

The Holy Ascension Cathedral (Russian Orthodox) in Unalaska town

Eagles perched atop the dome of the cathedral

The old Russian Orthodox cemetery

Typical wood houses of Unalaska town

The Grand Aleutian Hotel is the only place to dine

The barracks for the temporary fishermen during the summer season

A part of the dock area of Dutch Harbor

A part of the fishing fleet featured in "Deadliest Catch"

One of the many fine exhibits featured in the Aleutian Museum

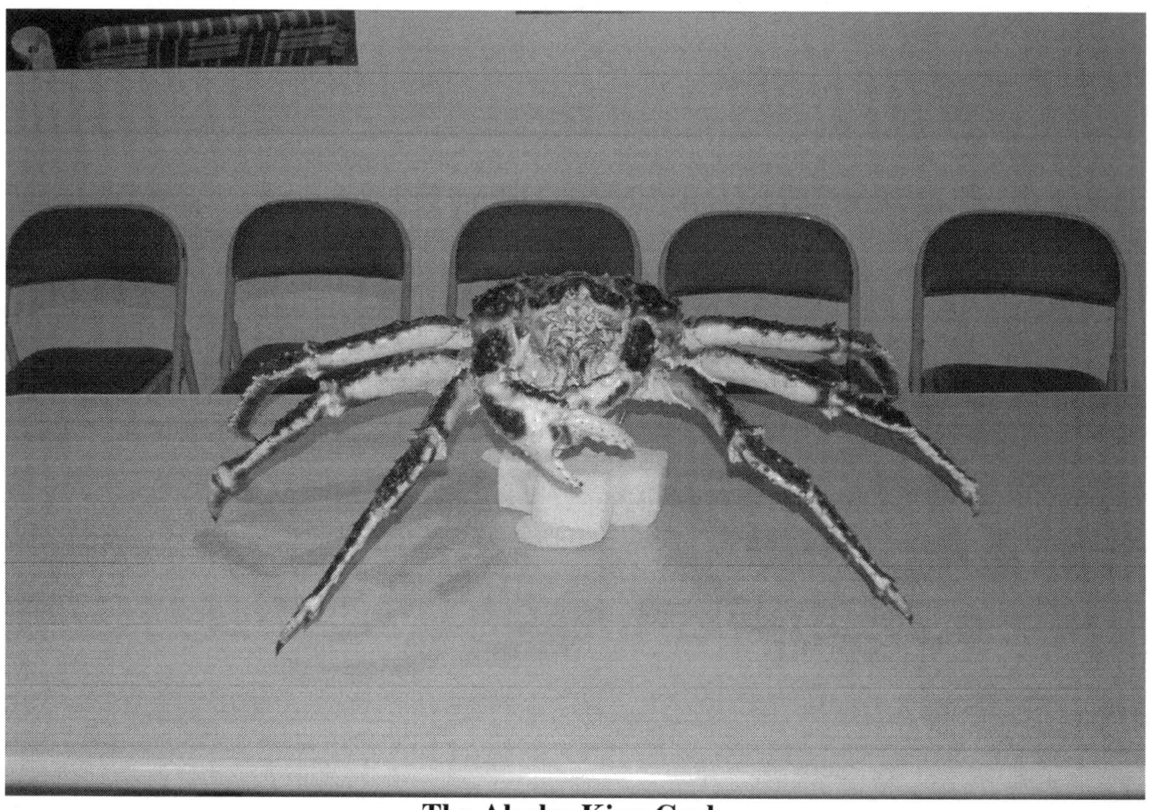

The Alaska King Crab

A SUPPLEMENT ON RUSSIA'S FAR EAST

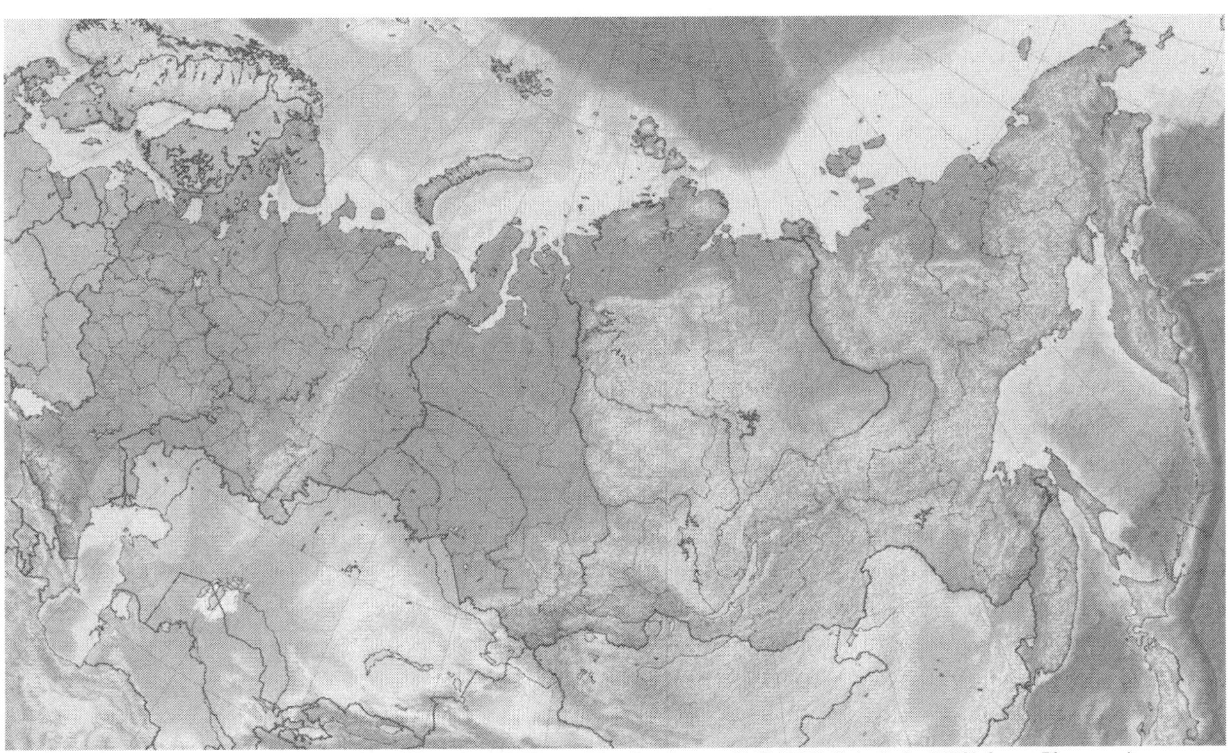

The vastness of Russia (Work of Uwe Dedering, CC BY SA 3.0, Wikimedia.org)

If your cruise has come as far west as Dutch Harbor, or if it is your first port in Alaska, it means you are on one of the repositioning cruises between Vancouver and Tokyo or Hong Kong. For those of you taking such a cruise, I have added this section on Petropavlovsk, Kamchatsky because of its very close ties to the history of Alaska.

WELCOME TO RUSSIA: This is a country I know very well. I studied Russian language, literature and culture during my University years, as this was at the height of the Cold War. And I have cruised in and out of Russian ports from Petropavlovsk to Sochi on the Black Sea, St. Petersburg on the Baltic Sea and Archangelsk on the Arctic Ocean. I have also visited many inland cities, the most important being Moscow. I have visited the country a total of 51 times at the writing of this book, so I know it quite well.

There is an old Tsarist saying notes that, "Russia is not a country, it's a world." Ever since the expansions brought about by Tsar Peter the Great in the early 1700's, Russia has been the world's largest nation. Even though the former Soviet Union split into 15 individual nations, Russia itself is still the world's largest country in physical size. It is hard to imagine Russia's scope. To imagine the vastness and scope of Russia, picture getting on a train in San Francisco and going to New York and then staying on the train while crossing the Atlantic Ocean, eventually reaching Paris, France. That gives one an idea of the east to west distance across Russia that one can travel by rail, from Moscow to Vladivostok. But Petropavlovsk where you will be visiting is still roughly 2,092 kilometers or 1,300 miles farther east than Vladivostok and around 1,126 kilometers or 700 miles farther north. The far eastern edge of

Siberia is where Russia meets Alaska and that is still farther east than Petropavlovsk. Yes Alaska is Russia's neighbor as hard as that may be to believe. There are two islands in the Bering Straits that are less than two miles apart. One belongs to the United States and the other to Russia. During the Cold War, soldiers stationed on these two islands would supposedly exchange visits over the frozen waters via snowmobile, sharing beer, vodka and cards, of course in secret. But neither side has ever been willing to admit to it.

Normally to do any independent exploring in Russia, most nationalities require a visa from the Russian government. Only if one is coming by ship, staying on the ship and then taking sponsored tours is the visa requirement waived, but only for the length of time you are on tour. Petropavlovsk is so isolated from the rest of the country, and the Kamchatka Peninsula has no roads or railway lines, there is no place you can go on your own. If you wanted to board the daily flight to Moscow you would need to show your passport and then the visa would be required. Therefore, because of the isolation of Kamchatka the government has relaxed its strict policies and you are able to leave the ship and explore the city on your own without a visa or organized tour. This is a frontier location and it will give you a unique look into one aspect of life in Russia. When in Petropavlovsk, you are only two hours by air from Anchorage, but nearly 10 hours by non-stop jet to Moscow. So this is the Far East of Russia, truly its distant frontier region.

PETROPAVLOVSK KAMCHATSKY ПЕТРОПАВЛОВСК КАМЧАТСИЙ

Your ship will be visiting just a miniscule piece of this vast nation, but an area that is as remote from Moscow or St. Petersburg as you can possibly get. If roads existed, which they do not, it would be around 16,000 kilometers or 10,000 road miles to journey overland to Moscow. The Kamchatka Peninsula juts south from the Asian mainland for nearly1,287 kilometers or 800 miles. It was formed along one of the earth's major plate boundaries by intensive volcanic and tectonic activity, which continues to this day. The peninsula is spectacular with its multiplicity of snow covered volcanic cones piercing the sky. It is thickly forested in spruce and fir, a land that is part of the great Russian Taiga. There are hundreds of white water rivers plunging outward on both sides of Kamchatka to the sea. And these rivers are home to salmon, otters and many other aquatic species. The land is home to bears, lynx, wolverine, deer, mink, sable, Arctic fox and a great variety of fur bearing animals. And the skies are filled with Steller's and golden eagles. The government of Russia has realized the great value of this remote land for its tourist potential. Numerous national parks have been created and there are many natural wonders such as geyser filled valleys that have been given UNESCO World Heritage status. In addition to volcanic activity, Kamchatka is subject to massive earthquakes that can occur anywhere on the peninsula and with great magnitudes.

This is a cold land because of both its northern latitude and its proximity to the main Siberian landmass. During winter great cold high pressure systems develop, bringing waves of bitter bone chilling air south to mix with the moist, warmer air that comes off the North Pacific Drift. The combination of the two air masses creates conditions conducive to heavy snowfall. Add to this the lifting impact of the high volcanic peaks, and Kamchatka experiences both brutally cold and snowy winters.

Summer is mild, and the lowland meadows turn green, but strewn with wildflowers in a carpet of color while snow remains on the higher peaks. Kamchatka is magnificently beautiful, but unfortunately the major part of the peninsula is inaccessible other than by horseback or on foot. Roads are few in number and do not extend far out of the few coastal ports such as Petropavlovsk or Magadan.

A BRIEF HISTORY: To understand even this remote part of the country, it is first necessary to know something about Russian history. Brutal would be an understatement. Russians have known not only a harsh and unforgiving environment, but their history has been one of bloodshed, depravities committed by the Tsars and wars fought both internally and externally. Siberia was settled not by willing colonists, but for the most part by government edict or exiled Russians.

It was during the ninth century that Slavonic tribes began to settle in the Ukraine, Belarus and in the Valdai Hills around what is now Moscow. Previously, Scythians inhabited the land, dating back to the third century BC, later having been overrun by the Germanic Goths, ancient enemies of Rome. The Slavonic people are believed to have originated in the rugged mountains of the Balkans, slowly migrating out onto the Steppes of the Ukraine. The first actual Russian state does not occur until around 850, its name being the Grand Principality of Rus, taken from the ancient Viking colonial leader Rurik. When the Principality collapses in 1132, central Russia is divided into small city-states that often warred with one another. In the middle of the 13th century, much of Russia falls under the domination of the Mongol hordes. By 1462, the Grand Principality of Muscovy emerged, given its commanding position over the headwaters of the Volga River.

The first leader of the Principality to forcibly unite all of the various fiefdoms into one large nation was Ivan IV, known as the Terrible who proclaims himself Tsar of all the Russias. The term Tsar being taken from Caesar, a reference to the grand rulers of ancient Rome. From 1533 to 1584, he consolidated his power in a brutal reign that is filled with murders and intrigues. During a rage, the Tsar clubbed his own son and heir to death, just one example of what occurred during his reign.

Following the death of Ivan, Russia was plunged into a series of court intrigues, a Polish invasion and finally it emerged still unified under the first of the Romanoff Tsars, Mikhail in 1613. But it was under the rule of Mikhail's grandson, Peter I, ultimately known as Peter the Great, that Russia becomes a world power. Tsar Peter ruled from 1696 to 1725. During his reign, he decreed that the Boyars, court nobles, must wear more western style dress, shave off their beards and become more accustomed to the ways of the outside world. The Tsar set

off on a journey of several years, visiting the Netherlands to learn about shipbuilding and then to England and France where he saw grand and elegant lifestyles.

Upon returning to Russia, he decided that the capital must be moved from its inland location in Moscow to a window on the Gulf of Finland from which it will be possible to travel by sea to the western nations of Europe. Peter pressed into service thousands of craftsmen to drain the swampy ground and began erecting a new capital, but one whose architecture would be patterned after that of Paris. And thus began the development of the city of St. Petersburg. The Tsar forced the nobility to move to the new city, and he commanded them to build palatial homes. At the same time that he was developing his new city, he also oversaw the expansion of his empire into the reaches of Siberia and down into the steppe and desert lands of Central Asia.

The Kamchatka Peninsula was still beyond the easternmost Russian outposts, explored first in 1651. By 1699, much of the peninsula had been explored and the native people found to be very hostile. By the 1730's, there were a few outposts on the peninsula mainly for trapping of valuable fur bearing animals. Vitus Bering established a port in 1740 to act as back up with supplies prior to setting out across the sea that now carries his name. He ultimately mapped and explored coastal Alaska to claim it for the Tsar. The port he established was named for his two ships St. Peter and St. Paul and thus the name Petropavlovsk. After Bering's voyages, the government saw the Kamchatka Peninsula as a perfect location for exile, and thus many of its early settlers were sent there to labor camps or to live off the land far removed from Mother Russia.

At the same time that Kamchatka was serving as a place of exile, the city of St. Petersburg got its greatest boost in terms of architectural construction and grandeur under the Empress Catherine, known as Catherine the Great. Apart from Peter, she becomes the most famous of all Russian rulers, and she was not even Russian. She was born a German princess in a rather obscure backwater principality, but she was sent to Russia to marry the nephew and heir of the Empress Elizabeth, daughter of Peter the Great. Catherine was baptized into the Orthodox Church and quickly learned the court intrigues in the palace. Her husband was not a willing partner, and to this day it is unclear if the son she bore was truly his. In 1762, a palace coup deposed her feeble husband, and with the support of the military, she was proclaimed Empress of Russia. She ruled in autocratic fashion until her death in 1796. She was responsible for many cultural reforms, and she expanded the empire to the Black Sea and deep into Siberia.

But Catherine's greatest accomplishments were in St. Petersburg. She expanded the Winter Palace into its present state of glory, adding a great art collection, which is today second only to the Louvre in Paris. She also expanded what was a small summer palace south of the city into one of the world's most splendid palaces – Tsarskoye Selo. Catherine brought a grand European elegance to the city, and this curried great favor among the nobility. However, her palace love affairs with military officers and politicians meant that nobody in government was on solid ground. By the time of her death, St. Petersburg was considered to be one of the glittering capitals of Europe.

Following Catherine's death, the next succession of Tsars varied from totally autocratic to somewhat benevolent. In 1812, the forces of Tsar Alexander I combined with an unusually brutal winter defeated Napoleon, ending the greatest threat of its day to the Russian Empire. The next major war in the 1850's was over the Crimean Peninsula, but it also impacted Kamchatka, as French and British forces laid siege to this remote outpost, but they were unable to dislodge the tenacious Russians and finally gave up.

In 1861, Tsar Alexander II freed millions of peasant serfs from their indentured service to the landed nobility. This of course ultimately led to his assassination and to a terribly autocratic rule by his son, Tsar Alexander III. His rule was the first of many underlying factors that would lead to the downfall of the House of Romanoff. The Russian government divested itself of Alaska in 1867 when it was sold to the United States. This placed Petropavlovsk in the position of being unimportant now that it lost its Alaska connection.

In the late 19th century, Tsar Nicholas II and his beautiful wife Tsarina Alexandra were to be the last of the Romanoff line and the end of an era for Russia. His uncle, King Edward VII of the United Kingdom, had warned him that he needed to establish a parliamentary system of government and end autocratic rule. The Tsar tried the concept, but when the Duma (parliament) appeared to show a degree of independence, he closed it down. The Tsar embroiled Russia in a war with Japan that Theodore Roosevelt had to negotiate a peace treaty to conclude in 1905, and this made the Tsar quite unpopular.

There was the issue regarding the young heir who suffered from hemophilia. A Siberian monk by the name of Rasputin was able to convince the Tsarina that he had mystical powers to heal. At times Rasputin was able to help the young Tsarevich, but in so doing, he wheedled his way into the inner circle, and there were fears among the nobility that he had a profound influence upon both the Tsar and the Tsarina. It was decided among a group of nobles that Rasputin had to die. He was invited one night to the Usupov Palace, served poisoned sweets and wine, which he survived. He was later shot and finally thrown into the Neva River. Ultimately he died, and nobody was ever apprehended for the crime.

In 1914, Russia entered the war against Germany and the Austro-Hungarian Empire because of their longstanding pledge to defend Serbia. The war was a disaster and the Tsar was unable to muster sufficient loyalty to keep troops from deserting the front. Finally in February 1917, he was forced to abdicate, and a provisional government was established. A Bolshevik named Vladimir Ilich Ulyanov, later to call himself Vladimir Lenin, inspired riots in St. Petersburg and Moscow. In October 1917, the Bolshevik forces stormed the Winter Palace and the provisional government collapsed. The Tsar and his family were exiled to Siberia, and in 1918, they were all grouped together for what was supposedly an official photograph before being moved to another location. But they were brutally executed by firing squad and their bodies were then soaked in acid, burned and buried. Thus the Communists felt assured that there would be no turning back.

The bodies of the Tsar and his family were discovered in the early 1990's, identified through DNA, matching them to Prince Phillip of the United Kingdom. They were then returned to

St. Petersburg and given a formal state burial in the Peter and Paul Cathedral, as was befitting a Tsar.

Lenin's victory was followed by years of bloody civil war, which ended in 1922 with the creation of the Union of Soviet Socialists Republics. The last of the fighting took place in the Far East around the city of Vladivostok, but Kamchatka was so isolated and unimportant that it was not impacted. The capital of the new Soviet Union was moved back to the Kremlin in Moscow, leaving St. Petersburg as a second-class city. When Vladimir Lenin died in 1924, the city of St. Petersburg was renamed Leningrad in his honor, and that name lasted until 1991.

This dictatorial and monolithic state would last until the end of 1990. The Soviet Union became a powerful state, but at the expense of its people. Freedoms were highly limited, especially after Lenin died in 1924 and Joseph Stalin came to power. It is now known that his various purges and incarcerations in the notorious gulags of Siberia cost the lives of over 20,000,000 Russians. Magadan in the northern part of Kamchatka had one such gulag and the town was later considered as a place of exile. Only during World War II, when Nazi Germany invaded Russia, did Stalin find that there was true support among the masses. He did engender a certain fatherly image that the Russians seemed to need to aid in their victory over the Germans. Of course they did receive massive foreign aid from the United States and the United Kingdom. Red Army determination once again combined with a brutal winter helped to defeat Germany and ultimately turn the tide of the war, but at a cost of another 20,000,000 lives.

During the war, the Nazi forces attempted to take the city of Leningrad, but were held at bay by a tenacious people. The Germans surrounded the city and for nearly three years they attempted to starve it into submission. The city was bombarded and people died of not only explosions, but also of starvation and cold. Only during winter could the Red Army supply the city by driving convoys of trucks over the frozen Lake Ladoga to the east. This was one of the most terrible of sieges in modern history.

World War II was far removed from Kamchatka, but Petropavlovsk was used as a naval base of operation in the invasion of the Kuril Islands of far northern Japan very late in the war. Following World War II, as Russia and the United States entered the Cold War, Kamchatka was officially declared a military zone and no foreign visitors were allowed on the peninsula. The ban on foreigners fell with the Soviet Union and today foreign tourism is a growing activity. The largest nuclear submarine base in Russia is located across Avacha Bay from the city. You can catch a glimpse of it from the ship during arrival or departure.

The Soviet Union became the Cold War enemy of the United States, especially after it too developed nuclear weapons during the 1950's. Several dictatorial leaders ruled after Stalin's death in 1953, the two most famous being Nikita Khrushchev and Leonid Brezhnev. During the 1980's, a new and moderate leader came to power. His name of course was Mikhail Gorbachev, the man who began to open the doors through his policies of glasnost and perestroika, openness and restructuring. But it was too late to restructure the system, as the Soviet Union was over extended and starting to crumble. The end came on December 31,

1990, when the Union of Soviet Socialist Republics was dissolved and the Russian Federation emerged.

The people of Russia have known bitter hardship throughout their long history. Yes there are many glories, and both Moscow and St. Petersburg display the opulence and elegance of a romantic era of tsarist life. But for the average Russian, just earning enough to survive has always been the primary goal. So to this day, there is a somber quality to the Russian personality. It is true that Russians love to sing and dance, and there is an exuberance to their style of folk dancing that pierces the soul. But these expressions were reserved for weddings and special occasions. Most of the music that one hears is melancholy and tugs at the heartstrings. It is a deep and moving part of the Russian soul.

VISITING PETROPAVLOVSK: The maps of Petropavlovsk at the end of this commentary shows you that this city of around 180,000 is quite spread out. The old city center stretches northeast along the shore from the main docks where ship's tenders bring passengers on shore. Although the harbor is deep, there has not been a dock dock adequate to berth a cruise ship. There have been plans to build a dock capable of handling cruise ships, but I have not been able to find any information regarding this possibility. As of 2018, cruise ships stopping in Petropavlovsk were still tendering passengers to the shore. It is an easy walk into the city center from the tender drop off, but many cruise lines operate shuttle busses that take guests farther inland and drop them at the new shopping mall and public marketplace about three kilometers or two miles from the docks.

The city itself spreads over numerous hills, some of which are quite steep. The backdrop for the city is very representative of Kamchatka - two mighty snowcapped volcanic cones. These two brooding mountains are both essentially active and do spew molten lava and ash on a reoccurring basis. Essentially the city is in ongoing danger, as it is inevitable that one of these two mountains will someday erupt with catastrophic force. But for now they are magnificent and do provide a degree of excitement with their small eruptions. Koriyaisky is a near perfect cone that tops out at 3,456 meters or 11,339 feet while its neighbor Avachinsky is less well formed and is only 2,741 meters or 8,993 feet in height. The last major eruption occurred in 2008 when Koryaksky sent up an ash cloud over 3,660 meters or 12,000 feet into the atmosphere.

Given the dispersed pattern of development of Petropavlovsk and its very hilly topography, it is especially difficult to do much walking and be able to see the major sights. But most cruise lines will offer a tour of the city that only lasts around two to three hours and still leaves you time to walk around on your own.

* There are no private cars with driver/guides available, but there are rental cars at the city's airport. However, I strongly urge you not to attempt driving on your own unless you are capable of reading the signs in the Cyrillic alphabet and likewise understanding the language. You do not want to get into a traffic accident in Russia.

* There is taxi service and drivers will take guests on a tour of the city, but the guest must be able to speak Russian since it is very, very unlikely that the driver will speak English. If you

are able to speak the language, then contact Taxi Petropavlovsky-Kamchatsky by phone at + 7 415 221 21 21 to make arrangements. You can also contact Vezitaki, which has a web page at *www.kamchatka.vezitaksi.com* **for information. But again, their web page is written in Russian using the Cyrillic alphabet.**

The prominent sights in the city include (listed alphabetically):

*** Galant City Shopping Mall and Marketplace - Located just to the northeast of the docks, this modern facility gives you a chance to see the types of food and merchandise available in this remote city. You will find food prices very high on items from European Russia, but reasonable on salmon, halibut and the red salmon caviar. It is open daily from 11 AM to 8 PM. The exact address should you venture to use a taxi is Ulitsa Pogranichnaya # 2, which written in Cyrillic is Улица Пограничная.**

*** Kamchatka Military History Museum – Located just south of the Vitus Bering Monument on Ulitsa Radiosvyazi #69 just off of the main street known as Ulitsa Leninskaya, this museum is dedicated to the role of the military on the peninsula. The role of the military has been very critical in the development of Petropavlovsk. Many of the major exhibits now have descriptions in English for the benefit of foreign visitors. And the staff is very friendly and helpful. No specific hours are given for the museum, but when a cruise ship is in port, it will be open.**

*** Kamchatka Museum of Local Lore - A good place in which to learn about the native people and the Russian settlers of this remote outpost. It is located at Leningradskaya Ulitsa #20 and open Wednesday thru Sunday from 10:30 AM to 6 PM, but closed on the last Friday of each month for servicing. There is some information provided in English.**

*** Memorial Complex Sopki Nikolskoye - A memorial cemetery to the lives lost during the British/French assault on Petropavlovsk during the Crimean War. It sits above Krasincev Street in the lower downtown area, but difficult to find on your own unless you can read the Cyrillic sign, but it is within walking distance of the Monument to Vitus Bering. Turn right at the sign for the street, which looks like this – Красинсев. The monument sits above the street on the hill and is easy to spot.**

*** Monument to Vitus Bering - Located near the dock, this monument is dedicated to the founder of the city and the greatest of the explorers of Alaska. It is located along the waterfront opposite the dock where the cruise ship tenders will put you ashore.**

*** Trinity Cathedral - Sitting atop a hill, this white and blue traditional Orthodox cathedral lends that true Russian architectural flavor to the city skyline. You may only see the cathedral from the outside, as it is not open when no services are being held. It is located on Vladivostokskaya Ulitsa #18. It is always a photo stop on the motor coach tours of the city.**

*** Science Museum of Vulcanology - Here you can see instruments at work monitoring the two major volcanoes. You will also learn about the volcanic history of Kamchatka and the**

many eruptions that have occurred in the last 50 years. It is located at Bul'var Piypa #9 and is open from 7 AM to 10 PM daily.

SIGHTS OUTSIDE OF PETROPAVLOVSK: There are spectacular sights to be seen outside of the city, but you will need to be signed up for one of the exploratory tours, as there are no private guides and cars available unless you have your travel agent book a private excursion through one of the small tour operators in Petropavlovsk. If you are the type who wants to be on your own and not part of a larger ship sponsored group, then the best way to accomplish this is through your travel agency well before leaving home. One company that has been used by people I know is Red River Kamchatka Tour Company. You may wish to check their web page at *www.kamchatkaredrivers.com* **for further details.**

Local taxi drivers generally do not speak or understand English and making last minute arrangements would be quite difficult. The important sights outside of the city include:

*** Avachinsky and Koryaiksky Volcanoes - Some cruise lines offer regular tours for limited numbers of guests utilizing giant snow cats that will take you right up into the lower slopes of either or both of the two great volcanoes. These two mountains dominate the skyline from almost any vantage point in Petropavlovsk. They are both active and eruptions can occur at any time. The snow cat exploration sells out fast, as space is limited. If getting up close to two mighty volcanic peaks is something you would be interested in doing, book as early as possible with your cruise line.**

*** Koryak Village – Some cruise lines offer a culturally based tour outside of Petropavlovsk to a native Koryak village, home to a native group of people who once lived by hunting, fishing and gathering. Today they still keep alive their traditional songs, dances and craft activities. A visit to their village is a true cultural experience and although they are orienting their presentation to please visitors, there is a great degree of authenticity.**

*** Mutnovsky Volcano – This may be included in a ship's itinerary. This is one of the most active volcanoes in southern Kamchatka. And at is base is an active geyser field with numerous erupting geysers and hot springs. The volcano is only 2,322 meters or 7,618 feet high, but it can be quite active, its last major eruption was in 2000. It only takes about two hours to reach and is therefore a popular attraction.**

*** Paratunskiye Hot Springs - This modest hot spring resort takes advantage of the steaming hot waters that are the result of the region's intense volcanic activity. The resort is a short distance outside of the city and may be included on your ship's planned tours. If it is not and you want to visit, you would need the services of a local taxi, which could pose a language problem.**

DINING OUT: Petropavlovsk is a remote city that receives very few foreign visitors, therefore the few restaurants that do exist are not easily capable of serving guests who do not have at least a modest knowledge of how to speak or read Russian. It is doubtful if any would even have a menu written in English or any other language. But for those with a sense of adventure, I can at least make the following recommendation that is within walking

distance of the cruise tender dock or where the majority of ship shuttles drop off in the upper city (shown alphabetically):

*** Cafe Grill Ugli - Located at Leningradskaya Ulitsa #82, this restaurant does offer good traditional Russian cuisine with polite service. And some of its waiters are capable of serving guests who only speak English. They are open from Noon to Midnight daily and you will find this to be a good place to sample Russian cuisine.**

*** Grand Café – Located at Ulitsa Pogranichnaya #1/1 , which is in the Galant City Shopping Mall where many ship shuttles stop, this is a traditional Russian restaurant with a modern vibe in its décor. The cuisine is very traditional and many consider it to be the best Russian restaurant in the city. It is open daily from 10 AM to 8 PM.**

& Petrovskiy – This restaurant is just north of the tender drop off, located on Ulitsa Leningradskaya # 27. It is a very lovely restaurant and offers traditional Russian and Central European cuisine. And they have a menu written in English even though most of the staff do not speak English. The service, atmosphere and cuisine will all please any ship guest. They open at 8 AM and stay open well past Midnight. Look for the big sign across the façade of the building, which reads in Cyrillic Петровский.

FINAL WORDS: For those who have never visited Russia, this will be a unique introduction to the country via its back door. For those who have been to Moscow or St. Petersburg, a visit to Petropavlovsk will show you a different side of Russia, one that is more earthy and unsophisticated. I have personally traveled extensively in Russia and I do know the language well enough to be out with a Russian only speaking guide or visit a restaurant. But even for those of you who do not know the language, you will find the Russian people very willing to be accommodating, so give it a try. Petropavlovsk is a frontier city and people are very eager to have foreign visitors, as it is a new adventure for them.

MAPS OF PETROPAVLOVSK

THE GREATER PETROPAVLOVSK AREA

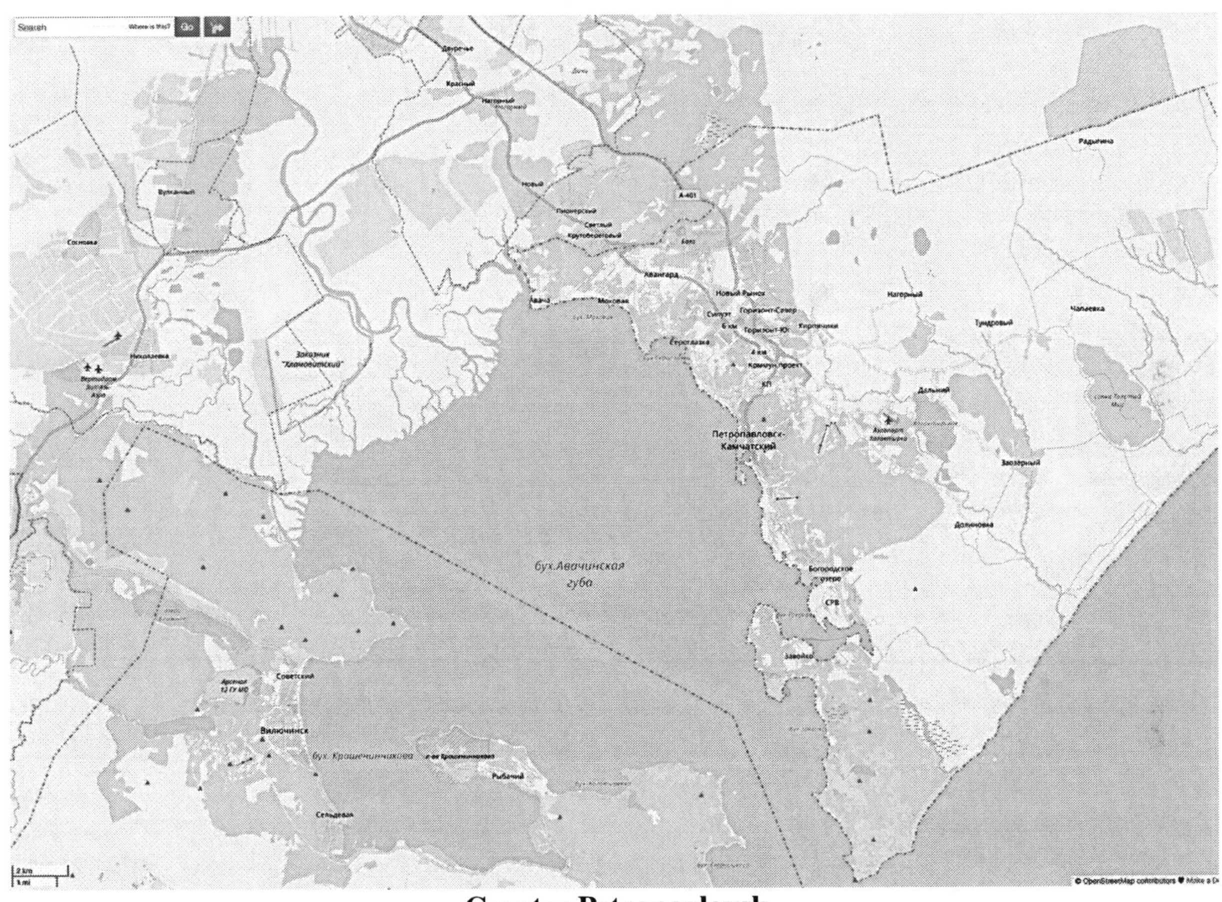

Greater Petropavlovsk

This map is best viewed directly from OpenStreetMap.com on your personal device where it can be expanded or one specific area can be enlarged. Given the format of this book, it is impossible to display maps with the level of detail you might wish to have while actually out exploring the city. But the OpenStreetMap maps used directly are the tool I always rely upon.

THE CITY OF PETROPAVLOVSK

The city of Petropavlovsk

This map is best viewed directly from OpenStreetMap.com on your personal device where it can be expanded or one specific area can be enlarged. Given the format of this book, it is impossible to display maps with the level of detail you might wish to have while actually out exploring the city. But the OpenStreetMap maps used directly are the tool I always rely upon.

THE PORT AND OLD TOWN CORE OF PETROPAVLOVSK

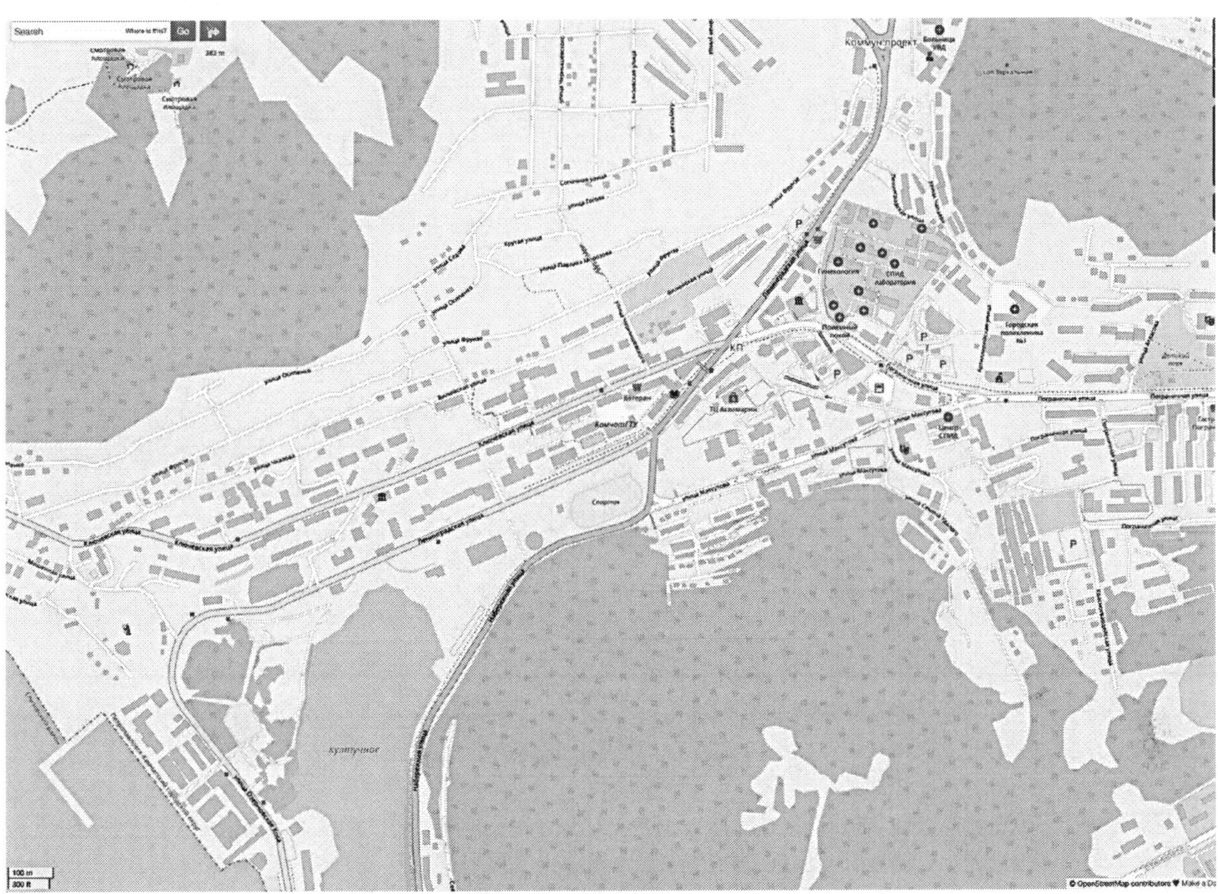

The port area and old downtown core

This map is best viewed directly from OpenStreetMap.com on your personal device where it can be expanded or one specific area can be enlarged. Given the format of this book, it is impossible to display maps with the level of detail you might wish to have while actually out exploring the city. But the OpenStreetMap maps used directly are the tool I always rely upon.

THE NEWER UPTOWN OF PETROPAVLOVSK

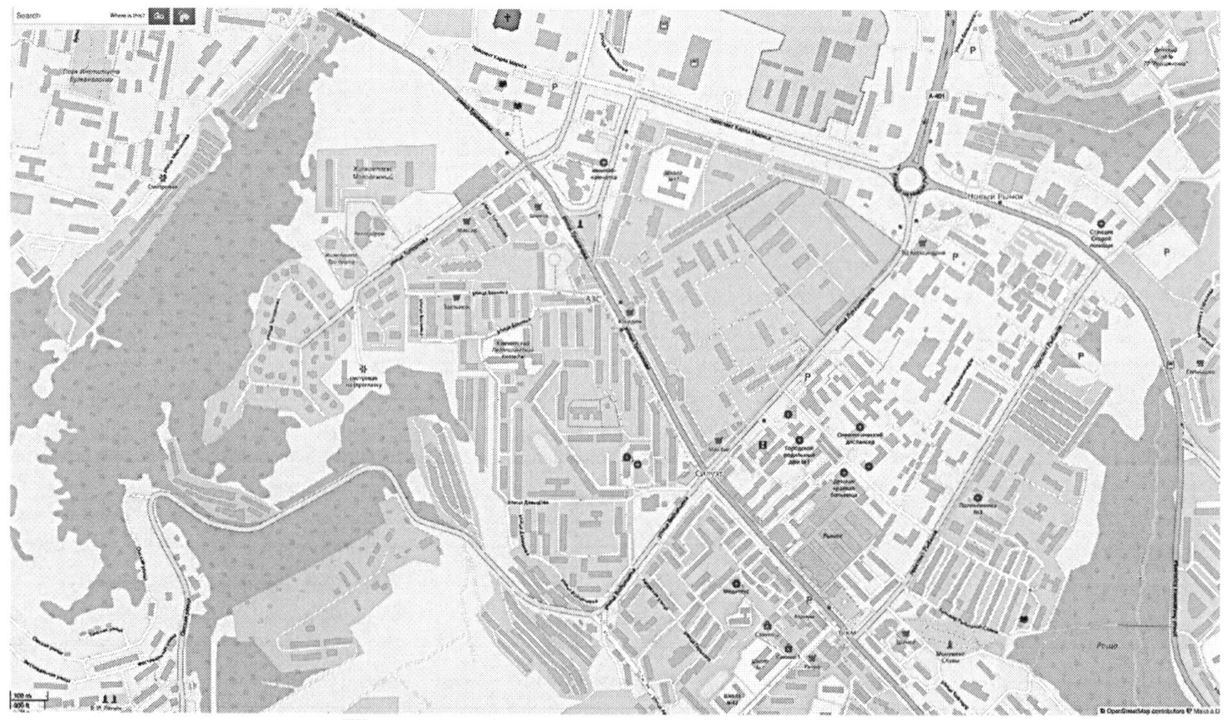

The newer uptown area of Petropavlovsk

This map is best viewed directly from OpenStreetMap.com on your personal device where it can be expanded or one specific area can be enlarged. Given the format of this book, it is impossible to display maps with the level of detail you might wish to have while actually out exploring the city. But the OpenStreetMap maps used directly are the tool I always rely upon.

Avacha Bay with Petropavlovsk and its two volcanoes at sunrise

The two massive and active volcanoes dominate over the city

The city center and the fishing fleet of Petropavlovsk

In the old city center of Petropavlovsk

The old city center is rapidly modernizing

The historic old wood church in the city center

The monument to St. Peter and St. Paul and the founding of Petropavlovsk

On the main road to the newer uptown city center with Koriyaiski Volcano looming

In the upper city there is a mix of old Soviet and new buildings

This is the uptown shopping area

The new Holy Trinity Cathedral overlooks the uptown

The two volcanic cones overshadow suburban Petropavlovsk

Inside the large public market where produce is flown in at great cost

Honey is always a major market commodity in Russia

This sign outside of Petropavlovsk says, "Here begins Russia"

A small dacha or country house outside of Petropavlovsk

Overlooking a part of the Russian submarine base

High above the city snow lingers into springtime

EXPLORATION CRUISES

This book has not included the more highly specialized naturalist exploration cruises that are offered to Alaska on board very small vessels operated by companies that specialize in adventure cruising. These are cruises on small vessels where a limited number of guests will explore fjords and islands that cannot accommodate larger vessels. These cruises are for those who are seeking to get closer to nature and do not mind "roughing it" to a degree, often going onshore in open zodiacs, hiking or wading into locations where you can see wildlife up close in a way that would not be possible on the more luxury oriented cruises.

As a travel author I have not personally experienced this type of exploration in Alaska or other wild areas primarily because I am at the age where there is simply too much exertion required. Therefore I do not feel competent to include any detailed accounting of the locales or activities available since anything I would write would be of a second hand nature. Among those carriers that engage in exploration cruises Silversea is the only major five-star cruise line that does offer three small ships designed for adventure cruising, but still provides the ultimate in luxury and comfort.

I recommend that if this is the type of Alaska adventure you are seeking, you should search on line for adventure cruises. You can then obtain more information regarding their offerings. The vast majority of cruisers visiting Alaska are either more senior, or they are younger with small to teenage children. These cruises appeal more to the age group of 20 to 40, married or single and without children. Often the guests have done one or more such expeditions in Antarctica, the Galapagos , Greenland or the Amazon.

ABOUT THE AUTHOR

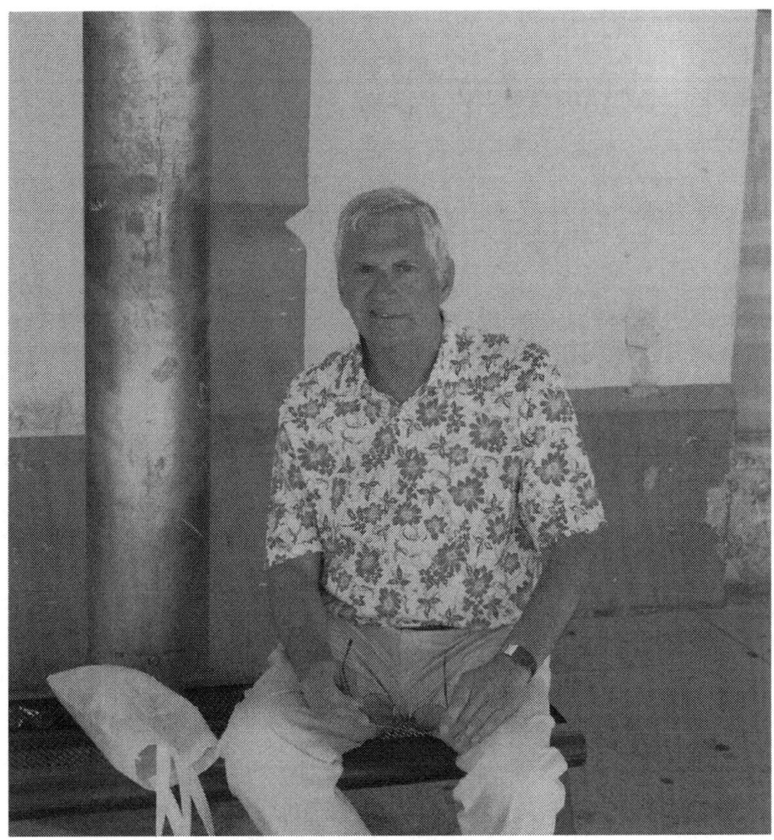

Dr. Lew Deitch

I am Canadian and a semi-retired professor of geography with over 46 years of teaching experience. During my distinguished career, I directed the Honors Program at Northern Arizona University and developed many programs relating to the study of contemporary world affairs. I am an honors graduate of The University of California, Los Angeles, earned my Master of Arts at The University of Arizona and completed my doctorate in geography at The University of New England in Australia. I am a globetrotter, having visited 96 countries on all continents except Antarctica. My primary focus is upon human landscapes, especially such topics as local architecture, foods, clothing and folk music.

I enjoy being in front of an audience, and have spoken to thousands of people at civic and professional organizations. I have been lecturing on board ships for a major five star cruise line since 2008. I love to introduce people to exciting new places both by means of presenting vividly illustrated talks and through

serving as a tour consultant for ports of call. I am also an avid writer, and for years I have written my own text books used in my university classes. Now I have turned my attention to writing travel companions, books that will introduce you to the country you are visiting, but not serving as a touring book like the major guides you find in all of the bookstores.

I also love languages, and my skills include a conversational knowledge of German, Russian and Spanish.

I am a dual Canadian-American, holding passports of both countries. I was raised in California, have lived and worked in Canada and Australia. Arizona has been my permanent home since 1974. One exciting aspect of my life was the ten-year period during which I volunteered my time as an Arizona Highway Patrol reserve trooper, working out on the streets and highways and also developing new safety and enforcement programs for use statewide. I presently live just outside of Phoenix in the beautiful resort city of Scottsdale.

TO CONTACT ME, PLEASE CHECK OUT MY WEB PAGE FOR MORE INFORMATION AT:
http://www.doctorlew.com

Made in the USA
San Bernardino, CA
03 March 2020